The Meal

The Mental
and the Material

Thought Economy and Society

♦

MAURICE   GODELIER

Translated by Martin Thom

VERSO

London · New York

This English-language edition first published by Verso 1986
© Verso 1986, 1988, 2011

First published as *L'Idéel et le matériel*
© Librarie Arthème Fayard 1984
All rights reserved

The moral rights of the author have been asserted

3 5 7 9 10 8 6 4 2

Verso
UK: 6 Meard Street, London W1F 0EG
US: 20 Jay Street, Suite 1010, Brooklyn, NY 11201
www.versobooks.com

Verso is the imprint of New Left Books

ISBN-13: 978-1-84467-790-0

British Library Cataloguing in Publication Data
A catalogue record for this book is available from the British Library

Library of Congress Cataloging-in-Publication Data
A catalog record for this book is available from the Library of Congress

Printed in the US by Maple Vail

Contents

For Claude Lévi-Strauss

Publisher's Note

The title of Godelier's book in French is *L'idéel et le matériel*. We have translated — for lack of a better alternative — the word 'idéel' as 'mental' but we are aware that this partly distorts what Maurice Godelier intended by using the word 'idéel', which is rarely used in French except in philosophical discourse. Godelier's intention was to take into account thought in all its forms and processes, conscious and unconscious, cognitive and non-cognitive. 'Mental' tends to underplay the unconscious aspects of thought and to reduce its conscious aspects to abstract and intellectual representations alone.

Verso

Preface
The Mental and the Material

My point of departure in this book lies in a fact, and a hypothesis.

The fact is this: human beings, in contrast to other social animals, do not just live in society, they *produce society in order to live*. In the course of their existence, they invent new ways of thinking and of acting — both upon themselves and upon the nature which surrounds them. They therefore produce culture and create history (or History).

Of course other social animals too are the product of a history, but it is one they have not made: that of the natural evolution of living matter, and of the animal and vegetable species which nature has engendered in the course of the earth's existence and which thereafter enter into its composition.

This fact is not just like any other, for an account of it involves an analysis of both the evolution of nature and the specificity of man within that nature. All else in this sense lies in its light or shadow. If we wish to explain the human race and its history, to develop the natural or the human sciences, we cannot but take this reality as our starting-point.

But how can a fact be thought without a hypothesis to interpret it? One such hypothesis does exist — which, though not new, I believe to possess a tremendous explanatory potential. It may be stated as follows: *human beings have a history because they transform nature*. It is indeed this capacity which defines them as human. Of all the forces which set them in movement and prompt them to invent new forms of society, the most profound is

their ability to transform their relations *with* nature by transforming *nature itself*. It is the same capacity which gives them the
material means to stabilize this movement, fixing it for a shorter
or longer period in a new form of society, or to develop and
extend certain of the new forms of social life so invented far
beyond their birth-place. It is not difficult to find data which
illustrate this hypothesis.

Is there a better example of human action on nature than
domesticated plants and animals — a domestication, begun
about 10,000 BC, which then soon became the starting-point for
an irreversible development of multiple forms of agriculture and
stockbreeding that in their turn wrought profound changes in
social life? Was it not within certain of these agricultural or agropastoral societies that the first stratifications of caste or class and
the first forms of State emerged (about 3,500 BC) in Mesopotamia,
then in China, in Egypt, in Peru, in Mexico? The people of those
times were much the same as ourselves today, individuals belonging to the species *Homo Sapiens* which does not seem to have
evolved much biologically in the last fifty thousand years.

If we go further back, to the several million years in the course
of which certain of our prehominid ancestors were gradually
transformed into *Homo Sapiens*, we learn from palaeontologists
and prehistorians that these transformations were associated with
an evolution which led the bodies of our ancestors to stand
upright, their hands to become free, and their brain to develop,
endowing them — beyond their new physical reach — with the
powers of the word and the tool.

Yet long before these latest discoveries of palaeontology and
archaeology, the scientific value of our initial hypothesis was well
acknowledged. Its history in Western thought has not yet been
written. Here we need only recall that the same idea is to be
found around 1750 in the work of the Physiocrats Quesnay and
Mirabeau in France, and in that of Lord Kames in Scotland — as
of his successor in the chair of Moral Philosophy at the University
of Glasgow, Adam Smith. In the nineteenth century, it can be
traced, in more or less diffuse or emphatic form, in the writings of
Darwin, Spencer and Morgan, as well as of Marx — who, though
he made it the starting-point of his theory, had no monopoly on
it.[1]

---

1. The idea of a transformation of nature by human beings has no meaning
in the majority of cultures where, as J.-P. Vernant has remarked of Greek thinking

At the beginning of the twentieth century, this tradition looked very vulnerable to the cumulative criticisms of the evolutionism which had dominated the sciences of the previous century.[2] History could no longer be presented as a linear continuation of a biological evolution which, advancing from the lower to the higher, had propelled man to the summit of nature and Western man to the summit of history. It is no secret today how far evolutionary ideologies of this sort served to underwrite that Occidental racism which legitimized the subordination and exploitation of colonized peoples, and a general attitude of contempt and destruction towards other cultures.[3]

However, purified of all the premises and limitations of evolutionism, the ideas of a natural evolution and of a human history founded on the capacity of men and women to transform inner nature and outer nature alike were to re-emerge in a still vital and scientifically valid form. The work of Claude Lévi-Strauss is a case in point. He can hardly be accused of evolutionism, yet in him we find the assertion that the 'theory of superstructures, scarcely touched upon by Marx', to which he wishes to make a contribution, does not 'undermine that law of order [which is] the incontestable primacy of the infrastructures'.[4] Such is my point of departure too, in the attempts below to explore the relations between thought, the economy and society, and to analyse the respective weight of the mental and the material in the production of social relations, in the motion of societies, in history at large.

Both the difficulty and the import of this undertaking are evident enough. How, and to what extent, do the material realities of external nature and those of human creation or transformation act upon the organization of social life and, above all,

---

about the origin and nature of the *technai*, it would be reckoned sacrilegious — a blasphemy against the divine order of nature. See, however, the fascinating work of an author who died too soon, Ronald Meek, *Social Science and the Ignoble Savage*, Cambridge 1976, and, more recently, Charles Woolfson, *The Labour Theory of Culture*, London 1982.

2. See L.T. Hobhouse, G.C. Wheeler and M. Ginsberg, *The Material Culture of the Simpler Peoples. An Essay in Correlation*, London 1965 (first edition 1915); Julian H. Steward, *The Theory of Culture Change. The Methodology of Multilinear Evolution*, Chicago and London 1955, and *Evolution and Ecology. Essay on Social Transformation*, Chicago and London 1955.

3. Eric R. Wolf, *Europe and the People without History*, Berkeley and London 1982.

4. Claude Lévi-Strauss, *The Savage Mind*, London 1962, p. 130.

the production of new forms of society? What indeed is meant by 'material realities'? On closer examination, we must distinguish between several types of materiality according to whether their existence and operation do or do not imply the existence of human beings.

First, there is that infinite part of nature which still remains outside the direct or indirect sway of humankind, but never ceases to affect it: the climate, the nature of the subsoil, etc. Secondly, there is that part of nature which has been transformed by human intervention, but indirectly, without the latter's agents having either intended or anticipated the consequences of their action: erosion of the soil, changes in vegetation due to repeated use of bush fires for hunting, agriculture, stockbreeding and so on. Thirdly, there is of course that part of nature which has been directly transformed by human beings and cannot thereafter be reproduced without their attention, energy and labour. Most salient here are those domesticated plants and animals which, until very recently, constituted the chief element in our subsistence. If separated from us and left to themselves, these plants and animals either survive precariously, or become wild again, or are incapable of reproducing and disappear.

Finally, two more parts of nature transformed by human beings for their own use in the process of producing their material conditions of existence should be noted. Tools and weapons made out of wood, bone, stone, etc. constitute so many external organs extending the reach of the human body and adding their powers to its. (This is not true of machines which do not function as an extension of our bodies.) Then there are all those elements of nature which, detached from it by human action, serve in either their original form or after transformation as material support for the production of social life in all its dimensions: the wood, bone, stone, leather and metals employed for the construction of simple shelters or sumptuous temples, schools or banks, statues of men or of gods. Tools, weapons, monuments and objects of every sort are the material supports for a mode of social life. Once abandoned, they fall into ruins — inert and silent residues of history, prey to the cupidity or imagination of the archaeologists of subsequent epochs.

The boundary between nature and culture, the distinction between the material and the mental, tend moreover to dissolve once we approach that part of nature which is directly subordinated to humanity — that is, produced or reproduced by it (domestic animals and plants, tools, weapons, clothes). Although external to us this nature is not external to culture, society or history. It is that part of nature which is transformed by human action and thought. It is a reality which is simultaneously material and mental. It owes its existence to conscious human action on nature — action which can neither exist nor be reproduced without the intervention not simply of consciousness, but of every kind of thought, conscious and unconscious, individual and collective, historical and non-historical.[5] This part of nature is appropriated, humanized, become society: it is history inscribed in nature.

There are, then, five kinds of materiality of which we may attain knowledge and in some instances control; and the effects of each on us are markedly different. For nature acts on us incessantly yet distinctly, according to whether we do or do not have knowledge or mastery of it. In the first part of this book I shall be looking at different forms of material and social appropriation of nature, and trying to identify the effects on the organization of different economic and social systems of the material constraints imposed by the conditions of reproduction of the natural ecosystems in which these societies are immersed, and upon which they work in order to reproduce themselves.

The notion of adaptation refers to the different strategies which humanity has invented to exploit the resources of nature and confront the ecological constraints which weigh upon the reproduction of both natural and human resources. To adapt oneself is to submit to constraints, to take them into account, in order to amplify their positive and attenuate their negative effects, for instance by regulating the movement of individuals and groups, limiting their number, inventing means of food storage, etc.: in short, by opposing a material and social practice to the material constraints of nature.

Of course the species which surround us have also been able to survive only by in a measure adapting themselves to the resources and constraints of their environment. But unlike ourselves, none is capable of assuming conscious and social control of part of the objective conditions of its existence. The processes of human adaptation are themselves contradictory, and stable only within certain limits — limits which reveal the content

5. See chapter 4: 'The Role of Thought in the Reproduction of Social Relations'.

both of their relations to nature and their social relations, whose properties derive neither from their will nor their consciousness. But at the same time these processes of adaptation imply from the outset the development of representations and interpretations of nature shared by the members of a particular society, and the organization of various forms of individual and collective interventions in nature which depend upon these representations and interpretations. Separate analyses are thus needed of the impact of profoundly different materialities upon the organization of social life and the production of society — some of which have an orgin external to humanity, in that nature which is prior to it, whilst others derive from humanity and its history, and have an origin internal to a particular form of society which they presuppose.

There is of course a link between these distinct materialities, since those derivative from human beings were invented to act (to react) upon those derivative from nature. But the difficulty is to discover the relations between the material (and mental) forces which humanity invents in a given period and the social relations which serve as a direct framework and support for its action on nature. Or, to employ Marx's terminology, what are the relations between the material and intellectual productive forces of a society reproducing itself within a determinate ecosystem, and the social relations which function therein as 'relations of production'?

The difficulty derives from the fact that a society never exists by halves or in pieces. A society always exists as a whole — that is, as an articulated ensemble of relations and functions, all of which are *simultaneously necessary* for its existence as such, but whose importance for its reproduction is variable. That is why the reproduction of any given society cannot continue beyond certain variations or alterations in the social relations which constitute it and the material base upon which it depends.

Thus it is by abstraction that thought may separate the various parts of a whole, the productive forces from the relations of production, and divide these two realities (thenceforth habitually called the 'infrastructure') from the remainder of social relations (which then become 'superstructures'). In passing, it is worth noting that 'infrastructure' and 'superstructures' are very poor translations of *Grundlage* and *Überbau*, the terms actually used by Marx. The *Überbau* is a construction, an edifice which rises up on foundations, *Grundlage*; and it is a house we live in, not the found-

ations. So another translation of Marx, far from reducing the
superstructures to an impoverished reality, could have emphasized their importance.

Be this as it may, what thought aims to do when it separates
the parts of a whole by abstraction and seeks to analyse the
relations between them is to reconstruct the movement whereby
the relation between the parts forming this whole was originally
established — so as to discover if this process was limited to the
establishment of a correspondence in some sense imposed from
the outside, to a reciprocal adjustment of elements of social practice initially alien to each other, or if on the contrary it was
something more: the simultaneous generation of elements of
social life from the outset internally correspondent to each other,
through a dynamic originating in human intervention within
nature.

It is obvious that in history these two eventualities are not
mutually exclusive. The first will tend to reflect the responses of a
society under external pressure or intrusion. The second is more
likely to involve a situation of internal pressure endogenous to the
society. In the former case, the production of new social relations
is in a certain sense a secondary and derivative process — the
resultant of an encounter (which can be wholly accidental) and
adjustment between heterogeneous pre-existent realities,
although they must be partially compatible with each other. The
latter case, on the other hand, in some sense presents us with the
question of the actual mechanisms involved in the original generation of new social relations, with the primary mechanism of the
production of society (if such a mechanism exists). Marx's
thought still remains so original and fundamental to the development of the social sciences precisely because he treated this hypothesis as central.

But it is clear what becomes of history when thought opts for
one or the other of these two possibilities, or both at once. In the
first case, the role of chance seems to prevail over that of necessity
in the generation of society and the dynamic of history; in the
second, it is the other way around. In actual fact, since the two
cases are not mutually exclusive, history cannot be reduced to
either of them. It is born of their admixture, from their conjuga-
tion.

In reality what varies is the respective role of chance and
necessity in the circumstances surrounding the birth and the
maintenance (be it ephemeral or durable) of new forms of social

practice, new ways of organizing society. But what is invariably present, constituting as it were the *minimum of unintentional necessity* operative in and upon every society, forging and propelling history, is the action of the properties of social relations themselves, with their uneven disposition to arise and to disappear. Of course it is the action of human beings themselves which causes their social relations to emerge and to dissolve. But it is neither from their volition nor their consciousness that the properties of these relations, or their ability within certain limits to reproduce themselves, are born. And it is the ineluctable necessity of submitting to these properties that sets in motion and guides the processes of erosion, destruction and reciprocal adjustment which ultimately render the presence and action of social relations born separately or collectively compatible within one and the same social totality (i.e. a particular society) — subject to the material constraints of the nature which surrounds that society, of the ecosystem in which it is immersed, whose pressures never cease to operate.

But if not all the components of social life have the same weight in the production and reproduction of society; if there exists a hierarchy of social relations depending upon the function or functions each assumes in this process; if the mental-material relations of humanity with nature and the relations of human beings with each other which serve as support and framework for their material action on nature have more weight than the other elements of social practice in the process of production of society; in short, if there exists what Lévi-Strauss terms 'an incontestable primacy of the infrastructures' — then we must conclude that the part played in history by necessity cannot be reduced to that minimum of unintentional necessity operative in and on every society, but is considerably in excess of it — yet without ever suppressing the existence and importance of chance and contingency in history.

If history is above all the *genesis* of new forms of thought or society and the *passage* from one form of thought or society to another; if, alongside chance encounters and forced transitions, there also exists simultaneous geneses of distinct elements of social practice which correspond to each other because they represent a response to the same thrust coming from the actual interior of the society, rather than one arising and being imposed from the outside; and if in every epoch something like a primacy of infrastructures is operative, then it would seem difficult to argue that history is always no more than an effect of chance, an irreducible contingency. Yet this is what Lévi-Strauss asserts when he writes of the 'Greek miracle' and the transition from mythical thought to philosophy in Ancient Greece that it was simply 'a historical occurrence which means nothing except in so far as it was produced in this place and at this moment', for 'the passage was no more necessary here than there' and if history retains its 'front-row seat, it is the one it occupies by right because of its irreducible contingency.'[6] The idea of the primacy of the infrastructures borrowed from Marx has been shorn of an element indispensable to it, so that it loses what is effectively essential to its scope. I shall return to this point below, but meanwhile let me explain my own understanding of the distinction between infrastructure and superstructures.

This is not an easy question. It has occasioned many a disorder in theory, not to speak of action too. It is worth recalling how but a few years ago a number of disciples of Marx — Althusser at their head — made much ado of this pair of concepts, forcing them into some rigid, even burlesque, dance steps on the floor of a theory which deployed a good deal of philosophical abstraction and for that very reason doubtless intimidated and confused specialists working in more empirical disciplines, even on occasion men of action. Gradually, under the label 'Marx', a model emerged in the social sciences which represented society as a kind of cake composed of superimposed and unequal layers, the hardest of which (the infrastructure) supported the others (the superstructures). The latter became less and less firm as one approached the uppermost level, which comprised all those ideas and ideologies human beings have in their heads that reflect, in a partial and distorted manner, both the inner and the outer realities of their society.

These distortions were not held to derive solely from hazard, error or ignorance. To a great extent they were seen as imposed by the inherent need in every society for a legitimation of the place occupied by each individual in his own eyes within that society — and in the universe at large — such that this individual contributes from his post, be it inferior or superior to that of any other, to the reproduction of prevailing social relations and therewith of the entire social edifice.

In this perspective, the production and distribution of repre-

6. Claude Lévi-Strauss, *From Honey to Ashes*, London 1973, pp. 474-7.

sentations, at once distorted and distorting, of humanity, society and circumambient nature were supposed to establish — immediately and necessarily — between each individual and his or her 'real' infrastructural conditions of existence a whole series of 'imaginary' relations limiting and imprisoning thought and action in advance.

Strictly speaking, nothing in this theory was either new or indeed entirely false. Anyone with even a slight familiarity with history or anthropology, or just some ability to observe daily life, knows that individuals may entertain 'imaginary' relations with their real conditions of existence and thus with themselves and others. Everyone knows too that ideas can serve to legitimize a social order, to win acceptance for relations of domination or oppression between the estates, castes and classes that this order may contain or upon which it may entirely rest. But a 'theory' must also take into account the fact that these 'imaginary' relations are not imaginary for those who believe in them or act upon them, as also the fact that ideas which have traditionally served to legitimize a social order may tomorrow be turned against it and serve to destroy it. So not everything was false in this theory, but became so once confronted with all the different or opposite facts it had left on one side.

For my part, ten years or so before I had chosen to follow a different path. On coming into contact with the work of anthropologists and historians (concerned with Antiquity and the Middle Ages in particular), I found it impossible to adopt the notions of infrastructure and superstructure just as they were. Two facts in particular prompted me to examine the realities which these terms designated more closely, and in each case this examination forced me to pose the same question: what part do ideas and mental constructs play in social relations? What is the role of thought in the production and reproduction of society?[7]

The first of these facts was the realization that no material action of human beings upon nature, by which I mean no action which is intentional and pursued of their own volition, can be executed without setting to work mental realities, represent-

---

7. My first attempt at formulating my thoughts on this theme was an article published in *L'Homme* in 1978 and entitled 'The Mental Part of the Real'. The second part of the present work is an extended and reworked version of this text, together with the chapter mentioned above on the role of thought in the reproduction of social relations.

ations, judgements, principles of thought which can under no circumstances be simply reduced to reflections in thought of material relations originating outside it, prior to and independently of it.

Moreover, these mental realities are not all of one and the same kind. They include, alongside representations of nature and humanity itself, representations of the aims, means, stages and anticipated results of human activities on nature and in society — representations which simultaneously organize a sequence of actions and legitimize the location and status of their agents in society. Such ideas explain who should do what, when, how and why. In short, there is a mental component at the core of our material relations with nature. Three functions of thought mingle there: the representation, organization and legitimation of our relations with each other and with nature.

This is true not only of material activities, but also of all human practices and every social relation (kinship, authority, etc.). For there exists in every social relation a mental part that is both one of the actual conditions for the birth and reproduction of this relation, and at the same time its internal organizational schema, part of its armature, the portion of this relation which exists in thought and therefore belongs to thought.

Having said this, let me immediately anticipate wilful misinterpretations or accusations in bad faith. To assert that every social relation exists both in thought and outside it in no way implies that everything in this relation is reducible or deducible from thought. It is merely to affirm that thought does not exist as an instance separate from social relations, a superstructure in which the other components of social reality are reflected after the event and in deformed fashion — that is, a reality originating outside and independently of thought and upon which it may only react all the less effectively for commencing from distorted representations of the real.

Nevertheless, this does not mean either that everything in thought may be reduced to the social and historical conditions of its exercise, and therefore to its content, or that it may be deduced from them. For our thought is not unaffected by the fact that we have a body, a brain and, thanks to them, the capacity to apprehend and construct relations, relations between relations and so on — in short, that we have the capacity to think. In the exercise of thought there is always something that transcends the historical moment and the material and social conditions of its exercise, something which refers to a reality and history other than that of the thinker, something rooted in the history of nature which is at once anterior and exterior, if also interior to humanity, since it has endowed us with a material organism (the body) and an organ (the brain) that enables us to think. As Lévi-Strauss puts it, behind the structure of the mind there is the structure of the brain. But in that case, why assimilate (as does Lévi-Strauss) mythical thought, which is socially and historically determined through and through (at any rate in so far as it dominates other forms of thought in primitive society, such as those implied by their 'science of the concrete'), to 'savage' thought or thought in the wild state — that is, to the set of functional conditions and principles of thought with which we are all endowed by the effects of a history which is not our own?[8]

Is it not because for Lévi-Strauss human history only truly begins with the emergence of 'hot' societies whose logic and motion rest upon the existence of social contradictions between estates, castes or classes that have nothing in common with the contradictions of the more egalitarian 'cold' societies before the domestication of plants, animals, or indeed thought itself? Yet I cannot see any theoretical reason to consider the forms of life and thought characteristic of hunters, gatherers and fishers as more natural than those of the agriculturalists and stockbreeders who succeeded them, amongst whom developed here and there relations of domination and exploitation which we today call estates, castes and classes.

Thus analysis of the conditions and functions of thought, and of the part played by mental constructions in social reality (much wider than that of consciousness and its representations), led me to look again at the problem of the origin and evolution of relations between estates, castes and classes, and of the birth and development of the State — issues which I consider at the end of chapter 3 and throughout chapter 7. Without seeking to be provocative or paradoxical, I have come to the conclusion that the first class relations[9] and the first forms of the State probably emerged less from the exercise of violence by a minority which imposed them on the rest of society, than from the co-operation

---

8. See Claude Lévi-Strauss, *Totemism*, London, 1964, pp. 90-1.

9. I use the term 'class' here in a generic sense, subsuming relations between estates or between castes (compare the Appendix to chapter 7, which is devoted to the two meanings — generic and specific — of the word 'class' in Marx).

of all, including those who suffered the duress of the new forms of domination and exploitation they brought with them.

Examination of new ethnographic, historical and archaeological materials, chosen for the light they shed on the workings of both classless societies and societies stratified by estate, caste or class, has demonstrated time and time again that of the two forces on which power rests, in either kind of society, the strongest and most effective in guaranteeing the long-term maintenance of that power is not violence in all the forms deployed by the dominant to control the dominated, but consent in all the forms in which the dominated acquiesce in their own domination. Such consent involves a certain co-operation in the reproduction of this domination. Violence certainly suffices to institute new social relations, but it alone will not guarantee their enduring reproduction. Consent is the portion of power added by the dominated to that which the dominant directly exercise over them. In the deepest sense, coercion and consent combine and collude, albeit in different ways, to the same end. They are not mutually exclusive.

What we need to be able to explain, therefore, is how social groups and individuals can in some measure co-operate in the production and reproduction of their own subordination, even exploitation. Unless one is to believe that castes, classes and States arise more or less at random through a fatal combination of the perverse desire of some to enslave and be served and the desire of others — more numerous — to be enslaved and to serve, in a current cut-rate socio-analysis conjuring up a cancerous proliferation of sado-masochistic relations, we must look elsewhere to understand the formation of classes and the State.[10]

I hold to the contrary view that new relations of inequality must have been a response to new problems which pitted society and thought against their own past forms. The response must have seemed advantageous to everyone — especially to those who had to bear the social costs of this development. What must have arisen was not some blind combination of perverse desires but rather a broad community of thought, an extensive sharing of the same representations, for the greatest possible number to contribute in mind and will to the production and reproduction of new divisions in society that would profoundly alter the practices

---

10. I refer here to the theses of Gilles Deleuze and Félix Guattari in *Anti-Oedipus*, New York 1977, and to those of Pierre Clastres in *Society against the State*, Oxford 1977.

of domination. We must therefore seek to use our theoretical imagination to penetrate the black box of those mechanisms which govern the distribution of the same representations among social groups with partially or profoundly opposed interests.

For there to be such shared conceptions, the exercise of power must appear as a *service* rendered by the dominant to the dominated that creates a *debt* of the latter to the former — which can only be discharged by the gift in return of their goods, their labour, their services or even their lives. For new relations of domination and exploitation to emerge and develop with the acquiescence, if not the co-operation, of those subjected to them, a new division of labour and an exclusive specialization of certain social groups in the production of specific services which seem to benefit the community as a whole must come to seem socially necessary and hence legitimate transformations.

I would reckon the most important of these services to be magical and religious practices designed to establish ritual control over a progressively domesticated nature. For the original general dependence of hunter-gatherers on untamed nature gradually gave way to a new sort of dependence, at once more complex and more fragile: people now depended on a particular portion of nature — domesticated plants and animals — which itself depended upon human know-how and intervention, individual or collective, for its own reproduction. Over some millennia a profound transformation in the material, social, affective and intellectual relations of human beings with nature, and with each other, occurred. A new field opened up for the exercise of magical and religious practices upon nature, and upon men and women. Over time, as populations grew and ecosystems changed, regressions to hunting and gathering, to former ways of living and thinking within an untamed nature, became ever more difficult and eventually impossible. The process had become irreversible.

At the same time, new material solidarities might be imposed when a lineage of agriculturalists suffered a bad harvest or pastoralists had their flock decimated by disease. New forms of mutual aid, but also of material and social dependence, unknown in smaller hunter-gatherer societies which relied on resources of the wild available throughout the year, would typically develop — in which it also became possible for some groups to accumulate labour and wealth more rapidly than others. The community's control over local groups and the arbitration between a

general interest and particular interests were bound to be modified in this sequence.

Such transformations of community structures were most
extensive among sedentarized populations, for pastoral and
nomadic populations, like hunter-gatherers, could always use
their mobility to attenuate or even surmount their material and
social contradictions. The drift towards the sedentarization of
human populations did not of course begin with agriculture.
Certain fisher-hunter-gatherer societies would settle on sites
where nature periodically built up exceptional quantities of
resources — say in fish or crustaceans. To take full advantage of
such resources, techniques for hauling large catches in high
season, and conserving the catch for consumption throughout the
year had to be invented. The Indians of the North-West Coast of
America and of Florida knew how to do this. Now it is precisely
among the Kwakiutl of the North-West and the Calusa of Florida
that we find stable social hierarchies with titles, ranks and even
(in the case of the Calusa) 'castes', at whose summit aristocracies
dominated common people whom they termed 'stinking dogs',
and even wielded rights of life or death over slaves.[11]

But we can learn still more from archaeology since it can now
situate in time and locate in space the sites and epochs in which
not only the first class societies but also the first forms of State
developed: Ancient Egypt, Mesopotamia, Mesoamerica, North
India, China. All these spaces, hitherto very sparsely populated
or even uninhabited, could only be put to the service of men and
gods by a considerable material and social effort — one beyond
the powers of the first agrarian or agropastoral societies of the
Neolithic Age. It was in these areas that the first towns
appeared,[12] built like the Neolithic villages around a ceremonial
centre. The gods who resided there were permanently served by
priests, craftsmen, domestics or slaves — in short, a population
which had become sedentary and was henceforth specialized in
intellectual or material tasks to the greater glory of the gods and
the benefit of men. This population in turn was supported by the
labour of the agricultural or agropastoral communities which

11. Compare John M. Goggin and William Sturtevant, 'The Calusa, a Stratified, non-Agricultural Society', in W. Goodenough, ed., *Explorations in Cultural
Anthropology*, New York 1964, pp. 179-220.

12. See the classic work by Robert Adams, *The Evolution of Urban Society. Early
Mesopotamia and Prehistoric Mexico*, London 1966.

either lived in the town or surrounded it, and identified with the reigning god or king. Here too the separation of functions and classes between priests, warriors and those whom we would today call labourers — agriculturalists, herdsmen, craftsmen, merchants — took shape. It was this separation which rendered the State necessary to recombine what had been separated, to reunify what had been divided, and to maintain each order, caste and class in its place within the hierarchy of visible and invisible forms composing the universe.

This is why the origins of the State lie in the world of the sacred, and why those who embody or direct it are either gods living among men, like the Pharaoh or the Inca,[13] or men so close to the gods that like the kings of Sumer they could couple each year with Inanna the Goddess of Love in the depths of her temple, performing with her direct and divine aid a fertility rite which rendered the wombs of women fertile and multiplied harvests and flocks.[14]

Yet the services performed by the sovereign do not wholly pertain to a domain which we would define as imaginary. Thus if we consult the list of sacred duties proper to the Sumerian monarch, we find that his first task was to defend the property of the city, the apanage of the god, to wage war and to protect his people. The second was to create, maintain and extend the system of irrigation canals which brought fertility, prosperity and well-being to the country. His third and last obligation was to establish the rule of justice, to ensure that the poor and weak

---

13. Compare Henri Frankfort, *Kingship and the Gods*, Chicago 1948: 'The ancient Near East considered Kingship the very basis of civilization. Only savages could live without a king. Security, peace and justice could not prevail without a ruler to champion them. If ever a political institution functioned with the assent of the governed, it was the monarchy which built the pyramids with forced labour and drained the Assyrian peasantry by ceaseless wars. But if we refer to Kingship as a political institution, we assume a point of view which would have been incomprehensible to the ancients. We imply that the human policy can be considered by itself. The ancients, however, experienced human life as part of a widely spreading network of connections which reached beyond the local and the national communities into the hidden depths of nature and the powers that rule nature ... Whatever was significant was embedded in the life of the cosmos, and it was precisely the king's function to maintain the harmony of that integration.' (p. 3.)

14. Compare S.N. Kramer, *Le Mariage Sacré*, Paris 1983, and particularly chapter 2, pp. 55-80.

were not oppressed by the rich and powerful.[15] The monarch's powers over the invisible world were therefore supposed to prove their worth in the visible world of his people's daily existence. It is this fusion of services, some of which appear to us today to be purely imaginary and others perfectly real, which above all explains the consent of the members of the community to the exercise of royal power and dominion.[16]

Here we see how profoundly the domestication of plants and animals and the development of new arts and trades in the end transformed the typical relations between societies of pre-Neolithic hunter-gatherers and nature. If we take, with all due caution, the Australian Aborigines as an example of how these long-vanished societies once functioned, we observe that in their societies too, just as in caste or class societies, not everyone has the same kind of access to the invisible powers which control the reproduction of untamed nature and of men and women; certain segments or clans have the task of acting on the Sun, others on the Moon, and still others on the Python that is master of the rain, and so on.[17] But all must play their part and co-operate to reproduce the order of the world. Likewise, when initiation ceremonies or fertility rites are held, everyone hunts, gathers and fishes, not for themselves but in order to reproduce the community as such, to communicate with the forces of the universe which sustain its existence. This additional material 'labour' is proffered by all in the service of all.

In societies divided into estates, castes or classes, functions are separated and access to the gods tends to be reserved to a few. Additional labour by all for all becomes the labour of almost all on behalf of those who henceforth incarnate the general interests of the community. The way is then open for the power consequent upon the function to become a power to exploit, and for the additional labour proffered in the service of all to become surplus labour.

It was in such contexts that law, mathematics and astronomy emerged and here and there philosophy replaced theology and

---

15. S.N. Kramer, p. 29.

16. Compare Henri Frankfort 1948: 'The power of the King over his subjects did not cease with death, and we must remember that this power was experienced not as a tyranny reluctantly endured but as a relationship which established for each subject his function and place in the world.' (p. 53.)

17. Compare C.G. von Brandenstein, 'The Meaning of Section and Section Names', *Oceania*, XVI (1), September 1970, pp. 39-49.

mythology.[18] It is hard to believe (as Lévi-Strauss asserts of the Greek world) that passage was 'no more necessary in this case than in any other'. By this he certainly cannot mean that all in the internal structure of a society is contingent, since for him within each structure that constitutes — along with other structures — a concrete society a strict determinism rules: that of the conditions of the operation of the structure itself. Furthermore, for Lévi-Strauss there obtain relations of correspondence and compatibility between any given structure and the others, without any internal necessity presiding over their coexistence within the same society — a coexistence which at most might rest on unverifiable relations of probability.

In Lévi-Strauss's work history seems to serve above all as a pretext or occasion for the play of the savage or tamed mind, by providing these with contradictory situations and 'structures of contradiction' to think.[19] Although I am in agreement with him on the second point, I cannot follow him on the first. For where outside the substance and wealth of contradictions, outside the contradictory situations and structures which human beings generate by acting upon nature and themselves, can we find the reasons why societies become divided and thought becomes opposed to itself — in short, why history consists more of necessity than chance?

Let us now return to the starting-point of our analysis — the need to reconsider the distinction between infrastructure and superstructures because of the active presence of thought at the very heart of our material activities. Social relations are not things. They do not exist without human intervention and action producing and reproducing them each day — which does not mean that they are always reproduced in a form identical to that of yesterday or the day before yesterday. All relations are realities in flux and motion, and in this movement they are daily deformed, altered or eroded to a greater or lesser degree, vanishing or metamorphosing to rhythms that may be imperceptible or brutal, according to the kind of society to which they belong. But since thought is not an instance separate from social relations, since a society has neither top nor bottom, since it does not consist of superimposed layers, we are forced to conclude that if

---

18. Compare the early work by H. Frankfort, J. Wilson and Th. Jacobsen, *Before Philosophy*, London 1949.

19. Claude Lévi-Strauss, *The Savage Mind*, p. 95.

the distinction between infrastructure and superstructures is to retain any meaning at all, it cannot be taken as a distinction between levels or instances, any more than between institutions. It was this conviction which served as the second starting-point for my reflections on the notion of infrastructure.

I shall not linger over this point. But we should note the important conclusions reached both by anthropologists and certain historians of Antiquity concerning the sites and forms of the economy in Ancient or non-Western societies. Whatever their ideology, most economists have a profoundly ethnocentric view of the economic. Their spontaneous impulse is to look in every society for 'economic' institutions and relations separate and distinct from other social relations, comparable to those of Western capitalist society, where the production and the exchange of goods take place in sites and institutions which serve as a support for the working of kinship relations, religious practices and political forms (family, Church, State). Karl Polanyi must take the credit for having shown that the economic does not always occupy the same sites and social relations throughout history, and that it changes its forms according to whether or not it is 'embedded' in the operation of kin or politico-religious relations. Whilst I think Polanyi's theory needs certain qualifications,[20] the debates it has provoked enable us to re-examine the notion of 'social relations of production' which for Marx define 'the economic structure', the foundations (*Grundlage*) upon which is raised the edifice (*Überbau*) of each society. I therefore propose to isolate relations of production from the totality of our material and mental relations with nature. As a first step, it is necessary to define relations of production in abstraction from any reference to particular societies. It then becomes clear that relations of production discharge one or all of the following three functions: determination of the social forms of access to resources and control of the conditions of production; organization of labour processes and allocation of members of society to them; determination of the social forms of circulation and redistribution of

---

20. See chapter 5, below. It was in 1962 that I became aware of Polanyi's work owing to a polemic then raging amongst anthropologists between the partisans and adversaries of substantive and formal definitions of the economy. Claude Meillassoux came under Polanyi's influence earlier, whilst in the United States. It was considerably later that Polanyi's work was debated in France, by a number of historians and anthropologists in *Annales. ESC*, November-December 1974.

the products of individual or collective labour. It is then possible to show that in certain societies kinship relations (the Australian Aborigines) or political relations (fifth-century Athens) or politico-religious relations (Ancient Egypt) also functioned as relations of production. This conclusion, which accords with Polanyi's theses, had never been seriously envisaged by Marxist anthropologists or historians. At the theoretical level it could be summarized as follows: the distinction between relations of production (the infrastructure minus the productive forces) and other social relations (the superstructures) is a distinction between functions and not, save in exceptional cases, a distinction between institutions. But the exceptional case exists: it may be found in our own socio-economic system. Moreover, it was this exception which made it possible in the nineteenth century to perceive the importance of material activities and 'economic' relations in the movement of societal production and reproduction more clearly — and so to cast new light upon the whole history (past and future) of humanity.

This analysis of social relations of production — their sites, forms and effects — allows one to reformulate the problem of what is called the 'domination' of such-and-such an institution (superstructure) over the global operation of a society. Among other things, it has led me to oppose Louis Dumont's positions in this regard,[21] for I believe that more than religion itself was required for religion to dominate the social life and mould the social hierarchies of ancient India, with its kingdoms and caste system.

For while in every society there exist social relations which organize the workings of kinship, the mechanisms of authority and of power, and the channels of communication with gods and ancestors, yet kin, political or religious relations are not dominant in every society. Why then should one set of relations be dominant in one place and a different set in another? I believe I have shown below that a set of social relations dominates when they function simultaneously as social relations *of production*, as the social framework and support for the material process of appropriation of nature.

It is in this perspective that I have engaged in a critical but non-polemical dialogue with Edouard Will[22] — to show that

---

21. See chapter 3.
22. See chapter 6.

some light can be thrown on the historical data he has so intelligently reconstituted for us, by bringing out both the existence of an original economic system peculiar to fifth-century Athens and a few other commercial cities and the reasons for the domination in them of what we somewhat ethnocentrically perceive today as 'political' relations. I hope that the relevant specialists will forgive my temerity here, which must expose me to their criticisms. But such are the rules of the game, and I accept them.

Should it turn out that social relations which simultaneously assume other functions dominate the reproduction of a society *because* they function as relations of *production*, the first steps would have been taken towards proving Marx's hypothesis that different social relations have an unequal weight in the generation of society, according to the nature of the functions they assume within this process: or, more precisely, that the social relations which serve as a framework for the material appropriation of nature and thus for the production of the material conditions of existence play a determinant role in the last instance in the formation of society.

But we then encounter a formidable question which was never posed by Polanyi himself: for what reasons and in what conditions do kinship relations or political relations assume the functions of social relations of production? Why and how do social relations of production change both site and form in the course of history? How far do these topological and morphological changes modify their impact upon the operation and motion of societies? If we were to pursue Marx's hypothesis to its logical conclusion, we would have to be able to demonstrate that relations of production are connected with historical transformations in the material and intellectual capacities of human beings to act upon the nature which surrounds them. We have seen that this hypothesis, when considered from a fairly lofty perspective, seemed valid for an analysis of the historical transformations wrought by the advent of the domestication of plants and animals. But looked at more closely, things are not so simple and the hypothesis has yet to be proven.

If, for example, kinship relations function as relations of production in numerous societies whose material existence depends upon either hunting, agriculture or stockbreeding, can this range of material bases actually explain the diversity of kinship relations which prevail in them? The truth is that one cannot and probably should not attempt such a correlation, because the main function of kinship relations is to reproduce human beings *socially* by acting upon them, and not to produce their material conditions of existence by acting upon nature. This issue therefore remains an open one which involves our interpretations of kinship as much as of economic structures.

Here I rejoin Claude Lévi-Strauss, although taking my distance from him on one essential point. For when he examines the effects of the infrastructures of a society on its thought,[23] whether of the Murngin of Australia or the Salish, Chilcotin and Bella Bella Indians of the North-West Coast of North America, what is missing from his inventory of the infrastructure is any reference to social relations of production. In his remarkable analyses, Lévi-Strauss explores three components of the infrastructure: the material, ecological and technological conditions of social existence; the various forms of knowledge of nature (the mental dimension of productive forces); and the number of human beings (demography). Relations of production are conspicuous by their absence.[24]

There is a sense in which the concept is missing because kinship relations assume their function in the societies with whose thought Lévi-Strauss is concerned, and he deals with them elsewhere and in another way. But he is then treating kinship in terms of its principal function, separating this from its other — economic and political — functions. An ethnocentric vision of the economy is thereby perpetuated, which does not preclude a valid structural analysis of kinship or mythology, but limits its scope and in some measure arrests its progress.

I hope the reader will not misinterpret my debate with Lévi-Strauss. We owe to him the development and application of the structural method to the analysis of social facts as complex and important as kinship relations, types of thought and forms of art. In these vast domains, rife with pseudo-theories, Lévi-Strauss's findings earn all my admiration. In this volume I have adopted

---

23. See Claude Lévi-Strauss, *The View from Afar*, Oxford 1985, chapter 7, 'Structuralism and Ecology', pp. 101-20.

24. In *The Savage Mind*, p. 130, Lévi-Strauss declares that 'The development of the study of infrastructurs proper is a task which must be left to history — with the aid of demography, technology, historical geography and ethnography'. With regard to the effect of the infrastructure on the mythology of the Murngin, he writes: 'The primacy of the infrastructure is thus in a sense confirmed, for the geography and climate, together with their repercussions on the biological plane, present native thought with a contradictory state of affairs.' (pp. 93-4.)

the structural method for an exploration of domains untouched by him. I think it is a mistake to argue that it is the structural method as such which is Lévi-Strauss's stumbling-block:[25] it is rather he himself, and not his method, which has stopped his thought short before '[certain] major phenomena which have no place in this programme'.[26] But this stoppage has had effects which Lévi-Strauss himself has emphasized: '... since my aim here is to outline a theory of superstructures, reasons of method require that they should be singled out for attention and that major phenomena which have no place in this programme should seem to be left in brackets or given second place.'[27] One therefore cannot reproach him, as too many critics have frivolously done, for having chosen his own particular field in the current intellectual division of labour in the human sciences.

Finally, I wish to extend my thanks to Marie-Élisabeth Handman. Whatever clarity there is in this book, whatever proportions there is in its construction, is largely owing to her. A little over half the present work had already been published in various places in the form of articles; the rest was still in manuscript, its thought still groping and its style that of a rough draft. All the texts have been rewritten and, with the exception of chapter 2 on the appropriation of nature, all have been reworked and restructured in the light of my present concerns. As for the unpublished texts, they had to be given an appropriate form, shortened, polished and modified. At every stage in this work, Marie-Élisabeth Handman showed unstinting generosity in posing questions which forced me to clarify the substance of my argument, and a merciless rigour in urging me to prune and concentrate a form which we both wished to be as limpid as possible. That form has declined to reply on a public essentially composed of a handful of professional accomplices. Its difficult aim has been to deliver up a body of thought in its entirety to be shared. Let me here express my thanks to her.

Maurice Godelier
Paris
13 February 1984

---

25. See Henri Lefebvre, *L'Idéologie Structuraliste*, Paris 1971, especially 'Claude Lévi-Strauss et le nouvel éléatisme', pp. 45-110.
26. *The Savage Mind*, p. 117.
27. *Ibid.*

Part One
The Material and Social
Appropriation of Nature

1

Ecosystems and Social Systems

Since the beginning of the 1970s, the world economy has been in a state of massive, flagrant and undisguised crisis. It no longer goes without saying that the economic development of some can promote the development of others, nor even that it will maintain their standard of living. Furthermore, it has become increasingly evident that an economic rationality founded exclusively on the principle of short-term profits gives rise to gigantic wastage of the planet's resources and is accompanied by growing pollution of the environment which it is ever more urgent to combat and reduce. Wastage, pollution, inflation and austerity have become the distinguishing features of a global situation which, over the last ten years, has seen inequalities become still more extreme and the gulf between the industrial, developed countries and the others grow wider and wider.

It is therefore more necessary than ever to analyse the conditions of reproduction and non-reproduction of the economic and social systems which coexist on our planet's surface and which, one and all, are subject to the domination of either the capitalist or the 'socialist' system. This I shall endeavour to do, relying on the data gathered by anthropologists who have studied societies which have been more and more dislocated, disrupted sometimes to the point of annihilation, by the expansion of industrial societies.

Before proceeding, a few points must be clarified. The reader will recall my point that the natural environment is never either a

27

variable completely independent of man or a constant factor. Rather, it is a reality which humanity transforms to a greater or lesser extent by its various ways of acting upon nature and appropriating its resources. Nevertheless an ecosystem is invariably a totality which is only reproduced within certain limits and which imposes on humanity several series of specific material constraints.

Next, it is crucial to bear in mind that the main obstacle encountered by the theoretical thinking of economists and sociologists has been — and still is — the ethnocentrism implicit in their conception of the relations between economy and society. Their ruling conception is inspired by Talcott Parsons' model, in which society is seen as a global system articulating economic, political, religious, etc. sub-systems with specialized functions. This theoretical representation more or less corresponds to the structure of industrial and market capitalist societies, wherein the economy appears as an autonomous or quasi-autonomous subsystem with its own laws of operation, while the other levels of society appear to be 'exogenous' variables which intervene from outside in the reproduction of the economic conditions of social existence. But such a conception of the economy impedes recognition of the logics peculiar to non-capitalist societies.

In fact, the economy does not occupy the same place in these societies, and consequently does not assume the same forms and experience the same type of development. At this point we can appreciate the fundamental contribution made by historians and anthropologists. Indeed, the results of their enquiries demonstrate that in certain types of society kinship relations can function from the inside as social relations of production, whilst in others, conversely, politics plays this role, and in yet others it can be played by religion. By 'function as social relations of production' I mean: assume the functions of determining access to and control over the means of production and the social product for the groups and individuals comprising a particular type of society, and organizing the process of production as well as the process of distribution of products. In the second part of this work I shall give a number of examples to substantiate this assertion. For the time being, let me simply state that so far, theoreticians of the economy have hardly concerned themselves with discovering the reasons and conditions responsible in history for displacement of the site of the function of production relations in various human societies and, along with such changes in site, for metamorphosis in their forms and effects. A theory accounting for these reasons and conditions, which must largely depend on the results of studies by anthropologists, historians and sociologists, still remains to be constructed.

Hierarchy of Functions or Hierarchy of Institutions?

I have just stressed the importance of criticizing and eliminating the empirical and ethnocentric prejudices which, though merely implicit, are still operative in the contemporary social sciences. I am referring to the spontaneous tendency to conduct analysis of the functioning and evolutionary conditions of non-capitalist social systems according to a view and definition of the site and forms of the economy which corresponds to the situation in industrial capitalist societies, whose wealth depends upon the production and sale of commodities. Yet historians and anthropologists who seek precisely to demonstrate the specific character and original rationality of the societies they study run a different risk — namely, confusing hierarchy of functions with hierarchy of institutions. On realizing that in a given society kinship, politics or religion play an apparently dominant role, they conclude that the economy has only a secondary role in its functioning and evolution. However, when kinship functions as a relation of production, it is not kinship such as it exists in capitalist society; the same applies to religion and politics. One could therefore advance a quite contrary hypothesis and suggest that kinship, religion or politics only dominate if they function simultaneously as relations of production, as 'infrastructure'.

This returns us to Marx's central hypothesis: the determinant role played by economic structures for understanding the functional and evolutionary logic of different types of society. But the manner in which I shall refashion this hypothesis means that we are no longer prevented from recognizing and explaining the dominant role played in a particular society by what seem to be kinship relations, political structure or religious organization. To my mind, only this kind of approach enables us to overcome the complementary and opposed difficulties encountered, on the one hand, by 'reductionist economic theories which, like vulgar materialism, reduce all non-economic structures to mere epiphenomena of societies' material infrastructure, and on the other hand by the various empiricist sociological theories which discern in the diverse aspects of a society's functioning only the consequences of religion or politics or kinship, depending upon the form of social practice dominant there. In fact, the distinction between infrastructure and superstructure is nothing but a distinction within a hierarchy of functions and 'structural' causalities[1] which guarantee the conditions of the society's reproduction as such. In no sense does it prejudge either the nature of the social relations which in each case assume responsibility for these functions (kinship, politics, religion, etc.), or the number of functions for which these social relations may serve as supports. A dynamic and global conception of the conditions of reproduction of different types of society therefore involves discovering the hierarchy of constraints and functions which enable this reproduction to take place. Each level of social organization has specific effects on the functioning and reproduction of the whole of society and, in consequence, upon the relations of humanity with nature. As we shall see below, it is only for considering the interplay of all the levels of functioning of an economic and social system that one can uncover the logic of the different modes of representation and perception of the environment encountered in different types of society.

For the individuals and the groups belonging to a given society, these modes of representation constitute a system of 'information' about the properties of their social relations and their relations with the environment. Now, as the theoretical notions I have just expounded — regarding the diversity of sites the social relations of production may occupy, which in turn entails a diversity in their forms and modes of representation, on the one hand, and on the other the determinant role played by the relations of production in our understanding of social evolution — also enable us to analyse the problem of the diverse 'capacities for information' about the properties of their social system offered to the individuals by the (always specific) content of the production relations.

It is only by taking stock of what I shall call the transparency and opacity of the properties of social systems that one can understand the conduct of individuals and groups within these

---

1. By 'structure' I mean the framework and the logic governing the functioning of a social relation. By 'structural causality' I mean the series of effects produced by this structure both upon its internal components and upon the structure of social relations which are connected to it.

systems and account for the forms and measure the efficacy of their interventions in their particular systems.

This poses the problem of the role of human beings' conscious action upon the evolution of their social systems, the problem of the relation between the rational intentionality of individuals' behaviour and the unintentional rationality of the appearance and disappearance of these systems — in fact, of the movement of history.

Information and Social Systems

When scientific analysis has managed to distinguish the particular characteristics of human beings' relations with each other and with nature which establish the specificity of a society, it is necessary to ask what information concerning the properties of these relations — through their representations, ideologies and culture — the individuals and groups comprising the society have at their disposal.

How are these properties discovered, if indeed they are? In what forms are they then represented and thought? What in the functioning of a social relation, etc. remains opaque and never becomes conscious? It is crucial that all these domains be explored by the human sciences, but as yet, unfortunately, the latter have not penetrated very far. I shall do no more here than present a number of relevant ethnographic examples.

For my first example, I shall consider the representations which members of Inca society prior to the Spanish conquest made of the role and nature of the Great Inca, son of the Sun. For them, the Inca controlled the conditions of reproduction of both nature and society. Because he was son of the Sun, he could vouchsafe prosperity by guaranteeing the fertility of both the fields and of women. We should consider the type of information about the functioning of their social relations available to the members of Inca society in terms of these social representations, for it was from this standpoint that they consciously acted upon their system. The forms of conscious regulation of the economy and the relation with nature in various types of society therefore cannot be understood without constructing a theory of the transparency and opacity these relations assume in the consciousness of their members.

We thus find ourselves faced both with the problems of the perception of the natural and social environment and with that of the motivations and forms of individual and group action in the various types of society.

Both series of problems require some examination of what we mean by the 'ideology' of a society — that is, of the members. I hold that we should distinguish between at least two types and two forms of ideology which also have quite distinct consequences. On the one hand, it is generally supposed that an ideology appears as the surface of social relations, as a set of more or less adequate representations of such relations in social consciousness. For instance, people speak of the ideology of the working class in nineteenth-century England, and study the effects up on this class's representations of the accelerated process of industrialization and urbanization.

In the case of the Incas, on the other hand, religion does not merely constitute the surface of, but is in some way internal to, economic and political relations, — part of their internal armature. Indeed, belief in the supernatural efficacy of the Inca — common to the dominated peasantry and the dominant class alike — was one of the main sources of the dependence which, in the case of the peasants, informed their relation with the Inca and the State. Once each individual or local community thought it owed its existence to the supernatural power of the Inca, they felt obliged to supply him with labour and produce, to glorify him and repay part of what he had done (in a manner which is predominantly symbolic and imaginary for us) to ensure the reproduction and prosperity of all. In this example, religious ideology not only constitutes the surface of things, but their interior too. Indeed, the dependence recognized by the Indian peasants vis-à-vis the Inca at once founded and legitimized the unequal access of both parties to the means of production and social wealth. Religion thus functioned on the inside as an element of the production relations determining the type of information available to the members of society for acting upon the conditions of their system's reproduction. In turn, the type of information determined the real import of the actions undertaken by groups or individuals to maintain or transform their social system. Thus, when faced with a crisis situation threatening the actual reproduction of their society (severe drought or civil war, for example), the Indians of the Inca Empire necessarily responded by intensifying their religious sacrifices. A huge number of fabrics, precious or ordinary, were burnt on the *huacas*, the sacred residences of the ancestors and gods; llamas were sacrificed, and maize beer was sprinkled everywhere. Since the general form of their social relations involved the dominance of political and religious institutions, the Incas' response to these exceptional circumstances largely consisted in a very extensive effort, at once material and mental, to consume both the material resources and the time the society had at its disposal. Sooner or later, however, the constraints weighing upon the society had to be yielded to, clearing a way, more or less easily and rapidly, through all the initiatives taken by the individuals and groups of which the society was composed.

I shall give another example of a society's 'phantasmic' response to a contradictory situation threatening its reproduction. In the middle of the nineteenth century, following the Whites' systematic destruction of the herds of bison which were the main resource of the tribes of mounted hunters in North America, there appeared a Sun Cult which gradually spread to all the tribes on the Prairie. They placed in the gods their hopes of seeing the bison 'darken the plains again' — but to no avail.

The cargo cults which developed in Melanesia after the arrival of the Whites provide another instance of this same phenomenon. In many regions the tribes spontaneously built landing-strips to incite their ancestors to bring the wealth the Whites had stolen from them. There have been other cases, as in the Solomon Islands, where tribes of fishers have been known to build boats which did not float to set off in search of the wealth and the powers the Whites had seized.

In these three examples, the meaning of the situations and contradictions confronted by each society manifests itself as a specific relation of transparency and opacity. It is therefore readily apparent that one condition for the further progress of the social sciences is the development of a coherent theory both of the diverse forms economic relations assume and of the capacities for transmitting information these forms imply.

The Problem of Social Perception of the Natural Environment

We need to analyse a little more closely the systems of representation which individuals and groups, as members of a given society, make of their own environment, since it is on the basis of these representations that they act upon this environment.

A particularly revealing example is provided by the contrasting representations made of the same environment by the Mbuti

Pygmies, hunter-gatherers, and the Bantu, slash-and-burn agriculturists. These two groups live in the Equatorial African forest of the Congo. According to the typology of natural eco-systems developed by David Harris, this forest is an example of a 'generalized' ecosystem, i.e. one characterized by the presence of many species each of which is represented by a small number of individuals. These ecosystems are opposed to the so-called 'specialized' ecosystems where a small number of species coexist, each being represented by a very large number of individuals, as was the case with the savannas of North America when the bison was the dominant animal species.

For the Pygmies, the forest represents a friendly, hospitable and benevolent reality. They feel wholly secure there. They contrast the forest with the spaces cleared by the Bantu, which appear to them to be a hostile world where the heat is over-whelming, the water polluted and deadly, and illnesses are numerous. For the Bantu, on the other hand, the forest is a hostile, inhospitable and deadly reality into whose depths they venture only rarely and always at great risk. They see it as being peopled by demons and maleficent spirits, with the Pygmies, if not the incarnation of such spirits, at least their representatives. This contrast primarily corresponds to two ways of using the forest based upon different economic and technical systems. For the Pygmies, who are hunter-gatherers, the forest holds no secrets. They easily and rapidly find their bearings there. Even if they shift their camp from month to month, it is always within the same territory. Each band live in a stable relation to the forest, which harbours in its depths all the animal and vegetable species they exploit in order to survive — especially antelopes and a wide variety of vegetables. In the forest they are protected from the sun and the springs are abundant and pure (unlike the wells sunk in the middle of the Bantu villages). Furthermore, for them the forest is not merely a collection of vegetable species, animals and human beings (the Mbuti themselves), but also a supernatural, ubiquitous, omniscient and omnipotent reality upon which the maintenance of their life depends. For this reason, they perceive the game they catch and the produce they gather as so many *gifts* lavished upon them by the Forest, to which they therefore owe all the love and recognition expressed in their rituals.

Conversely, for the Bantu agriculturists the forest is an obsta-cle which must be cleared with axes if manioc and maize are to be cultivated. This is an arduous form of work, ever liable to be frustrated by the very exuberance of the vegetation which is always encroaching upon the gardens. Moreover, once cleared the soil rapidly loses its fertility. They therefore have to move, to seek out another territory where the processes of production can be reviewed. Consequently, the Bantu find themselves condemned to confront not only the virgin forest yet again, but also other Bantu groups which, being subject to the same constraints, have identical requirements. A Bantu agriculturist does not know the forest well and rarely ventures into its depths for fear of getting lost and dying there. If all these practical reasons are borne in mind, it is easier to understand why for the Bantu the forest remains a terrifying reality peopled by hostile spirits or supernatural beings.

On the basis of this contrast between two distinct ways of perceiving and representing the environment, we can venture several observations of a theoretical nature. In the last analysis, this contrast is based on the existence of two technical and economic systems which depend for their functioning on opposite sorts of constraints, and have distinct effects upon nature. The Mbuti impose a levy upon the natural resources and do not effect a major transformation of nature; whereas the Bantu agriculturists are obliged, before planting their tubers and domesticated cereals, to transform nature by creating an artificial ecosystem (fields, gardens) which can only be maintained in effective operation through a considerable investment of human energy.

This example serves to demonstrate that the social perception of an environment consists not only of more or less exact representations of the constraints upon the functioning of technical and economic systems, but also of value judgements (positive, negative or neutral) and phantasmic beliefs. An environment always has imaginary aspects, for it is the place where the dead exist, the house of supernatural powers (be they benevolent or malevolent) believed to control the conditions of reproduction of nature and society. Such representations render meaningful forms of behaviour and active intervention in nature that may well appear totally irrational to a Western observer. Livestock is not simply meat, milk or leather, and trees are not just wood or fruit. Every programme of economic development which fails to take into account the real content of the traditional representations a society makes of its own environment and resources is bound to suffer very serious setbacks. Numerous failures encountered in the so-called underdeveloped countries witness to this.

Analysis of diverse societies, multiple forms of representation of the environment must therefore be regarded as an operational necessity in the implementation of a programme of material and social intervention in nature, and may well be a crucial factor in ensuring its success. This research is urgent and should be conducted as much by anthropologists as by agronomists, technology experts, geographers and ecologists, and indeed, where archives exist, with the aid of historians as well. Such work presents considerable difficulties whose complexity may be appreciated if we return to the example of the Pygmies and the forms of their perception of the environment.

According to Colin Turnbull, the representation of the forest as benevolent and lavish is common to all the Mbuti Pygmies. But each year, with the arrival of the honey-gathering season, there emerges a kind of contrast between the representations entertained by the members of the bands which hunt with nets and those of the bands of archers. For the hunters who use nets and who cooperate the whole year round, practising a form of collective hunt, this season entails the division of the band into several sub-bands which harvest the honey in different parts of the territory. The gathering of the honey is a task for men, because most of the hives are in trees and climbing trees is a strictly masculine activity.

For those who hunt with nets, this season is regarded as one of abundance in honey and game alike. For those who hunt with bows, in contrast, it is regarded as a difficult season. How is one to account for the fact that the environment may be perceived as lavish in game or as miserly when, from the viewpoint of a foreign observer, there is no significiant variation in the quantity of game available? The explanation advanced by Colin Turnbull has important implications but in order to understand it, we must return to the differences in economic and social organization between bow-hunters and net-hunters.

The latter live in bands of from forty to two hundred individuals of both sexes for ten months of the year. A certain number of problems and contradictions between the individuals and families comprising the bands accrue from this prolonged cooperation. Consequently, owing to the splitting-up which occurs, the honey-gathering period allows conflicts to be assuaged and resolved by the imposition of distance between the opposed individuals. Thus it is that at the end of this separation period, the sub-groups are ready to resume their communal life and reconstitute the band. This is what the Mbuti call a 'good' separation because it does not endanger the reproduction of the band as such.

The members of a band of bow-hunters, on the other hand, live a separated and isolated existence for ten months in small groups of three or four families. The men use ambushes to hunt their prey but although there is intense cooperation between these hunters, cooperative forms involving the collective effort of the whole band such as we find in the case of the net-hunters are non-existent. In the course of the year the difficulties and social problems created by the prolonged separation of the different sub-groups comprising a given band accumulate. The honey-gathering period provides an occasion for reassembling the whole band. It then organizes a collective bow hunt, called a *begbé*, whose form reproduces the net hunt of the other bands. The bow-hunters arrange themselves in a semi-circle, some distance from each other, and, like their counterparts among the net-hunters, the women beat the game towards them. Technical reasons alone hardly explain this modification in the form of the bow hunt. In fact, a hunt of the *begbé* type is not simply a material activity concerned with production, but also a symbolic activity, a 'labour' upon the group's social contradictions whose aim is to restore the band's unity and reproduce the social conditions which enable it to function.

The reader will now appreciate the difficulties encountered in analysing in depth systems of environmental representation. In order to resolve them, all the levels of the society being studied must be taken into account; the specific constraints operative at each of these levels, together with their effects upon the articulation of the whole, must be discovered. It is only by grasping the contrasting effects of these constraints that one can essay an interpretation of the fact that they affect their environment positively and negatively at the time of the honey season — which in a way contradicts another fact, namely, that in general both are imbued with the characteristics of the milieu within which they exist to a remarkable degree.

This example has again confronted us with what has been termed a relation of transparency and opacity in the properties of a social system. We are better able to guess at the real efficacy of the Mbutis' interventions in their social system and natural environment. Their institutions and ideology appear to be responses adapted to a set of specific constraints; but one would guess that their possibilities of adapting to certain variations in these constraints are limited. The existence of such limits already enables us to intuit that it is pointless conceiving of adaptation as a process without contradictions, and that we should, on the contrary, conceive both it and failure to adapt as two aspects of one and the same dynamic reality, arising from its own contradictions.

The Problem of the Limits of Societies' Adaptation to their Environment and the Notion of 'Economic Rationality'

Over the last twenty years, anthropology has turned to a detailed study of the various social forms of adaptation to specific ecosystems. A new theoretical current has been created which is opposed to traditional Anglo-Saxon cultural anthropology and has chosen to call itself cultural ecology or human ecology. Taking the much older works of Leslie White and above all of Julian Steward as their starting point, numerous anthropologists have stressed the necessity and urgency of a careful study of societies' 'material' bases and a reinterpretation of all human cultures which conceives them as specific processes of adaptation to determinate environments.

On the methodological level, these anthropologists, while reasserting that each society should be analyzed as a totality, also hold that it should be regarded as a sub-system of a more extensive totality — a particular ecosystem wherein human, animal and vegetable populations coexist in a system of biological and energy-source interrelations. In order to analyze the conditions underlying the functioning and reproduction of such ecosystems, and in order to reconstitute the structures of energy flows, the mechanisms of self-regulation, feedback, etc., they appeal to systems theory and communication theory. The approach, methods and theoretical possibilities of traditional functionalism have thus been given a new direction. We were now much better placed to consider the problem of comparing social systems — a problem which traditional functionalists either refused to face or faced with difficulty. In addition, there arose the problem of a new evolutionary schema for societies — one which was multilinear in contrast to most of those current in the nineteenth-century.

I will give a brief summary here of some aspects of the positive discoveries that were rapidly made. For example, it became apparent that the adult members of Bushman hunter-gatherer bands in the Kalahari desert only needed to work approximately four hours a day to collect or produce the resources required to satisfy the socially-recognized needs of all members of the bands (including a large number of old people and young children who did not participate in the production process). These facts quickly demolished the notion of primitive hunters as people living on the edge of scarcity without the leisure to progress towards civilization. Turning the old ideas on their head, Marshall Sahlins even went so far as to proclaim that these hunter-gatherer societies were the only real 'societies of abundance', since their social needs were wholly satisfied and hence the means to satisfy them were not scarce. I shall return to this extreme conclusion for it requires some modification and criticism.

I shall now analyse a little more closely the results of the works of Richard Lee and his team on the !Kung Bushmen. These populations, which live in a specialized semi-arid ecosystem with very strict constraints, do not exploit all the resources of food potentially at their disposal. The Bushmen have identified and named 220 animal species (mammals, birds, insects, etc.), of which 54 are regarded as edible but only 10 are hunted on a regular basis. They have also identified and named 200 vegetable species, of which only 80 are considered edible. Amongst all these resources, the fruit of the *mongongo* tree (*Ricinodendron rautanei* Schinz, Euphorbia) constitutes a practically inexhaustible supply of food.

Why are the Bushmen so selective in their eating habits? Those who have attempted to isolate their criteria have observed that they involve a combination of four different elements ranked in descending order of importance: taste, recognized nutritional value, abundance and, finally, the ease with which a particular food can be procured. On the basis of this scale of preferences and other constraints, such as the absence of storage procedures, researchers have been able to understand how the Bushmen utilize their environment. They practise a strategy whose principle can be formulated as follows: at all seasons the members of a camp seek to gather and hunt their favoured foods in locations as close as possible to the water hole where they have pitched camp. This sheds new light on the Bushmen's movement from camp to camp and their use of the environment: in general they remain in the same place for as long as they need undertake no more than a day's march to go hunting and gathering and to transport the water they require whilst engaged in these activities. The crucial element in this strategy is therefore the increase in the labour-cost needed for completing the outward and return journeys between the camp and the zones where the natural resources are.

But this general principle is modified as dry seasons alternate with wet ones. Between November and April, the waterholes are numerous, the food abundant, the distance between water and food minimal; between May and July — the beginning of the dry season — food is still plentiful but life is centred upon eight permanent waterholes; between August and October, resources around the eight permanent waterholes become more and more scarce and the distance between water and food is therefore at its greatest.

One of the first lessons we can draw from the example of the Bushmen is that so-called primitive man does not continually live at the limits of his system's possibilities on the brink of famine or catastrophe. The Bushmen under-exploit the alimentary potential of their environment. This is also true of the Mbuti Pygmies. They do not catch the fish with which their rivers are teeming. They kill neither chimpanzees nor birds. They rarely kill wild buffalo, because they do not like their flesh. Numerous ecological corners of their environment are thus left unexploited.

But amongst the Bushmen, as amongst the Australian Aborigines and other populations living in semi-desert areas, there is one overriding constraint, i.e. procuring a regular supply of water. Whilst animal and vegetable food is often more plentiful than is necessary, water remains scarce, since there is no means of sinking wells to reach the water-table or of constructing dams to retain the surface water. I am therefore loth to describe societies of this sort as 'societies of abundance', as does Marshall Sahlins. For the technological impossibility of circumventing the water constraint dictates nomadism, limits the size of the social groups gathered around the waterholes, and thereby determines many aspects of their social life. We can see from this that the strategic aspect of the relation between man and environment involves both the level of technique and that of the structure of the social organization of production.[2]

The example of the Bushmen enables us to bring out another

2. I shall develop this theme at greater length in chapter 3, 'The Mental Part of the Real'.

fact of theoretical significance, since it points to the existence of multiple forms of 'economic rationality'. Indeed, we have just seen how the Bushmen not only have a very complex representation of the exploitable resources in their environment, but in order to exploit them implement a strategy which aims to satisfy their hierarchy of preferences at the lowest cost in labour.

These facts serve to refute the thesis of Karl Polanyi and George Dalton according to which optimization strategies only have meaning and are only possible in capitalist market societies. For them, only an economic system of this sort — which all the factors of production (land, labour, raw materials) have a price — makes possible an optimal use of resources based upon calculation and comparison between the costs of all the available production methods. This is not to deny that in many societies, land and labour are not scarce and that, consequently, the use made of resources is quite distinct from that practised in a capitalist system and may even appear irrational to an economist familiar with that system.

What the example of the Bushmen (and of others which I propose to analyse below) demonstrates is that each economic and social system determines a specific mode of exploitation of natural resources and implementation of human labour-power, and consequently determines specific norms for the 'good' and 'bad' employment of these resources and this power — i.e. a specific, original form of *intentional* economic rationality. By intentional rationality I mean a system of consciously elaborated and applied social rules for the optimum attainment of a set of objectives. One only has to call to mind Roman agronomic treatises by such writers as Cato, Varro, Posidonius, or Columella, or the medieval English agronomists (not to mention Indian or Chinese economic treatises) to see that the problem of the optimal management of an estate, whether relying on the labour of slaves or peasants bound to the soil, has at various different historical periods been the object of lively discussion and profound and quite conscious elaboration.

Consideration of the manner in which the white trappers and the Montagnais Naskapi Indians of the Labrador peninsula[3]

---

3. See E. Leacock, 'The Montagnais "Hunting Territory" and the Fur Trade', *America Anthropologist* 56 (5), 1954 part 2 (supplement); 'Matrilocality in a Simple Hunting Economy (Montagnais-Naskapi)', *Southern Journal of Anthropology* 11, 1955, pp. 31-47.

organize their labour and exploit their environmental resources (animals with precious fur) will enable us to register the differences — the contrast — between the two models of economic rationality and two types of economic and social organization. The ecological context is the same, the techniques are the same, and the aim of the hunt is the same — to produce commodities for the market in luxury goods constituted by the furrieries. Where, then, does the difference lie?

The white trappers do not bring their families to the hunting grounds during the long winter season. Women and children remain at the trading-post, near to the trade counters and the school. Save for that which he must set aside to hunt for food, the trapper devotes all his time to hunting animals for their skins.

The Indians, on the other hand, are loth to leave their families at the trading-post. Consequently, they are obliged to make at least two journeys at the start of the winter season, to transport provisions to their hunting territory. Later in the season they have to hunt to ensure that their families are fed. All in all, they are unable to devote anything like the same amount of time as the white trappers to commercial hunting. The latter are therefore able to lay much longer trapping lines and thus exploit a much larger territory. But the length of these lines obliges the trappers to invest a considerable amount of labour in watching over them to prevent the furs of snared animals being damaged by predators.

For his part, the white trapper, belongs entirely to a monetary economy and is imbued with the desire to maximize his material profits. He has more of a tendency to behave like a predator and exploit natural resources to the maximum. The Indian, by contrast, is less likely to abuse these resources. This is not necessarily because he wants to guarantee their reproduction, but because he places paramount importance upon the reproduction of his social relations and the maintenance of a particular way of life. Here we are not concerned (or at least not only concerned) with different choices between 'values', contrasted in the abstract, in the consciousness of Indians and Whites. In maintaining a family life on the hunting grounds, the Indian is not necessarily seeking more or less faithfully to reproduce a traditional way of life. Rather, his behaviour reflects the need to maintain certain social relations — both as kinsman and as neighbour — which guarantee him protection, reciprocity, cooperation and cultural continuity despite the transformations occasioned by the development of a market economy.

Through these differences in the use of resources, in efficacy or in rationality — as the economists would say — social structures are in fact brought into contrast. The white trapper, like the Indian, *reproduces* his society in his economic activity and treatment of the environment. The former belongs to an economic system wholly oriented towards monetary profit and in which traditional familial solidarities have disappeared; the individual is isolated in his own society by this society and, having no alternative, he accepts his condition as natural. The latter still belongs to a society whose ultimate end is to reproduce itself as such, and not to accumulate material goods and profits. Kinship and neighbourly relations constitute the general social framework for the individual's existence and protection, against both the rigours of nature and the destruction caused by the Whites.

The behavioural norms of the white trapper, like those of the Indian trapper, are therefore 'rational' in the sense that they in each case are 'adapted' to specific constraints, i.e. those of their respective economic and social relations. How, then, should 'adaptation' be understood?

Above all, this notion designates the material and social logic of exploitation of resources, and the conditions of its reproduction. However, the existence of 'constraining limits' to the reproduction of technical and economic systems explains why the preservation of a particular technique and way of life beyond these limits transforms them into wholly 'maladapted' practices. The example of the Yakuts, Altaic tribes which were driven back by the Mongols towards the sub-Arctic Siberian zone in the Middle Ages bear this out. Being nomadic pastoralists and horse-breeders, for them the horse was not only an economic resource but also a prestige item, the symbol of a way of life. For a long time they strove to keep up horse breeding in an ecological context which rendered the task extremely difficult. Given that the summer season was too short for them to harvest sufficient fodder for the whole winter, the Yakuts resorted to trying to feed their horses on meat and fish remnants. This obstinate insistence upon maintaining at any price a way of life ill-adapted to the environmental possibilities should primarily be seen as a reflection of the strength of a tradition, the weight of a past with its own values and habits of social organization. Ultimately meeting with failure, these populations were forced to imitate the way of life of the reindeer breeders surrounding them. Only in this way could they survive into modern times.

Let me give another example of the wealth of results already obtained by an 'ecological' approach in anthropology: the comparative study of a number of nomadic pastoral societies in East Africa. For many years, anthropologists had accepted Herskovits's arguments and maintained that African stockbreeders suffered from a veritable 'cattle complex' which was first and foremost an expression of a 'cultural' choice, of values 'differing from those of the Europeans', rather than of specific ecological and economic constraints. Indeed, a whole set of these stockbreeders' practices seemed, and still do seem to Europeans to be profoundly irrational. In these societies, livestock is a form of wealth which is apparently accumulated in order to acquire a social status, prestige, a position in the social hierarchy, rather than to guarantee a living to, or the material enrichment of, its owners. Although livestock may often be sold as a commodity, thereby procuring monetary profit, it is more often exchanged on a non-commodity basis to seal a marriage alliance and rights over a lineage.

Cattle, sheep and goats form huge herds whose meat is only consumed on ceremonial occasions. Cattle are used as beasts of burden and only supply a very meagre amount of dairy produce. Some European observers have come to the conclusion that these various 'irrational' forms of exploitation of livestock are explained by fact that for the African stockbreeder, livestock was basically associated with rituals performed at the time of his birth, his marriage and his death, that it symbolized the status of his lineage and that this is why he was attached to it by what was primarily an affective, even a mystical, tie.

The works of Deshler, Dyson-Hudson, Gulliver and Jacobs shed more light on these 'cultural features' and 'ideological' aspects. We have discovered that we were a little too hasty in declaring that livestock was only a prestige item, and the many occasions which it was exchanged, entirely without ceremony, against the agricultural and artisanal products of sedentary peoples have been listed. We are now better able to understand that the lack of meat-preservation techniques meant that the slaughter and eating of cattle had to assume a collective aspect. Since it is impossible for a unit of domestic production to preserve and consume the quantity of meat supplied by a single cow, this has to be shared out amongst the other units making up the group. This distribution is conducted according to the networks of reciprocal obligation obtaining between individuals and groups. It reactivates and reinforces them. In a technical, economic and social context of this sort, the slaughter and eating of cattle therefore necessarily assumes an exceptional social character. We are concerned with acts which express and condense numerous material and mental[4] aspects of human beings' relations as much amongst themselves as with nature. We are concerned with acts and moments of social life 'loaded' (even overloaded) with 'meaning' and consequently in 'symbolic' relation with the totality of the social organization.

To borrow the expression Marcel Mauss coined to designate this class of social facts, we are concerned with 'total' social facts, in the sense that they summarize and express — and therefore totalize in an exceptional moment, in a particular configuration of social life — the organizational principles underlying a given way of life. A particular practice is required to stage and live out the exceptional character of these acts, load them with meaning, and express the full scope of what is involved. This is 'ceremonial' practice.

However, the exceptional ceremonial character of the slaughter of cattle and the redistribution of the meat by each unit of production does not mean that the entire group does not regularly eat meat and often in significant quantities, since for one reason or another every family is led to sacrifice one of its animals.

These same anthropologists have cast new light upon another fact which seemed equally irrational to Europeans: the presence in Africa of huge herds — often comprising a significant number of old animals — whose size eventually led to overgrazing of pastures and a deterioration in vegetation and soil. These facts used to be explained by reference to the emotional attachment of owners to old animals they could not bring themselves to sacrifice, or — more banal still — to the owner's pride in showing off enormous herds. After detailed analysis of the environmental constraints under which the Dodoth of Uganda lived, it has emerged that the loss of cattle attributable to the scarcity of water regularly totalled ten to fifteen per cent of the herd a year, that the young animals vital to herd reproduction were particularly hard hit, and that, owing to the poor quality of pasture, they took six or seven years to attain full adult size, eventually produc-

---

4. The mental universe is the system of ideas, values, beliefs and representations constitutive of a society.

ing twenty times less milk than a European dairy cow.

In these conditions, one can much more readily understand why African pastoralists should attach such importance to the number of cattle in their herd, and one can more easily grasp the reasons for their complex and parsimonious strategy in the use of meat, milk, and even the blood of their cattle. Far from being the expression of an irrational or thoughtless practice, the large number of cattle was a response to the constraints weighing upon herd reproduction. A man with sixty cows has a much better chance of facing up to exceptional droughts or epizootic diseases, and therefore reproducing his material (and with them, his social and political) conditions of existence, than a man with only a herd of six to ten cows at his disposal.

The contradictory character of adaptive processes is apparent in this case too. The great size of the herds is certainly an intelligent response to the constraints the pastoralists have to confront it; but this intelligent response entails a risk of destroying the system's conditions of reproduction. By multiplying his own animals, each stockbreeder causes the society's herd to expand beyond the feasible levels of balanced reproduction of resources in pasture grass. The very expansion of the system — its adaptive success — entails its disappearance in the long run — although this disappearance is necessarily preceded by a more or less drawn-out period of maladaptation, when other solutions can be investigated and accepted. Amongst the pastoralists of East Africa, we find that agriculture assumes more importance as the pastoral economy runs into difficulties. Consequently, the society evolves towards a different model of social organization which corresponds to the exigencies of partial sedentarization required by agricultural production. One is then witness to a vast cycle of economic and social transformations in which adaptation and maladaptation to the same environment alternate.

If we pursue our enquiries in another direction, and consider the work done by anthropologists, agronomists and ecologists in Oceania, South-East Asia, Amazonia and tropical Africa among agriculturalists producing tubers (yams, manioc, taro, sweet potato, etc.), we find glaring proof of the 'pro-cereal' prejudices of Westerners — their ignorance of and contempt for the adaptive value of exotic agricultural systems. It has turned out that the clearing techniques peculiar to slash-and-burn agriculture were particularly well-adapted to tropical conditions, in which the ecological cycles are very rapid, the nutrients are not mixed with the soil, and the heat means that humus formation is very slow. If the natural vegetation is destroyed, the cycle is interrupted and the soil will not be very fertile. By practising slash-and-burn, by multiplying the number of species planted in a field and selecting plants which, because they grow in tiers, break the full force of the rain and protect the soil, tropical agriculturists have created artificial ecosystems which are adapted to the environment and which in some respects reproduce the diversity of the natural ecosystem. Studies by Conklin (1954), Geertz (1963) and Rappaport (1967) have shown that the grubbers of South-East Asia and Oceania had transformed the natural forest into one which could be 'harvested', whilst at the same time largely preserving the reproductive capacities of the natural ecosystem and their own society. But this reproductive capacity had its limits and the very success of these systems brought about their eventual disappearance. When the population increased, the fallow period gradually had to be shortened, and this caused the soil to lose fertility. In some cases, it became altogether impossible to return to the secondary forest and a savanna, covered with scrub, which was difficult to cultivate replaced the former forest. The system was therefore being transformed and tending towards the selection of more intensive practices, but on more restricted areas (terrace cultivation, irrigation, and so on). Production per area increased, but the productivity of labour fell. Here too we are concerned with an adaptation-maladaptation cycle which can lead to a system's complete disappearance and its replacement by another in a profoundly transformed ecological context. This is also the case with the Chimbu of New Guinea, who have been studied by Brookfield and Brown.

As a final example of complex adaptation, I shall take the 'vertical' economy of the Andean societies, established before the Spanish conquest.[5] In his ethnological and historical analysis of the evolution of successive economic and political systems in the Andes during the pre-Columbian period, John Murra (1972) has demonstrated that the principle underlying this evolution was an increasingly complex adaptation to a great many ecological levels. The Inca State had developed to a quite unprecedented degree this model of exploitation of numerous ecological stages, whose origin is lost in the night of pre-Inca times. Each com-

---

5. See J.V. Murra, *El 'control vertical' de un maximo de pisos ecologicos en la economia de las sociedades andinas*, Huanuco (Peru) 1972.

munity exploited the zones around its residential centre (where the dwellings and the ceremonial, political and religious sites were), some very distant zones located at a high altitude where llama and vicuña breeding took place and where the salt mines were worked, and finally some zones located in the hot valleys where cotton was grown, coca harvested, tropical woods were to be found, and so on. Each community was therefore divided into three or more groups which exploited these different ecological corners; but these groups did not constitute autonomous social units. Therewith, an extensive intertwining of colonies belonging to distinct communities obliged them to coexist in the outlying ecological zones. These strategies of adaptation to an environment with extremely diversified resources have lent their peculiar character to the pre-Inca Andean societies. The modes of government and the minimal development of commercial exchanges reflected the fact that all these societies were based upon the same model, constituted by a ring of ecological and economic islands linked to a common centre.

Although the Incas did not put an end to this very ancient pre-Inca model, they did alter the scale and content of its operation. By developing specialised crafts, creating huge communication networks and transferring entire populations from one region to another, they did however create a social system which became more and more independent of the local ecological contexts. Thus, whilst the pre-Inca societies constituted so many centres which were largely autonomous and adapted to a local ecological diversity, the Inca Empire became an economic and social reality organized upon the basis of a centre whose power and fragility were equally unique. This was the fragile equilibrium the Spanish conquest was so swiftly and irremediably to shatter.

By means of all these examples of hunter-gatherers, nomadic pastoralists, slash-and-burn agriculturists and intensive agriculturists, we can appreciate the specific but very diverse limits to the reproduction of social systems and, through them, of the environments to which they were originally adapted. Once again we can see that a central contemporary problem for the human sciences is the construction of a comparative theory of the conditions of reproduction and non-reproduction of economic and social systems.

However, we must also consider the negative aspects of the studies written by those neo-functionalists who owe their allegiance to 'cultural ecology' and seek their origin. It generally derives from a reductionist conception of the complex relations pertaining between economy and society. The diversity of social relations and the complexity of ideological practices are never wholly recognized as such. Thus, Rada and Neville Dyson-Hudson, authors of valuable studies of the Ugandan Karimojong pastoralists, write of the boys' initiation rituals and their identification with the animal given to them upon this occasion:

> These are cultural elaborations of a central reality — namely, that livestock are their principal source of subsistence. In the first and last instance, the role of livestock in the Karimojongs' life is to transform the energy stored in the grass and brush of the tribal lands into a form of energy readily available to men.[6]

I would question whether this 'energetic' explanation of religion and symbolic practice can account for the multiple functions of religion in Karimojong society. Such statements converge with polemical ones made by Marvin Harris (1968), who is quite happy to present himself as the aggressive leader of this 'cultural neo-materialism' and who, having undertaken to 'desacralize' the sacred cows of India, declared:

> I have written this paper because I believe the irrational non-economic, and exotic aspects of the Indian cattle complex are greatly overemphasized at the expense of rational, economic, and mundane interpretations. ... insofar as the beef-eating taboo helps discourage growth of beef-producing industries, it is part of an ecological adjustment which maximizes rather than minimizes the calorie and protein output of the productive process.[7]

To me this is a variant of 'vulgar' materialism, — economism — which demotes all social relations to the rank of epiphenomena accompanying economic relations, which are themselves reduced to a set of adaptive techniques to the natural and biological environment. The deeper rationality of social relations is thereby reduced to that of adaptive advantages whose content, as Claude Lévi-Strauss had earlier noted in relation to Malinowski's functionalism, often resolves itself into the simplest of truisms. As soon as a society exists, it functions, and it is banal to say that a

---

6. Rada and Neville Dyson-Hudson, *Subsistence Herding in Uganda*, Kampala 1969, p. 76.
7. M. Harris, 'The Cultural Ecology of India's Sacred Cattle', *Current Anthropology* 7:1, 1966, pp. 51, 57.

variable is adaptive because it has a function in a system. As Marshall Sahlins himself puts it:

> 'Proof that a certain trait or cultural arrangement has positive economic value is not an adequate explanation of its existence or even of its presence. The *problématique* of adaptive advantage does not specify a uniquely correct answer. As principle of causality in general and economic performance in particular, "adaptive advantage" is indeterminate: stipulating grossly what is impossible but rendering suitable anything that is possible.'[8]

From this kind of perspective, the reasons for the dominance of kinship relations or political and religious relations in a particular society remain almost impermeable to analysis.

I shall approach this problem in the following manner. In the first place, I hold that social relations come to dominate the functioning and motion of certain societies, neither by chance nor through the number of functions they integrate, but through *the nature* of the functions which they assume. To be more precise, I shall advance the hypothesis — one I shall attempt to substantiate below[9] — that social relations become dominant when they serve as framework and direct social support for the process of appropriation of nature — in short, when, whatever their other functions, they function as relations of production. To be sure, this hypothesis is inspired by Marx, but it is worth noting that it is not to be found in his work in this form.

A further hypothesis, which *was* explicitly advanced by Marx but is much more difficult to verify, may be put as follows: at certain periods of their development, there existed relations of correspondence between the material and the social conditions of the process of appropriation of nature. This same development, to whose effects should be added those occasioned by the development of the social contradictions contained in the relations of production, entailed in the (more or less) long run the erosion, and then the disappearance of these relations of correspondence and reciprocal overall compatibility. An epoch of transition to a new type of society, based upon new relations of men with nature, then ensued. According to Marx, if we could reconstruct this contradictory dynamic, we should possess a guiding

---

8. M. Sahlins, 'Economic Anthropology and Anthropological Economics', *Social Science Information* 8:5, 1969, pp. 29-30.

9. See chapters 3 and 5.

thread with which to penetrate more clearly into the diversity of forms of family, government, religion, art, etc., and into their succession. In short, we should begin to have a better understanding of the logics underlying the functioning and evolution of societies.

The difficulties which arise when one attempts to verify these hypotheses vis-à-vis the societies anthropologists have been studying for over a century can be imagined. For more often than not, the work of an anthropologist involves being a researcher who, to be sure, immerses himself for a long time in a given society, but who conducts his research alone. Hence he (or she) single-handedly, and more or less systematically, collects multiple data on the material and social life of a population whose past remains largely unknown, erased from collective memory and oral tradition. Most of the time, the anthropologist is more inclined to analyse the complexity of kinship relations or ritual practices than of material life, for the study of which he is not always well prepared. When, therefore, we seek to understand the ecological constraints weighing upon the society an anthropologist has studied and, more broadly, the material constraints linked to production techniques, demographic pressure, etc., we find that precise measurement is lacking. Admittedly, there are certain exceptions, such as the works of Conklin upon the Hanunoo of the Philippines or those of Rappaport on the Tsembaga of New Guninea to which I referred above.

However, even if more precise measurements and data are at hand, there is still the theoretical problem of how to discover the relations of correspondence or non-correspondence — if, indeed, these exist — between the material (and intellectual) conditions and the social conditions for the appropriation of nature. For when an observer begins to analyse the aspects of material and social life (i.e. to isolate them from one another), he finds that everything is offered to observation at once, and that all aspects exist in advance with all their interrelations. To attempt to discover the effects of the material conditions of the appropriation of nature upon the society's mode of organization and the 'rebound' effects of these organizational modes upon these material conditions, is abstractly to separate some of a society's components from the rest. Moreover, in some respects it is to aspire to be present at the reciprocal generation of all that particular society's components, to be present when they are positioned within the empirically observed totality, whose deeper logic would now become apparent, reconstructed by thought. This approach appears to be a kind of 'logical' genesis of the observed reality, the genesis of a social logic which should retrospectively illuminate the real historical process which combined a material base and social relations in that order and then constantly reproduced them in a more or less modified form. How is the scientific value of such a reconstruction to be verified? Verficiation is possible, but only if the *current* transformations of the societies in which anthropologists work are studied with great care, repeatedly, and over a long period of time. In such analyses, which need to be conducted in the largest possible number of contemporary societies, processes (by no means infinite in number) of destructuration-restructuration of social relations under the impact of industrialization, demographic pressure, modifications of the natural environment, etc. emerge time and time again.

The attempts of anthropologists to reconstitute history (i.e. the mechanisms of destructuration-restructuration which, in the past, have engendered such-and-such a type of society, such-and-such a combination of social relations) will only have real explanatory value when the theoretical imagination possesses a pool of precise information on these contemporary processes. The historian, on the other hand, seems better placed than the anthropologist to reconstitute these long-term processes of structural transformation, at any rate if he has a plentiful supply of documents furnishing precise data on material and social life. However, he has a handicap from which the anthropologist does not suffer, since he has no means of observing the daily production and reproduction of social relations and their articulation in a practice which, in various different forms, is more or less self-conscious.

But there is another series of difficulties which anthropologists must confront, and which constitute a formidable obstacle to those who opt for a 'Marxist' approach to social logics. For until very recently, there were numerous societies which knew neither castes nor hierarchized classes. Now, in this type of society the relations of production do not exist in a separate and distinct state, as they do in a capitalist or "socialist" society where the production process is seen to operate in an institution — the enterprise — separated off from family, church or party. The production process is undertaken and proceeds within social relations whose main priority is other functions, e.g. producing relations of marriage and descent between individuals and groups, and thus producing *kinship* relations in the society. We are therefore faced with the problem of trying to understand why and how certain secondary functions of these kinship relations can affect the society's deep structure, since this structure depends above all on the *primary* function of these relations — i.e. acting upon individuals and groups to enable them to reproduce themselves socially (through 'kinship' relations) and not acting upon nature to produce their material conditions of existence. How is the effect of one function upon another within the same relation to be analysed? How can the effect on the structuration of these relations of the action of a second (but not secondary) function upon a first function, the effect of the transformation of the operative conditions of a function upon the other's conditions of realization and upon the evolution of the global structure of these relations, be made plain?

I do not have an answer to all these questions; but it was necessary to pose them. However, I would like to present in another form an earlier analysis which took these same questions as its starting-point and was based upon data collected among the Mbuti Pygmies of Zaïre by Colin Turnbull.[10] The particular interest of this example consists in the fact that it concerns a society of hunter-gatherers whose material life, some thirty years ago, still depended by and large upon the exploitation of a natural environment relatively undisturbed by human beings. This provided an opportunity to reconstitute the role and measure the weight of material conditions of existence, in other words, to measure the action of ecological constraints as regards nature, and the action of technical constraints as regards human kind, upon the organization of society.

A large part of the Mbuti's subsistence derived from hunting and gathering. We know from the testimony of the captain of an Egyptian expedition beyond the sources of the Nile that the Mbuti have been in the Congo forest since the second millennium BC, but they have not been alone for several centuries. Groups of Bantu agriculturists progressively invaded portions of their territory and cleared gardens in the forest. The Pygmies yielded ground and on each occasion retreated ever deeper into the forest. However, they did not lead an entirely autarkic existence there. They used to exchange game or services with the neighbours encroaching upon their domain — agreeing, for

---

10. See Colin Turnbull, *Wayward Servants*, London 1966.

instance, to protect gardens planted with banana trees against the devastation inflicted by herds of elephants or bands of monkeys — in return for agricultural products and especially iron, with which they fashioned their arrowheads. For centuries these Pygmies had also been dealing in ivory from the tusks of elephants with Arab merchants from the East coast of Africa.

The Mbuti mainly used to hunt antelope. They did very little fishing, even though their rivers were plentifully stocked. They did not kill monkeys, and killed wild buffalo only rarely. Thus they did not exploit all the resources of their ecosystem. Most bands practised net hunting; some hunted with bows and a few with assegais. We do not know the reasons for this range of choice in hunting techniques, but it would appear that bow hunting was generally practised in those parts of the forest where the vegetation was less dense. The important point to bear in mind is that all the Mbuti knew how to make bows, nets and assegais. Each net belonged to a married man and the hunt entailed the men holding their nets end to end in a huge arc, concealed in the undergrowth, towards which the women and children drove the game, which was then killed with assegais. Thus the hunt was collective. It brought together a certain number of nuclear families and combined the efforts of each in a division of labour based upon gender and generation. According to Turnbull, the Mbuti reckoned that a hunt was less effective if conducted with fewer than seven or eight, or with more than twenty-five or thirty, nets. This experiential datum would have helped to fix the number of families associated in a local band within these limits, and would thus have had an effect upon the distribution of the population among the bands, taking into account local variations in natural resources together with other, more properly social factors of course.

These material — ecological and technological — conditions would seem to induce three sorts of effects in the society's mode of organization:

1) Neither an individual nor a nuclear family can in any lasting sense, produce their material conditions of existence singlehandedly. They have to cooperate with a number of other individuals and families, and the form of this cooperation varies according to gender and generation. It is obligatory to belong to a community and everyone is obliged, moreoever, to act in such a way as to reproduce the conditions of existence of this community while producing his own.

2) Space is distributed among these communities, each of them exploiting a territory whose bounds are known to the neighbouring bands. In the process of appropriation of natural resources, the band as such — independently of the variations it may undergo in its internal composition — always maintains ultimate control over these resources, no matter what rights individuals or nuclear families operating separately upon the common territory may acquire over them through initiatives distinct from those of the band. Thus it is that for a certain period of time a hunter retains a right over a honey hive he has himself discovered in the course of a hunt or a journey; but he will lose this right if he does not come to harvest the honey.

3) The variations in natural resources according to season and territory are sometimes so great that families will leave one band and join up with another, where they have friends or, most often, kin — people related either by blood or by marriage. These departures can be definitive, and the local bands are therefore not closed social units reproduced on the same site on the basis of the same families. The theoretical difficulties begin here: this reciprocal social openness between the various bands and this state of flux, are *not only* a response to the necessity of adjusting human relations to natural resources. Simultaneously, they serve as a means of adjusting the relations between men when a conflict erupts within a band. One or two families will then choose to live elsewhere, where there are kin prepared to welcome them temporarily or indefinitely. Material constraints partly account for the flexibility of Mbuti residence rules perhaps, but there are many other motives unconnected to either ecological constraints or conflicts deriving from opposed material interests; bands will split up after a case of adultery for example. What makes analysis difficult is the fact that social relations are 'overdetermined', i.e. determined in the same direction for distinct reasons which are sometimes even partially opposed. There are not, as Althusser supposes, too many causes for the one effect. There are several distinct causes which, for reasons and via mechanisms still to be discovered, act with an unequal weight in the same direction.

There is another, still more formidable difficulty. We have just seen how kinship relations constitute an essential axis of the cooperation between individuals and families within and between the bands. What light can the three material constraints just described shed upon this role played by kinship relations?

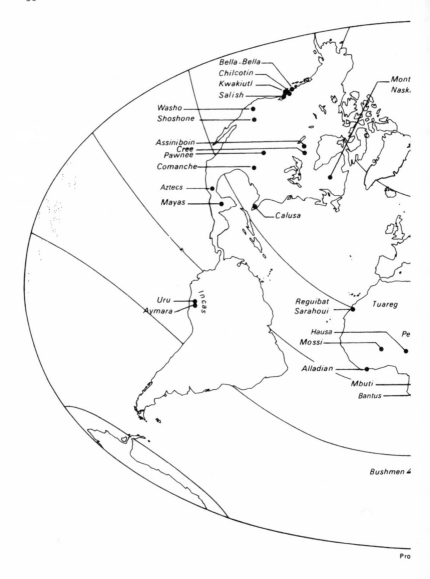

Bella-Bella
Chilcotin
Kwakiutl
Salish
Washo
Shoshone
Assiniboin
Cree
Pawnee
Comanche
Aztecs
Mayas
Calusa
Uru
Aymara
Incas
Mont
Nask.
Reguibat
Sarahoui
Tuareg
Hausa
Mossi
Pe
Alladian
Mbuti
Bantus
Bushmen
Pro

Yakuts

Mongols

Naga
Chin
Katchin
Wa
Hanunoo

Chimbu
Tsembaga
Baruya
Siane
Maenge
Trobriand
Tikopia

Assur
Sumer
Rwala
Bakhtiári

Nuer
So
Dodoth
Karimojong
Kingdom of the Ankole
Masai
Hadza

Murngin
Aranda

rtin

Regions and peoples cited in the text

Let me resume our analysis from another angle. Mbuti forms of knowledge of nature are very complex, but the material objects and technical procedures which they utilize are simple. Every man and woman, taking into account the division of labour between the sexes, is normally capable of making and using these objects. However, an individual cannot, on his own, produce his conditions of existing, in a *lasting* fashion; as we have seen, he must cooperate and add his capacities to others'. Thus, in this society where man and woman constitute the main productive forces operating upon nature, these forces are only fully effective when employed in common, through various forms of cooperation. We should undoubtedly come to the same conclusion if we analysed other societies of hunter-gatherers, such as the Australian Aborigines, or even the majority of societies of agriculturists, horticulturists and pastoralists. Despite the great diversity of techniques employed to produce his material conditions of existence, man remains the principal productive force in all these so-called primitive societies.

Bearing this in mind, the importance of controlling the process of production of human beings may more readily be gauged. As a biological process, it belongs to nature and cannot have varied throughout the course of history. But this process is subjected to social control, which establishes rules for marriage between the sexes and fixes the status of the children born of these marriages, — which, in short, effects this control through the production of kinship relations. We can therefore suppose that there exist several series of reasons which would enable us to explain, on the basis of the nature and internal composition of the productive forces at their disposal, the essential part played by kinship relations in societies where no complex social division of labour obtains (between estates, castes or classes). We can also suppose that the other essential element in the functioning of these societies is the organization of individual and group access to a portion of nature, to a territory, and the control over the processes of appropriation of the resources found there.

In demonstrating that amongst the Mbuti the productive forces invented by humankind and added to its own labour-power are much less important than the latter, we have high-lighted a fact characteristic of many societies with quite different modes of production and forms of appropriation of nature. But this gives rise to further problems. Whilst this fact illuminates the importance of kinship relations in all these societies, on the one hand it in no way explains the specific features of the Mbuti kinship system, and, on the other, it does not enable us to illuminate an aspect of kinship relations common to all societies — the incest taboo, which is the first condition of all kinship systems. For the prohibition of incest involves the active presence of something which cannot be effaced by the development and growth of the productive forces added by humankind to itself in the course of its history in order to act upon nature: the fact that human beings are not a species content to live in society, but a species which produces society in order to live — in other words, which invents new modes of organization and thought. Furthermore, it has this capacity because it is also capable of transforming its relations with nature. But this observation has even less to do with the specific features of the Mbuti kinship system. I must return to it on another occasion.[11]

According to Colin Turnbull, the Mbuti system is cognatic rather than lineal in aspect, but with a patrilineal bias. Whilst it is true that one often encounters groups of brothers living in one and the same band, in no sense do they constitute 'lineage segments'; and the maternal kin play an important role, as is borne out by the rite which dictates that on marrying a man receives from his mother and from his mother's brother the net which will allow him to assume his place within the band as a fully-fledged hunter. But he is forbidden to take a wife from the band whence his mother originally came, or indeed from that of his paternal grandfather's wife (i.e., his father's mother). Thus he cannot reproduce the ties of marriage-relationship of either his father or his paternal grandfather. Nor is he entitled to take a wife from bands whose territories are adjacent to his own. The logic of the system therefore obliges individuals to redirect their marriage relationships in every generation, and to go and seek their marriage-partners at a distance in both space and time. Ten years ago, I regarded the logic of this constantly open and fluctuating system as expressing a relation of 'structural compatibility' between the kinship system of the Mbuti and their mode of production. Indeed, I interpreted their need to constitute their local bands as social units open to each other as a consequence of their material conditions of existence. I no longer believe this to be the case.

---

11. The reader may care to consult the analyses contained in Godelier, *Perspectives in Marxist Anthropology*, Cambridge 1977.

For what these material conditions of existence impose, above all else, is a degree of fluidity in the rules governing membership of the local bands, and therefore in residence patterns. But there is an identical fluidity among Australian Aborigines, whose kinship system depends upon the existence of kinship groups (moieties, sections and sub-sections) with well-defined contours, which proceed, generation after generation, to form marriage-relationships with the same groups and which are therefore oriented in the same directions in time and space. Therefore the main point is not to explain the fluidity of residence rules and variations in the composition of Mbuti or Australian Aborigine local bands, but rather to account for the diversity of marriage and descent systems among the groups of nomadic hunter-gatherers which have survived up until our own time. I cannot yet see how to explain this diversity. We may note the existence of different, even opposed, social logics: the presence or absence of closed kinship groups; regular reproduction of marriage-relationships or their voluntary non-reproduction; distant marriage or close marriage (the closest being the so-called Arab marrriage). But we still do not possess the theoretical reasons which would enable us to explain why one or other of these systems is present in such-and-such a society. Moreover, these systems are not infinite in number. After all, there exist only four 'logical' possibilities for establishing social relations of descent: through men; through women; through men and through women in different ways; and through men and through women indiscriminately. All kinship systems pertain to one or other of these four main types. But what circumstances favour the appearance of a matrilineal system? Some have pointed to the role of women in societies practising extensive agriculture in Africa (the matrilineal belt of Africa), in Melanesia or in America; yet so many societies in these very same areas in fact have patrilineal systems! Others have then pointed to the role of men in stockbreeding, as if this would account for the overwhelming number of patrilineal systems amongst nomadic pastoralists. This correlation is largely proven, but one still has to account for the matrilineal elements in the Tuareg system. Others again have pointed to the role of men in an intensive agriculture combining stockbreeding and agriculture, such as has existed in Western Europe since Antiquity; but this combination does not exist in a number of strongly patrilineal Asian societies. What is one to make of bilineal systems? Of cognatic systems?[12]

Analysis of the Mbuti case, as of any other, thus does not depend solely upon the wealth of empirical information available or forthcoming about the ecosystem within which the Mbuti live. It also depends upon the theoretical progress made in the analysis of the circumstances which favoured the repeated appearance of one or other of the main types of kinship system. The chain of causes which would enable us, taking material conditions of existence and the nature of the material and intellectual productive forces as our starting-point to understand something more of the functioning of kinship systems then just the residence rules has still not been constructed. This 'something more' is the deep structures of these systems — those generated by their first function, which is to produce relations of descent and marriage between the individuals and the groups constituting a society. One could also investigate the links which exist between the material conditions of existence of the Mbuti and the forms of authority and power within the local bands. The contrast with certain Australian societies would be striking. There is a sharp difference, in fact, between the relatively slight inequality in status and power between men and women and between generations among the Mbuti, and the blatant domination enjoyed by the men in the Australian societies, which assumes the dual form of control over the circulation of women between kinship groups and the complex initiation systems which segregate boys and girls for years at a time. I shall not pursue this discussion any further here, for we are now touching upon another set of problems, that of the relations between the sexes in different societies.

The reader should not conclude from the fact that I have pointed out some of the difficulties which arise when one works on a particular case, that there is no theoretical interest in attempting an accurate analysis of the material, conditions of existence of the various populations coexisting on the earth's surface. I shall try to prove that precisely the opposite is true, using once again the studies by Richard Lee and Nancy Howell on the Bushmen of the Kalahari Desert. These studies are concerned with the interval between births, but they have been conducted in such a manner that they open up new perspectives

12. See Audrey Richards, ed., *Economic Development and Tribal Change*, Cambridge (N.J.); Audrey Richards, *Land, Labour and Diet in Northern Rhodesia*, Oxford 1939; Jack Goody and S.J. Tambiah, *Bridewealth and Dowry*, Cambridge 1973.

on the demographic and economic effects entailed by the sedentarization (whether voluntary or forced) of populations of nomadic
hunter-gatherers on several occasions in history.

Amongst the Bushmen, who live in a semi-arid milieu, the
women gather wild plants and fruits, supplying two-thirds of the
food annually consumed by their 'camp'. The camp will
normally number between ten and fifty individuals living less
than a mile from a waterhole. Richard Lee[13] has calculated that
on average an adult woman covers about 2,400 kilometres a year
on her economic activities and visits to other bands, and that she
goes half that distance carrying heavy loads of food, firewood and
of course children.

A Bushman child is weaned around the age of four. During its
first two years, it is constantly carried by its mother (2,400 kilometres). As the child grows, this figure decreases (1,800 kilometres or so in the third year, and 1,200 in the fourth). In the
course of four years, the woman thus covers a total distance of
7,800 kilometres, during which time the child's weight is added
to that of the other loads she carries. Given that the economic
activities a woman is engaged in — gathering and transporting
loads — necessarily involve a degree of mobility, the labour
expended in carrying children must be maintained within limits
compatible with the regular and effective performance of her
economic activities. Now, this depends upon all on the spacing of
births. It has been calculated that, over a period of ten years, if
the spacing between births is five years, a woman will have had
two children and the additional weight to be carried will have
been on average 7.8 kilograms. If the spacing were two years
(without taking into account the high rate of infant mortality), on
average the weight to be carried would be 17 kilograms and, for
four of these ten years, 21.2 kilograms.

Theoretically, an interval between births of at least three years
would be compatible with the material constraints imposed by
the Bushmen's mode of production, as the statistics themselves
seem to bear out. The Bushmen themselves are well aware of
such constraints, since they declare that 'a woman who brings
one child after another into the world, like an animal, will have a
permanent backache'. Furthermore, if there are twins, they kill
one of them at birth; they practise infanticide on children who

---

13. R.B. Lee, 'Kung Bushman Subsistence: an Input-Output Analysis', in
Ecological Essays, Ottawa 1966.

are born deformed; and they abstain from sexual relations during the twelve months following each birth. However, this conscious 'demographic policy' is not sufficient to explain why statistically the spacing between births is at least three years, since the women resume their sexual activity after a year's abstinence; one would expect them to become pregnant again almost immediately.

It seems that unintentional, biological factors intrude here, and in particular the fact that prolonged breast-feeding of children suppresses ovulation in women. Now, as Nancy Howell suggests[14], the wild foodstuffs consumed by the Bushmen do not include anything which is easily digestible by children, whereas the foods produced by agriculturists and stockbreeders (gruels, the milk of domestic animals, etc.) do. This means that the Bushmen, together with other hunter-gatherers, have no choice but to indulge in prolonged breast-feeding. The mother's milk is therefore not only an indispensable food, it is also the only food available to societies with this kind of technical base. Meggitt has made a similar observation regarding the Australian Aborigines, and Yengoyan has analysed the 'economic' aspect of this spacing: 'The prolonged period of breast-feeding not only forced the populations to limit their number, it also lessened the overall usefulness of a woman as an economic partner.'

Richard Lee suggests that the establishment of a sedentary mode of life, insofar as it makes the women less mobile, would itself be sufficient to eliminate the negative biological effects of the nomadic way of life upon the women's fertility level, and might well bring about a tendency to a rise in population and, *above all, an increase in food resources* thanks to the adoption of other material forms of production, such as agriculture and stockbreeding. This hypothesis has been borne out by Lancaster Jones's studies of the Australian Aborigines, used by Yengoyan as evidence for his hypothesis. Sedentarization in reserves and the change in alimentary regime with the arrival of food rations distributed by the Europeans have been accompanied by an explosion in the birthrate which, combined with the effects of medical supervision, has produced a rate of population growth far higher than that which we have been able to reconstruct for the pre-colonial period.

However, in terms of far wider historical perspectives, these studies also suggest that there may well have been exceptional

---

14. Nancy Howell, *Demography of the Dobe Area: !Kung,* New York 1979.

demographic growth amongst the Neolithic food-gatherers of the Near East, who exploited dense crops of wild graminaceae (the ancestors of our cereals), or amongst the populations settled on the river banks or on the coasts of the well-stocked seas in America or in South-East Asia.[15] The growth of these Neolithic populations must have accompanied their sedentarization on very rich sites and, assuming that this growth could have commenced without any increase in spontaneous natural resources, it clearly could not have been prolonged or amplified without the populations' active intervention in the reproduction of wild plants, to domesticate them, — without, that is, a transformation in the material and social conditions of production.

There therefore must have been a shift from one social form of production and existence to another. But it is no easy matter to analyse the relations of transformation existing between different forms of society. If it is difficult to distinguish between different social forms when they have superficial aspects in common, it is not any simpler to recognize similar social forms which have superficially different aspects. This is where a theoretical approach content to proceed case by case runs up against insuperable barriers. Edmund Leach has quite clearly shown with respect to the Kachin of Burma, that a ranked society, dominated by a chief — who is, or who claims to be, the last-born of the descendants of the last of the sons of the village's founding ancestor — may in certain circumstances become a society without an internal hierarchy or chief, or in different circumstances again become a society with a chiefship once more. The Kachin say of hierarchized societies that they are 'of the *gumlao* type' and they describe the societies without chiefs as being 'of the *gumsa* type'. Although the explanations advanced by Leach for these forms of reversible evolution do not seem to me to be adequate, since he regards the phenomenon as essentially ideological (the effect of successive choices of one or the other model of social organization which their value system allows to the Kachlin), the analysis of such examples is of crucial importance if we are to uncover the conditions for the transformation of social structures.

Adopting a similar perspective, Jonathan Friedman has attempted to demonstrate that the Kachin, Chin, Naga and Wa societies of Burma, which would at first sight seem to be profoundly different social and economic regimes, actually belong to

---

15. See Carl O. Sauer, *Agricultural Origins and Dispersal*, New York 1952.

the same group of transformations. Kachin society is hierarchized, aristocratic and scattered among thirty-populated
hamlets; Naga society is democratic and concentrated in large
villages. The former practises an extensive slash-and-burn
agriculture, the latter an intensive agriculture in a deforested
environment. Yet Jonathan Friedman maintains that there is an
internal relation between these different social forms which
derives from the fact that they all belong to a single system of
structural transformations. Analysis must therefore go beyond
visible differences in search of the invisible mechanisms which
generate these differences on the basis of the structural properties
of a single group of social relations.

The shift from one social form to another brings into operation
relations of incompatibility between new functions and old structures which appeared and were reproduced in quite other conditions. It takes the form of a contradictory development of
combined elements within these structures and of the development of contradictions between these structures within the
system in which they are articulated under the dominance of one
structure in particular. I should like to pause here for a moment
to consider the term 'contradiction'.

Contradictions and Evolution of Social Systems and of the Relations of Man with Nature

By revealing the form of regulation of systems known as retro-
action or feedback, cybernetics has posed the problem of the
existence of contradictions internal to systems (both physical and
social) in new terms. Retroactive mechanisms guarantee a
relative independence to a system vis-à-vis the variations in its
internal components and its external conditions of functioning.
One must distinguish between negative and positive feedback,
the former inducing a variation in the contrary direction to the
variation which occasioned the feedback, the latter inducing a
variation which proceeds in the same direction and amplifies its
effects.

The conditions for a system's reproduction is not therefore the
absence of contradictions in the interior of that system, but rather
the existence of a *regulation* of these contradictions which *provisionally maintains its unity*. A social system or a natural ecosystem are
therefore never, as functionalists old and new would claim,

wholly 'integrated' totalities. They are totalities whose unity is the 'provisionally stable' effect of the properties of structural compatibility between the elements which constitute a structure or the structures which constitute a system. For this reason, we have to distinguish between contradictions internal to a single level of the society's functioning and contradictions between that society's organizational levels. An example of this would be the contradictions peculiar to the political and economic organization of the Greek City: the opposition between free men and slaves on the one hand, and that between citizens and metics on the other. The development in the fifth and sixth centuries of commodity production, founded upon the labour of an ever increasing number of slaves and upon the greater prominence of metic merchants, constituted both the basis of the rise of Athens and the reason for its internal difficulties, which were to culminate, after the Peloponnesian War, in a withdrawal into itself and a kind of stagnation. The City State was later to enjoy a new lease of life, but at the price of a profound mutation in its political and economic regime inasmuch as it lost its independence and its original character and gradually came under the sway of the Macedonian kingdom. This marked the birth of a new, Hellenistic world wherein the traditional forms of the City were maintained for some time to come, but with a different content.

Let me make two important points quite clear. First, the notion of the unity of opposites adumbrated here should not in any way be confused with the metaphysical and unscientific notion of the unity of opposites as defined by Hegel. Admittedly, there is both complementarity and opposition between the masters and the slaves; but in no sense can the master be said to be simultaneously himself and his own slave, opposing himself to himself, and so on.[16]

Secondly, to speak of contradictions between social relations is a way of referring to the existence of relations of incompatibility between the properties of these relations, between their conditions of production and reproduction. As such, these contradictions are relations between properties of relations, and therefore relations of the second degree, which are lacking in purpose, in intentionality. As such, they are not occasioned by any human will. They appear when social relations arise, since they are

16. See G.W.F. Hegel, *The Phenomenology of Spirit*, translated by A.V. Miller, Oxford 1977.

nothing other than the objective limits to these relations' conditions of reproduction. To be more precise, they are simply the negative effects of the properties of social relations when the limits to the conditions of their reproduction are reached. They have negative effects upon these relations themselves, upon their internal structure and the elements which they combine. They have negative effects upon the articulation of these relations with the other social relations which, in combination with them, constitute a particular type of society. Thus we have contradictory development, a development of unintentional contradictions within the reproduction process of that society.

Unintentional contradictions have a determinant effect upon the evolution of societies. But they do not operate by themselves and are insufficient to explain this evolution. Evolution can only be realized through the active, conscious intervention of human beings who, depending upon the places they occupy in the particular society and the interests they think they ought to defend, seek to impel it in one direction or another. And to the extent that these places are distinct and these interests complementary or opposed, the conscious action of human beings necessarily takes charge of all or some of the contradictions contained in social relations. However, this conscious action is no less confronted by and subject to the objective properties of the social relations within and upon which it operates.

History is the product of an encounter between these two logics, between these two sets of intentional and unintentional forces, between the conscious action of human beings — which often breaks off and sometimes achieves its aim — and the uninterrupted action of the properties of their relations, an action lacking intention and properties without a goal. The degree of control by humanity over its own destiny therefore depends in the last instance upon its capacity to become aware of and, above all, to take charge of the unintentional part of its existence. The difference between history and the evolution of nature without humanity consists in the fact that no animal species is capable of taking charge of the objective conditions of its existence. Natural ecosystems are relatively stable totalities composed of vegetable and animal populations whose relations evolve without any agency being able genuinely to act upon the causes of that evolution. They adapt themselves to their own effects.

By way of conclusion, I should like to append two examples of the evolution of societies which belong to a world which still survives or which has only recently drawn to a close.

As we have seen, Eleanor Leacock lived and worked among the Montagnais Naskapi Indians in 1950 and 1951, in an Algonquin group living in the centre and south-east of the Labrador peninsula in the north of Canada. In addition to her own personal observations, she used the records of the Jesuits who had been established in Canada since the seventeenth century,[17] and in particular Paul Le Jeune's account of his journey of 1633-34.[18] Eleanor Leacock has shown how this society of hunter-gatherers, composed of unstably-composed exogamic bands, with a kinship system that was probably cognatic with a matrilineal bias, and which enjoyed no exclusive rights over any hunting territory, had evolved towards a modern form of organization of bands, which had become patrilineal and exogamous and also far more stable in composition, and whose trappings territories for fur animals were claimed individually and handed down from father to son.

The old form of organization had been adapted to the hunting of big game (caribou), which required constant cooperation between the sexes and the different groups. During this period, small animals such as the fox were not pursued, because their fur was not thick enough to make hunting clothes and their flesh was not liked. With the development of the fur trade and hunting with traps, and with the setting up of permanent lines of traps, the bands' territories and personnel were stabilized, the labour process was individualized, the importance of men in this process increased, and a transition to patrilocality and patrilineality occurred. These transformations led to the constitution of endogamous bands and a reversal in the marriage rules. There was thus a transformation of all the internal elements which constituted the society's organizational structures, together with a reversal of their meaning. Yet the society's overall organization in bands has survived, although with the development of a monetary economy and the policy of 'social security' followed by the Canadian Government in its dealings with the Indians, it is today under threat.

Another particularly remarkable example of the effects upon societies' organization and reproduction of transformations in

17. See Eleanor Leacock, 'Matrilocality . . .', 1955.

18. Paul Le Jeune's account is in volumes VI, VIII, XII, XIV and XX of R.G. Thwaites, ed., *The Jesuit Relations and Allied Documents*, Cleveland 1906.

modes of production and material conditions of existence is provided by the formation and development of an original type of economy and society among the Plains Indians of North America from the seventeenth century onwards. In a very detailed analysis, Symes C. Oliver has shown how this type of society, whose hunting economy depended upon the horse (which had recently been introduced) and upon the rifle (which had come into use a little later) was adapted to the bison's particular ecology. This adaptation entailed two opposed constraints: dispersal of the bands during the winter months when the herds of bison had split up; concentration in the summer when the bison gathered in the plains to resume their migration. For each band, dispersal entailed independence for several months, whereas concentration entailed a degree of reciprocal dependence; for whilst a band attacking a huge herd singlehandedly would certainly secure its own means of existence, it would also drive the herd into headlong flight and thereby deprive the other bands of these same resources.

Accordingly what was required was a form of social organization which combined the flexibility and mobility of nomadic hunters with something analogous to the more centralized organization of agricultural tribal societies or, in short, a combination of agriculture and hunting. Now, what was particularly remarkable in the case of the Plains Indians was the fact that forms of social organization developed within tribes whose structures had originally been very different, even opposed, had come to converge and resemble each other more and more. Tribes from the North and the West such as the Cree, and Assiniboin and the Comanche, derived from groups which had previously practised hunting and gathering on foot and lived in bands whose composition was quite fluid. Tribes from the East and the South-East were originally populations of agriculturists which, in the South in particular along the Mississippi, had lived in settled villages, recognizing the authority of hereditary chiefs and priests.

In the course of a century, a new mode of production and social organization very quickly formed and spread through these tribes. The original social relations did not break down, however, but were transformed by the addition of new functions and the suppression or restructuring of the old ones. Those groups which had previously been sedentary horticulturists organized in chiefdoms were forced to adopt a more hierarchical organization, to impose the common discipline upon all the local bands which was requisite if the great collective summer hunts were to be successful.

In no sense did the old relations of production and other social relations suddenly disappear from the stage of history. Thanks to man's capacities for imitation, borrowing and invention, they instead underwent metamorphosis. In origin they were forms which registered and sites which revealed, in the context of the old social form of production and life, the effects of the transformations in the Indians' material conditions of existence.

In short, human intention and action always take root and encounter the limits of their effects in the unintentional properties and necessities of social relations and conditions of existence. History therefore explains nothing since it too must be explained. Moreover, if we are to understand it, we must have some means of referring it back to what is possible, of discovering the always limited number of transformations which a social structure, or a combination of such structures, considered in terms of the variations in their conditions of reproduction, may undergo.

This chapter is based on material used in two earlier articles. The first, 'Considérations théoriques et critiques sur le problème des rapports entre l'homme et son environnement', was drafted for the meeting on humankind and its environment held at Unesco in February 1974; it is reproduced with Unesco's agreement, (C) Unesco, 1974, in *Information sur les Sciences sociales* 13 (6) pp. 31-60. The second, 'Anthropologie et biologie: vers une coopération nouvelle', appeared in *Revue internationale des Sciences sociales* XXVI (4), 1974, pp. 666-90.

2

Territory and Property in Some Pre-Capitalist Societies

The problem of forms of property in nature, and of their foundation, has always been a subject for debate among theoreticians of
every kind, including theologians, philosophers, economists,
historians and, of course, lawyers. In the present context,
however, I shall set such theses and hypotheses to one side,
concentrating exclusively upon the materials accumulated by
anthropologists over the past few decades. I do not thereby mean
to disregard them or to imply that they have made no contribution to the debate; it is simply that it is not my brief to make an
inventory of them and to do each of them justice. Moreover, my
reliance upon contemporary anthropology does not preclude me
from acknowledging how, prior to becoming a scientific or even
an academic discipline in the latter half of the nineteenth
century, from Antiquity onwards (Herodotus, Tacitus and
others) anthropology has had a host of precursors (travellers,
military men, civil servants and missionaries) who, either because
they had a taste for it or because they were so commanded, took
the trouble to inform us about the ways of life and thought of
'savage and barbarous' nations as the latter became subject to the
laws of our own, 'civilized' nations. It was from their work that
the theoreticians would in turn take a few exotic examples to lend
more weight to their arguments and a sense of universality to
their conclusions.

What became of such exotic facts, which had originally been
observed (but how?) and reported (but in what terms, via what

concepts?) by a passing traveller or administrator, once they had been incorporated into 'theoretical' works? If you read Montesquieu, Rousseau or Adam Smith, you find that an exotic fact appears not as the point of departure for an enquiry focused upon it but to illustrate an idea or thesis which had been formulated prior to and independently of it. But there are also numerous occasions when acquaintance with new and exotic realities has led thinkers to arrive at conclusions which they would otherwise not have been able to formulate. Let me give a single, but famous example — John Locke. In chapter IV of his *Second Treatise on Civil Government* (1690), Locke posed precisely the problem of the diversity of forms of property in nature and their evolution. He argued that the earth was originally 'common' property, but that this had not prevented private property being formed on the basis of 'labour', for labour belongs 'in its own right' to each individual and 'has caused things to emerge from their common state'. I shall not linger here over this example, which reappears in the first and third parts of this text, but it is worth pausing to consider the proofs advanced by Locke in support of his thesis. For Locke, whilst invoking 'natural reason' and relying upon a passage in the Bible according to which God gave the earth in common first to Adam, and then to Noah and his sons, nevertheless asserts 'that there can be no clearer demonstration on this point than that which the various peoples of America offer us'.[1]

Why are the 'American' Indians accorded such significance, and why are the works which record their customs — an anthropology in all but name — accorded such a privileged theoretical

---

1. 'Whether we consider natural *Reason* ... or *Revelation* which gives us an account of those Grants God made of the World to *Adam*, and to *Noah*, and his Sons, 'tis very clear, that God, as King *David* says, *Psal.* CXV. xvj. *has given the Earth to the Children of Men*, given it to mankind in common. But this being supposed, it seems to some a very great difficulty, how any one should ever come to have a *Property* in any thing ... But I shall endeavour to shew, how Men might come to have a *property* in several parts of that which God gave to mankind in common, and that without any express compact of all the Commoners.

He that is nourished by the Acorns he pickt up under an Oak, or the Apples he gathered from the Trees in the Wood, has certainly appropriated them to himself. ... That *labour* put a distinction between them and common. That added something to them more than Nature the common Mother of all, had done; and so they became his private right ... The *labour* that was mine, removing them out of that common state they were in, hath *fixed* my *Property* in them.' John Locke, *Two Treatises on Government*, edited and introduced by Peter Laslett, 1960, Second Treatise, Chapter 5, 25-28.

role? It is simply because these ethnographic and historical realities are approached and deployed by Locke on the basis of an
analytical principle of general scope, which he takes to be as good
as proven, namely, that 'in the beginning all the world was [like]
America'. We can now clearly appreciate the reasons for the
value accorded to American examples and, more generally, to
anthropology. For they allow thought to enter into the presence
of the original forms of social life, of the origin of institutions, and
thereby to grasp the hidden principle of their subsequent evolution. The explicit theoretical principle which confers a general
relevance upon the use of anthropological materials is therefore
the hypothesis that the contemporary forms of social organization
encountered among savages correspond to the old, superseded
forms of social organization of civilized peoples. This hypothesis
regarding a correspondence between the present and the past,
between the ethnographic and the historical, legitimates a particular way of analysing and comparing social institutions.

Locke himself was not the author of this hypothesis, and his
originality lay only in having given it a simple, popular form and
making systematic philosophical use of it. It was first formulated
a century or so earlier by certain travellers or compilers of travellers' tales, such as Father José De Acosta, in his *Historia natural y
moral de las Indes* (1589). But it was already known to Antiquity in
the work of Herodotus, or in that of Thucydides, who asserted at
the beginning of his *Historiai* (narratives of enquiries and a historical treatise) that 'the Greeks lived in former times as the Barbarians live today'.[2] It also features in Aristotle's *Politics* and in
Lucretius's *De Rerum Natura*, and in both Porphyry and Varro.
Reinvented in the sixteenth century, this manner of analysing
exotic facts has been uninterruptedly practised up until our own
times. Father Lafitau used it in 1725 to demonstrate, in argument
against atheists, that all savage peoples had a religion and that
their gods resembled those of ancient Greece or the Egyptians.
Morgan, the founder of modern scientific anthropology, himself
used this same hypothesis in 1877 to compare (like Lafitau) the
customs of the Indians and those of the ancient Greeks and
Romans, and to show that the familial institutions of Antiquity,
the Greek *genos* and the Roman *gens*, are much more readily
understood once one grasps that they are institutions analogous
to an Iroquois tribal clan. The fixed idea behind this intellectual

---

2. Thucydides, I, 6.

approach was that there existed a unilinear evolution of social institutions dictated by principles that were either entirely supra-historical of (Father Lafitau) or, as in the case of Morgan who believed in God and in a plan by a supreme Intelligence) by principles which were in part supra-historical (the original impulse and the general direction) and in part immanent to this history (the determinant role, in the last analysis, of 'modes of subsistence'). It was only at the beginning of the twentieth century, with the general crisis of evolutionism in the social sciences, that this idea was subjected to criticism and rejected.

Nowadays we have to construct a much more complex theory of the evolution of social forms, for it would seem that whilst the transformation of forms of social organization is in general irreversible, the same forms may arise from wholly different points of departure and correspond to different historical necessities (as in the case of undifferentiated kinship systems which may be either the point of arrival or of departure for unilinear systems). Furthermore, no absolute referent exists, no particular line of evolution which has the privilege of displaying a supposedly universal line of humanity's evolution. Finally, even if one takes as a working hypothesis the idea that the historical (social, material and intellectual) conditions of action upon nature and production of a society's material base have a determinant effect upon that society's organization and transformations — whereby it is comparable to a certain number of others and together with them constitutes a type whose functional properties are peculiar to it, and whose evolutionary possibilities are specific and therefore finite, although the precise number of permutations may still be unknown to us — nothing allows one to allocate an obligatory form and evolution to these social conditions of production. Depending upon the particular case, relations of production, societies' economic structure, are to be sought in places or in forms which are wholly different from those in capitalist society, where the economic seems to be functionally and institutionally distinct from religion, kinship and politics — i.e. from the social relations designated by these terms.

After this long preamble, I should like to make two further points. I should like to remind the lay public that there is no theoretical criterion which defines the frontiers of anthropology and assigns it the study of some societies rather than others. Anthropology was constituted on the basis of a negative *de facto* situation. It was concerned with all those societies which, because they lacked written documents, interested neither historians nor economists. These societies, which were left on our hands as it were, were not necessarily all at the Antipodes. The village communities of Europe, the Albanian and Greek tribes, and so on — whose internal organization had never been of any interest to the nation states or foreign dynasties which pressed down upon them and were satisfied with making a written record of those of their customs that facilitated their control and exploitation — were close at hand and just as alien to nineteenth-century observers as the tribes of Papua or of Amazonia. There was only one way of coming to know them, and that was to go and see them, to live amongst them, to learn their languages and to record what one had learnt.

So it was not because they were primitive or barbarous that these societies became the object of anthropology. It was rather because a specific method had to be practised in order to get to know them — what anthropological jargon calls 'participant observation'. This was the concrete situation, based on an ignorance which for a number of reasons (military, missionary, economic) had to be overcome, together with the practical necessity of resorting to participant observation if one was to terminate this ignorance, which gradually constituted the experience of anthropologists and their field of action. Here we find a curious jumble of the last Bushman bands, hunter-gatherers of the Kalahari desert, the tribes of New Guinea, the pastoralists of Iran or Soviet Central Asia, the village communities of Peru, Java, India or Spain. The positive thing about these heteroclite materials, about this historical 'bazaar', is that it offers us an admirable vantage point from which to compare an immense range of processes of transformation of the forms of social life in a multitude of local conditions. Attempts to find order in so much diversity have necessitated complex and rigorous methods for the treatment of data, to reveal laws of combination and transformation generating stabilized internal arrangements, to apprehend social relations in terms of their 'structures'. Participant observation is therefore insufficient. It has to take turns with an analysis of field data which will highlight the structural logic involved.

Abstract and Concrete Appropriation of Nature

By property is meant a set of abstract rules governing access to and control, use, transfer and transmission of any and every social reality which can be the object of a dispute. Before analysing property insofar as this concerns a portion of nature, a territory, I want to emphasize five fundamental points.

The first point I want to make is that, in a formal sense, the concept of property may be applied to any tangible or intangible reality: land, water, a mask, ritual knowledge, secret magical formulae used to guarantee the fertility of plants or women, a rank, the names of the dead, and so on. Robert Lowie reminded us of this in 1928, in a famous article entitled 'Incorporeal Property in Primitive Society'. But it is just as important to emphasize that these 'realities' must be subject to dispute, i.e. they must seem to be a *condition* for the reproduction of human life.

Thus it is that amongst the So, a tribe in Uganda, only the oldest men of the various patrilineages are entitled to know and invoke the names of dead ancestors. They are also considered to be the requisite intermediaries between men and Bergen, a god who as they think, controls the rain and, with the rain, life — of livestock and men alike. The other, uninitiated men and all women are forbidden to pronounce these names on pain of death by witchcraft or through other forms of punishment inflicted by ancestors, spirits or gods, such as imagining oneself to be a monkey and climbing up trees, or eating one's own excrement.

It is thus the case that property rules — and this is my second point — always assume the form of normative rules, prescribing certain forms of conduct and proscribing others under pain of repression and sanctions.

These normative rules may apply either to all the members of a society or only to certain of them. But even when they apply to all, they generally tend to exclude the members of all other societies — whether neighbours or not — from these same rights and duties. To sum up, property rules are simultaneously prescriptive, proscriptive and repressive (threats of death or various kinds of punishment, either human or divine, physical or psychological, direct or indirect, immediate or deferred). But even when they apply only to certain members of a society (the medieval prohibition upon French peasants owning hunting dogs), if these rules are to be respected they must be understood by everyone and must therefore be taught to all. This is why all legal systems contain a principle analogous to that enshrined in French law: 'No one is supposed to be ignorant of the law.'

The 'law' is taught in enormously different ways. Amongst the Aranda, who are hunter-gatherers in Southern Australia, the young men used to learn from their elders which portions of the tribal territory, whether land or water, belonged to their kinship group, to their section, since their kinship system involved a division of the tribe into four exogamous sections. This teaching was transmitted during a long initiation journey lasting several months, in the course of which they would traverse every inch of the tribal territory from one end to the other in the company of old men belonging to the four sections. For days on end, their guides would teach each of the young men the tribe's frontiers and the limits of his own kinship group's territory, together with the resources in water, game and wild plants that they could hope to find in each part of these territories. In their turn, they would later need such knowledge when leading a group of families from well to well along the routes they followed in the course of their hunting and gathering. They were also taught where to find water and other resources in case of exceptional drought, and which solidarities and reciprocities to invoke.

But their education was by no means restricted to these lessons in ecology, economics or in political and kin solidarity. For each site, each irregularity in the terrain, each mountain, waterhole or oddly shaped rock had its own history, since they had appeared during the world's first moments, in Dream Time as the Aborigines call it, when the ancestor of one of the sections was turned into a lake, another into a cave, and another into the ancestor of the kangaroos or of the giant lizards, or even of the Australian wild dog, the dingo. Thus the long initiatory journey through hills and deserts served as an occasion for learning all the productive possibilities of the tribe's territory and, simultaneously for passing on the rights, which were thereby from generation to generation confirmed of the community and the groups and individuals comprising it over the territory's resources.

Another point I should like to make here — one of crucial importance but which has been little investigated — is that a society's property rules take the form of 'systems' which simultaneously depend upon several different, even opposed, but combined principles.

This runs counter to a thesis advanced by a number of eighteenth and nineteenth-century theoreticians who claimed that in the most primitive societies 'everything belonged to everyone', and that property (although one could equally well say the absence of any property) depended uon a single principle termed 'primitive communism'. In 1926 Malinowski found it an easy enough matter to demonstrate that this theory was inapplicable to the Trobriand Islanders of New Guinea, and he suggested that it was very probably inapplicable to any primitive society. More recent enquiries have provided ample proof of this last hypothesis.

It may be worth noting in passing that when Marx and Engels spoke of 'primitive communism', they never entertained such a simplistic thesis, for they always used to protest against what they called the idea of a primitive 'El Dorado' and tirelessly insisted upon the fact that even in the most primitive societies, there would seem to exist at least three forms of inequality: between men and women; between senior and junior generations; and between autochthons and foreigners. Modern anthropological data do not appear to invalidate the existence of these three forms of inequality, which may vary considerably in degree but are to be found in all classless societies. Furthermore, Marx and Engels subjected the idea of abstract equality between men to a far harsher criticism than that of Malinowski or, in the present day, that of Louis Dumont,[3] since they considered it a 'bourgeois' notion — i.e. one perfectly congruent with the constitutive inequalities of the class relations in bourgeois society, which struggled for the abolition of class privileges but never for the abolition of classes themselves. On this point, I would refer the reader to the *Critique of the Gotha Programme* (1875), to *Anti-Dühring* (1877), and to the three drafts of Marx's famous letter to Vera Zasulich (1881).

Be this as it may, it would seem undeniable today that there exist in all societies, to use Malinowski's own terms, 'systems of combined rights', i.e. systems combining collective and individual forms of appropriation. These forms vary with the 'reality' being appropriated and the material and intellectual means of control over nature available to a given society.

To illustrate this notion of a 'combined system' of rights resting upon distinct principles, I shall take the example of the Siane, a New Guinea society studied by Richard Salisbury. This tribe is divided into patrilineal clans, which are further divided into lineages placed under the authority of the elder brothers of the oldest generation. There is no central power and the society is governed

---

3. In *Homo Aequalis*, Paris 1977.

by the positive or negative, complementary or opposed relations between the clans and their representatives. Material life depends upon the production of wild plants and upon hunting wild pig, although the latter is of little significance.

Siane property rules regarding material and immaterial realities are of two kinds. In the first, a man has rights over an object in the same way as a father (*merafo*) has rights over his children; he is responsible for them before the community and his ancestors. To this category belong land, the sacred flutes and ritual knowledge — all inalienable sacred goods which therefore 'belong' *simultaneously* to the dead ancestors, to the living and to descendants yet to be born. In the second kind, a man or a woman has rights over an object if it is 'like his or her shadow (*amfonka*)'; to this category belong clothes, pigs, planted trees, axes and needles; these goods are personally appropriated and are alienable.

These two kinds of rule are in a hierarchical relation with each other. If someone is in a *merafo* relation to a portion of the tribal territory, the labour he expends in planting trees there gives him the right to appropriate them for himself (*amfonka*). We can interpret this relation as the product of two principles of social organization. On the one hand, the simple fact of belonging to the tribe, and therefore to one of its kinship groups, opens up rights and founds the system's first principle, whereas labour, whether individual or collective, is merely added on, as a second principle, to the first. Thus the common interests prevail over those of the individual whilst, at the level of power and forms of authority, the clan prevails over each of the lineages and each individual. As a member of the tribe, an individual has the right to hunt and to gather wild plants growing on the tribe's territory, but he only has the right to grow crops upon the cultivated lands of his own clan. As a member of a male house grouping together several lineages of his clan, he has more rights over some portions of his clan's territory than over others. And as member of a lineage, he will take precedence over the other members of his lineage in the use of certain plots of land, if it was his father or his great-grandfather who originally cleared them. When two individuals are in conflict over the use of a particular plot, the person with the greater number of rights of use in such a plot will take precedence.

Thus, membership of a group guarantees an individual access

to resources, and the relations of groups with each other multiply and distribute the number of possibilities open to the individual. His membership of a tribal group gives him hunting and gathering rights which do not provide him with sufficient to live; conversely, his membership of a clan, i.e. a descent group, guarantees him the essentials of his material (and political) means of existence, since it gives him access to some cultivatable land and since agriculture in this society furnishes what is essential in the way of material resources. The hierarchical relation within the system of property rules, subordinating *amfonka* to *merafo* rights therefore aims at limiting the contradictions of interest between the individuals and the various groups to which they belong and which control them.

Another interesting example of a 'combined system' is a situation in which different ethnic and political groups share distinct and complementary rights over the same resources. The Incas used to deprive the tribes they had subdued of any property right in their soil, which became the Inca's property. The land was then given back to the conquered tribes, who would hold permanent rights of use in it but with the obligation in return to cultivate a part of it for the State, in other words, for the Inca and his 'father' (the Sun-God) and for his priests. Many languages have distinct terms to designate these various rights which are piled up on a given reality. In French, we distinguish between *propriété* (the right to alienate something), *possession*, *droit d'usage*, and so on. In English, there is property, ownership and possession; in German, *Eigentum* and *Besitzung*.

My fourth point is that systems of property rights always distinguish the quality (and consequently the number) of those who possess rights and which rights they possess. This serves to define the equality or inequality of the members of the society in relation to the 'realities' to which these rights give access.

Thus, as we have seen, Siane rights in land and ritual knowledge are exclusively reserved for men. Amongst the Baruya of New Guinea, as amongst the Siane, hunting and agricultural territories are the undivided property of patrilineal lineages. However, amongst the Baruya an individual may not hunt throughout the tribal territory. The rights of undivided property are only transmitted through the men. Although after their marriage and throughout their lifetime — save if hatred divides brothers-in-law and the lineages via which they are related — the women retain the right to use their ancestors' land, they cannot transmit this right to their children since the latter belong to their father's lineage. On the other hand, they transmit to their daughters the magical formulae which enable one to raise pigs, together with the names given to pigs (a matrilineal element in a patrilineal society). Furthermore, only the men possess the sacred objects used during the initiation ceremonies to reproduce the strength of future warriors. The women are forbidden to see or touch them.[4] In other societies, by contrast, rights in land are transmitted exclusively through women (down the matrilineal line), whilst rights of succession to the throne or the chiefship in the same society will be transmitted through the men and down the patrilineal line.

In addition to these inequalities between the sexes and the generations, there is often an inequality of rights between a social minority and the rest of the population. In the Trobriand Islands, only the aristocracy has the right to practise the rituals which guarantee the fertility of the land and the waters (see Malinowski). We are concerned here with whole lineages enjoying a monopoly over ritual practice and not, as was the case with the So of Uganda, with a group of men who are lineage elders and initiates of the Keresan cult. In the case of the Trobrianders, the kinship groups (matrilineages) composing the society are not equivalent to each other but are ranked in a hierarchical order involving status differences in and property rights.

Finally, a form of property only exists when it serves as a rule for the concrete appropriation of reality. Property only really exists when it is rendered effective in and through a process of concrete appropriation. Property can only be reduced to a body of abstract rules at the cost of making it a set of velleities condemned to play the part of individual and collective fantasies. This is the fifth point that must be borne in mind if the various forms assumed by property in different societies are to be understood.

Society and Territory

By territory is meant a portion of nature and therefore space over

---

4. For a more detailed analysis of the rights of men and women in Baruya society and of their respective places in the process and relations of production, see Maurice Godelier, *La Production des Grands Hommes*, Paris 1982.

which a given society lays claim to and ensures, for all or some of its members, stable rights of access, control and use regarding all or some of the resources found there, and which it is desirous and capable of exploiting.

By 'space' one can as readily mean a stretch of land as of water and even, in recent times, of air; the 'exploitable' resources within these spaces can be encountered either in the soil itself or in the subsoil, on the surface of the waters or in their depths. Equally everyone knows that a natural reality, e.g. the power of the wind or the water, is not in itself a resource for humanity. It becomes such at a determinate historical epoch and for a definite period at the end of which, being either exhausted or abandoned, it is replaced by another. But a natural reality only ever becomes a resource for humanity through the combined effect of two conditions. First, it must be able to satisfy a human need either directly or indirectly and have some utility within a form of social life. Second, man must possess the technical means to separate it from the rest of nature and make it serve his own ends. This implies that a society has a particular interpretation of nature and that it combines these intellectual representations with material means in order to act upon a portion of this nature and make it serve the society's own physical and social reproduction.

What nature provides humanity with is firstly of course the nature of the human being, an animal species endowed with a body and obliged, in order to reproduce itself, to live in society. In addition, it provides this creature with material elements which can serve as: a) means of subsistence; b) means of labour and production (tools or raw materials with which to make them); c) finally, means to produce the material aspects of the human being's social relations, those which make up the determinate structure of a society (kinship relations, politico-religious relations, etc.). Into this latter category fall the shimmering feathers of birds of paradise and the clays or powdered minerals used to decorate one's body and to communicate with ancestors or spirits as well as the masks of carved wood and the temples and their stone altars where the gods reside. Need I remind the reader that the resources humanity levies from nature are very rarely utilizable just as they are, but must undergo a certain number of changes in form and state if they are to be transformed into 'consumable' realities? (e.g. the wild tubers or bitter domestic manioc from which the venomous juices must first be extracted if they are to be eaten.) When, moreover, each of these means of subsistence, production or reproduction of social relations has been consumed, production thereof must be recommenced.

Nature therefore presents itself to humanity in two forms, as two complementary but distinct realities (one could equally well say that they are two sides of the same reality): both in the form of the human being's 'organic' body — humanity's reality as a social animal species — and as the milieu which in a sense forms the human being's 'inorganic body (to employ Marx's excellent expression in the *Grundrisse der Kritik der politischen Ökonomie*). I shall therefore call 'territory' the portion of nature and space which a society claims as the site where its members are to find in perpetuity the material conditions and means of their existence. Of course, in no society, including our own (where various materialist visions of nature have been elaborated), does it seem possible to reduce natural realities to their sensible aspect. Everywhere human beings also represent them to themselves as being composed of forces and powers which elude the senses and which, so far as the reproduction of the human being is concerned, constitute its most important part. For this reason, all the forms of concrete activity invented by humanity whereby to appropriate material realities for itself simultaneously and necessarily contain and combine 'material' actions and forms of conduct enabling human beings to act upon their visible and tangible aspects, and actions which we should today call 'symbolic', that enable them to act upon their invisible background (rites preceding departure for the hunt, rites to guarantee the fertility of the soil, of women, etc.).

So what a society claims in appropriating a territory for itself is access to, and control and use of, both the visible realities and the invisible powers which constitute it and which seem to share between them mastery of the reproductive conditions of human life — both the human beings' own life and that of the resources upon which they depend. This is what the notion of 'property in a territory' seems to me to consist of. But this 'property' only fully exists when the members of a society use its rules to organize their concrete acts of appropriation. These forms of action on nature are invariably social forms, whether they are individual or collective, whether they are concerned with hunting, gathering, fishing, stockbreeding, agriculture, artisanal production or industry. In our society, we call these activities 'labour' and we term the organized development of each of them a 'labour process'. Hence one ought logically to consider the symbolic moments and

forms of behaviour that figure there and through which the
human being seeks to act upon the invisible forces controlling the
visible realities he strives to appropriate (rain, heat, game, plant,
etc.) as pertaining to labour and as an essential aspect of each
labour process. But it must be emphasized that the word 'labour'
does not exist in many languages, because the representations
corresponding to it do not exist either. Amongst the Maenge,
horticulturists in New Britain, horticultural activities are considered to be an 'exchange' with the dead and the gods, not a 'transformation' of nature and still less a transformation of 'human
nature'.[5] The latter is a commonplace notion in the West nowadays, but it appeared relatively late in our history, in the eighteenth century no doubt.

In short, the forms of property in a territory are an essential
part of what we call a society's economic structure, since they
constitute the legal — if not for everyone the legitimate — condition governing access to resources and the means of production.
These property forms are always combined with specific forms of
organization of the labour processes and of redistribution of the
products issuing from this process, their combination forming the
economic structure of a society, its mode of production and its
economic system. To describe and explain the various forms of
property in nature is, thanks to the collaboration of historians,
anthropologists and economists, to elaborate a reasoned history
of the economic systems which have succeeded each other in the
course of humanity's evolution.

The forms of property in a territory are therefore at once a
relation with nature and a relation between men. This latter has a
double aspect: it is both a relation between societies and a
relation within each society between the individuals and the
groups of which it is composed. The societies concerned are
generally neighbours, but not necessarily so — for example, the
colonial territories of France, Great Britain, Germany or Russia
and the respective metropolitan countries. For this reason, whatever the form — be it individual or collective — of any process of
concrete appropriation of nature, it is always that of a social
relation, the effect of a society's structure. The theoretical consequence of this fact is fundamental: the idea that the individual as
such, independently of the social group to which he belongs, is
everywhere and always the source of property rights in nature, is

---

5. See below, chapter 3.

quite without any scientific basis. Of course, such a notion is to be found in the ideology of certain societies during certain epochs, including ours, but even in the latter case, it is neither the source nor the ultimate foundation for the rights of the individual. Carl Brinkmann has put this point very well in the *Encyclopedia of the Social Sciences*, in the entry on 'Land Tenure':

> The vesting of land tenure in an individual as distinct from a social group, whether of contemporaries or of successive generations, is thus a very modern concept incapable of complete fulfillment even in a capitalist economy. But so also is land tenure as an individual right exclusive of other concurrent rights. What must seem a contradiction in terms to the property notion of Roman or of modern civil law — namely, that there may be two or more property rights in the same thing — is evidently the most general rule in the institutions governing the tenure of land.'[6]

A century before, Marx had said much the same thing, but in a more lapidary fashion: 'An isolated individual could no more have property in land and soil than he could speak.'[7]

Thus, nowhere — not even in the most developed of capitalist societies — does there exist individual property in land which the individual may himself wholly use and abuse. Everywhere there exists some kind of limitation upon his right, which is founded upon the prior existence of a communal right, a State, nation, crown and so on. The *ius uti et abutendi* defines a principle, a limit which is never wholly realized.

When, in the course of history, there have been individuals who have possessed a prior right to the whole of a territory and to all a society's resources, as was the case with the Pharaohs of Egypt or with the Inca, they never possessed it as an individual title, but because they were 'gods' and personified to a higher degree the 'sovereignty' of the State and the power of a dominant caste/class[8] over all the other groups and castes/classes in the society.

In these examples, a superior individual's 'property' is both the form and the effect of the concentration of landed property in the hands of a class and/or the State.

---

6. Carl Brinkman, 'Land Tenure', *Encyclopedia of the Social Sciences*, p. 74.

7. K. Marx, *Grundrisse*, Harmondsworth 1973, p. 485.

8. The word 'class' is understood here in its generic sense. See below, chapter 7, Appendix, pp. 245-52.

We can now proceed to give a rapid account of some forms of property in territory found in pre-capitalist societies.

Territory as a Relation between Societies

a) First of all, let me remind the reader that societies exist which seem not to 'possess' any territory of their own. This is the case with the Peul WoDaabe, transhumant pastoralists who nowadays live in Niger, and have been studied by Marguerite Dupire. They have slowly infiltrated the territory of a sedentary agricultural people, the Hausa, who allowed them to use their bush or fallow land in return for the payment of dues in livestock or services. Sometimes, when the Tuareg, themselves nomads, were in control of the sedentary populations onto whose territory the Peul had moved their flocks, the Peul would owe dues in livestock and services both to the Tuareg and to the sedentary populations. This form of collective transhumance does not therefore imply any appropriation of the pastures. And the paths of distinct pastoral peoples, be they Peul, Bella or Tuareg, over the territory of the same agricultural populations are intertwined and synchronized in a manner fixed by custom to avoid conflicts.

b) We know of cases such as that of the Bassari, a tribe from the South of Iran studied by Frederick Barth, where several pastoral nomadic societies use the same territory and the same watering places in rotation and in a definite order. Each tribe follows a path (*il-rah*), which it represents to itself as being a traditional right to use certain pastures at certain seasons of the year. By means of this kind of migration, the nomads are able to compensate for the seasonal variations in the region's ecological resources (torrid plains in the south, snow-clad mountains in the north) and they derive maximum advantage from it. This traditional right includes rights of passage over prepared paths or roads, grazing on uncultivated or fallow land, together with the use of both natural springs and rivers and irrigation canals, whether on the surface or under it (*ganats*).

In 1958, the Bassari tribe's seasonal displacement involved one hundred and fifty thousand people and over a million head of cattle. From winter into summer and from summer into winter, they had twice covered their *il-rah*, a tribal road almost five hundred kilometres long which had brought them from the coastal hills of the south (650 metres high) to the alpine zones of

Mount Kuhi-Bul in the north (4,000 metres high) — in short, a transhumance zone of more than 9,600 square kilometres. The Bassari are preceded in spring and followed in the autumn by the Kurdshuli-Lur tribe. This fluid system brings about a virtually continuous and almost maximal utilization of the resources of each locality and each season, providing for the future through a balanced adjustment between human and animal populations and local resources in grazing and water. This form of adjustment to technical and ecological constraints should not be taken to mean that there is no competition between the tribes. Whilst the total population of the region (human beings plus domestic animals) is determined by the maximum carrying capacity of the local pastures, the most powerful tribes do their utmost to make their own arrival on these pastures coincide with the time of their maximal productive capacity.

We are not dealing here with a mechanical ecological determinism, but with ecological and technological determinations (a lack of any procedures for storing fodder and so on) which require a response adapted to the level of the relations of production and power. These relations obviously imply a certain kind of policy in relation to the local sedentary communities through whose stubble-fields the nomads pass and with whom they exchange pastoral and artisanal products in return for agricultural and industrial ones.

Owen Lattimore has shown that an analogous system used to exist among the Mongol shepherds and that the power of the *khans* depended in part on their own tribe's capacity to regulate the succession of other tribes as these traversed the pastures and watering places which were the common property of the political confederation they constituted together.

c) The territorial structure of the Bassari is, moreover part of a more complex structure. The Bassari are in fact members of a tri-ethnic confederation called Khamseh (from the Arabic word for 'five'), which consists of five 'tribes': three Turkish-speaking tribes (Bahârihu, Nafar, Inân-Lu); one Iranian-speaking tribe (the Bassari); and one Arabic-speaking one. Now, these three ethnic and linguistic groups exploit tiers situated at different altitudes within the same ecosystems. In the upper part, the Turkish speakers breed Bactrian camels which are well adapted to the rigours of the high-altitude climate. Lower down, the Iranian speakers rear horses and small livestock. In the piedmount zones, the Arabic speakers live off the large-scale breeding of dromedaries.

d) Together with these instances of societies which simultaneously exploit adjacent territories, one should consider those societies which simultaneously exploit several separated territories. John Murra has presented us with an example of this — the Inca and pre-Inca Andean societies. The community of Chupaychu, as described by the Royal Visitor Inigo Ortiz at the time of his passage through the Huanuco region in 1559, was distributed as follows among three separate territories. At 3,200 metres there lived the nucleus of the population, which grew maize and tubers as its staple foodstuffs. The centre of local power was based there and the population belonged to only one ethnic group. Two kinds of peripheral centre served to complete the structure of the community. In the Puna, at 4,000 metres, some small groups extracted salt and engaged in the large-scale breeding of llamas and alpacas. In the Montaña, a zone situated several hundred metres above the Amazon basin, some other families cultivated cotton continuously and exploited resources in wood and coca. In the peripheral centres, the population was multi-ethnic and the space was simultaneously exploited by groups belonging to several tribes. However, the members of each community permanently domiciled in these peripheral centres, three or four days' march away from the various central nuclei, retained all their rights in the fields belonging to their central village. Each society thus formed a string of ecological and economic islands scattered around a centre.

The structure of the Altiplano kingdoms around Lake Titicaca was still more complicated. Using the account given by Garcia Diez de San Miguel of his visit in 1567, John Murra has shown how the kingdom of Lupaqa, which comprised around twenty thousand domestic units speaking Aymara and Uru, used to exploit several territories situated on the east and west slopes of the Andes, with the region of Lake Titicaca serving as its political and economic centre. In this case, in addition to the Amazonian forest's resources, there were those derived from the Pacific Ocean and the irrigated valleys of the coastal region. The distance between the central territory and its peripheral nuclei was from ten to fifteen days' march through alien territories. Considered as a whole, the Lupaqa kingdom seems to have had the same territorial structure as the Chupaychu community: a series of ecological and economic islands scattered at different altitudes around a centre in which two ethnic groups, the Aymara and the Uru, lived and shared resources; the population in the

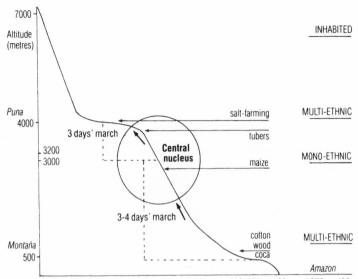

Territory of the Chupaychu: 2,500 to 3,000 domestic units in 1562. (After J. Murra, 1972, p.433.)

peripheral centres remained a multi-ethnic one. Alongside the tribal organization and ethnic diversity, there was also a 'class' difference, between a hereditary aristocracy and the mass of the common people. It was within this social framework that problems of access to resources in both the centre and the periphery were handled, and a policy pursued concerning war and peace and the conflicts and alliances between the ethnic groups and the kingdoms. At the same time, the society's economic structure had diversified and, alongside agriculturists and stockbreeders, specialized groups devoted themselves to the production of pottery or to metal-work in copper, silver and gold.

With the emergence of Tawantinsuyu, the Inca Empire of the 'Four Quarters' of the universe, there was a new transformation in the Andean territorial model. The State deported whole populations in order to break their resistance, or else it transferred communities of military colonists (*mitmaq*) across huge distances. These colonists, chosen from the most loyal tribes, were installed in strategic positions amongst those populations which showed signs of rebelling against the conqueror. Entire communities were thenceforth cut off from their traditional ecological environment and original ethnic group, and placed in the direct service of the State, with no choice but to co-operate in the reproduction

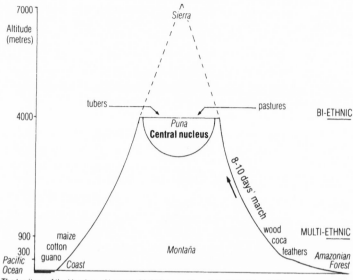

The territory of the kingdom of Lupapa: 20.000 domestic units in 1567. (After S. Murra, 1972, p.441.)

of relations of political domination. This reordering of territorial space expressed a new fashion of exploiting both nature and the peasants' labour-power, since from then on the limitations imposed by the diversity of regional ecosystems and the local character of forms of social organization and production were transcended to some degree.

These three examples provide particularly clear illustrations of the continuity and ruptures which could exist in the definition and use of nature as territory during the evolution which has transformed classless societies into class societies and state formations. Furthermore, we learn from contemporary archaeologists that this evolution first occurred in particular regions of the globe — Mesoamerica, Peru, Mesopotamia, ancient northern India and China.

Territory as a Relation between the Groups and Individuals Making up a Society: Territory as Object and Issue in Forms of Sharing within Societies

Forms of Property and Social Relations of Production

We have seen that the individuals and groups making up a particular society gain access to and appropriate natural resources by means of a *social form* of property (or of stable use) in a territory, a form which legitimizes such access and appropriation. Now, it can be shown that in every society the forms of property in territory assume the form of the social relations — whatever they may be — which function there as framework for production, i.e. as social relations of production.

An example may be helpful here. In certain Australian Aborigine tribes, it was legitimate for every individual belonging to one of his tribe's descent groups (moiety, section, sub-section, in the tribes which had these kinds of division) to hunt on all his kinship group's territories. Each individual also knew that in cases of necessity, when game and water disappeared altogether owing to exceptional drought, he could go and hunt on the lands — of his relatives, both those from whom his tribe had originally received his mother or those from whom he had received a wife in exchange for one of his sisters, whether real or classificatory.

We are faced here with what we have called 'abstract' property in nature, that is, a set of rules which everyone in a society must know and which each person learns in youth. These rules define the 'legitimate and normal' use of a territory and its resources, although they do make provision for exceptional circumstances when a local group's survival and, with it, the reproduction of the whole tribe is threatened. The term 'tribe' is used very loosely in ethnographic literature. It designates several groups which, by exclusively (or almost exclusively) inter-marrying, form a social unit (in extreme cases an endogamous one) and which recognize common interests and territory, which they may defend by force of arms.[9]

I should like to draw the reader's attention to three features of this system of abstract rules for appropriating nature. First, this 'property' in nature appears both to the Aborigines and to foreign observers as an aspect of kinship relations, an *attribute of kinship.* Second, it has the form of *communal* property of a group of kin engaged together in the egalitarian appropriation of resources. Third, the fact that each kinship group has precedence in the use of a portion of tribal territory does not mean that the other groups are totally excluded from it; the latter share certain rights in this fraction of territory through a system of reciprocal access and

---

9. See my analysis of the concept in *Perspectives in Marxist Anthropology*, Cambridge 1977.

cooperation. Precedence and continuous use are attributes of kinship by descent, while the rights guaranteeing reciprocal access, and which consequently are far from secondary — above all in periods of drought — derive from marriage relations.

This would seem to be the abstract model of the rules for appropriating nature. But how do things work out in practice, in concrete, daily appropriation, i.e. in the organization of hunting and gathering in the framework of local bands which live a nomadic existence on the tribal territory? For a long time anthropologists had given credence to Radcliffe-Brown (1931, 1952) who, without ever having really had first-hand experience of their life in the desert, had questioned many natives and obtained from them a description of their customs and practices. He had come to the conclusion that among the Australian Aborigines each patriclan had an 'exclusive' right to a particular territory, whose resources it alone exploited. That implied that each local band was a patrilineal group communally exploiting a territory bequeathed by its ancestors. But fieldwork done since 1930 by Elkin, Rose, Hiatt, Meggitt, Peterson, Turner and others, has shown that the local bands, far from being composed of members of a single patriclan, in fact consisted of men belonging to several patriclans and exploiting the resources of several territories. A lively polemic was unleashed against Radcliffe-Brown and his supporters (e.g. Stanner). Some, like Meggitt, went so far as to assert that a tribe's resources were common to all its members and concluded that the Aborigines had never had any notion of territory in the 'economic' sense of the term. For them, the territory peculiar to their section meant a series of sacred totemic sites created by the metamorphosis of a mythical ancestor, where the spirits of the clan ancestors remaining in perpetuity whilst awaiting their reincarnation in one or other of their descendants. If it seemed that a territory in the economic sense of the term existed for each section, this was because the members wished to be in permanent contact with their ancestors' spirits and therefore preferred to hunt around the sites where these spirits resided.

I do not wish to make dogmatic pronouncements regarding a specialist debate whose data change all the time. Nor do I wish to suggest, as Lévi-Strauss has done (in R. Lee and I. De Vore, 1968), that one can accept the positions of both schools on the grounds that they describe two different epochs in the evolution of the last bands of hunters subjected to increasing pressure from the Whites, who despoiled them of some of their lands and regrouped them in camps. In fact I hold that the distinction between abstract property and concrete appropriation will enable us to clarify the issue and to resolve certain contradictions. The fact that within a single local band we find families belonging to several sections means that in everyday life marriage relations are the condition for a wider cooperation than that obtained between the members of a single kinship group. The fact that such a band utilizes several totemic territories does not mean that these territories are not at the same time 'economic' territories. Proof of this seems to me to be provided by a detail in the organization of the hunt, which specialists have known about but which can hardly be said to have held their attention. Traditionally, when a composite band hunted with fire over several territories, the call to set fire to a corner of the bush would go out to a man belonging to the section which held sacred rights there. Would this not seem to indicate recognition of a precedence in the use of this territory, of a particular status enjoyed by this portion of the tribal territory resting upon a hereditary association between it and one of the kinship groups forming the tribe? Over and above the cooperation in 'labour' which confers certain rights to a share in the resources acquired through communal hunting or gathering, it seems that there are differences in the rights enjoyed by the hunters that are prior to their 'labour' and not reducible to it. The fact of belonging to a distinct kinship group with its own totems creates particular rights and duties for them vis-à-vis other groups. They are obliged to watch over the use and reproduction of the resources and realities in their charge, and which they actually or symbolically 'give' to other groups in the same situation. Often each group abstain from consuming the totemic animal or plant which it magically 'reproduce' for the others. Material obligation between groups obviously do not arise solely from their cooperation in labour, any more than they can be reduced to this form of cooperation.

We have touched here upon a point of great theoretical significance, for this example furnishes an instance of kinship relations which, as in every society, regulate descent, marriage and possibly the residence of the individuals who constitute a society, but which in addition and simultaneously regulate the abstract and concrete appropriation of nature; they are what, in our own western culture, one would call the society's economic structure and what Marxists would term social relations of production.

The term 'production' is by and large inadequate here, since the economic activities of the Australian Aborigines consist essentially in appropriating for themselves resources produced by nature and not by humanity (which nevertheless contributes to their reproduction through the systematic use of fire in hunting, which modifies the vegetal cover, and so on).

This returns us to the idea advanced in the previous chapter (pp. 28-31), namely, that the distinction between infrastructure and superstructure, between economy and kinship or religion, is a distinction involving functions and not institutions. The same institutions can function as economic structure and as kinship relations, and one must accept as an analytical principle that social relations are what they do, or rather what they make men do — and not what they appear to us to be.

Material and Social Forms of Appropriation of Nature: Some Examples

1. Hunter-Gatherer Societies

It may be useful to compare three societies living in very different ecosystems: a generalized ecosystem in the Equatorial forest (the Pygmies of Zaire) and two specialized ecosystems, the scrub of the Kalahari (Bushmen) and the desert expanses of southern Australia (Aranda).

The Bushmen of Botswana and South Africa exploit the wild resources of the Kalahari desert's more humid zones, where there are permanent watering places which enable them to survive during the dry season. In 1964-65 Richard Lee studied a group of !Kung Bushmen who lived in a region named after one of the six permanent watering places to be found there, the Dobe region in the north-west of Botswana. Of 336 individuals recorded, some 248, divided into 14 camps of 9 to 29 persons, then lived in this region. In the dry season these 14 camps were set up near the 6 watering places; 5 gathered at the same spot, so that there was a total of 94 persons based there, with additional occasional visitors (13 in all). All told, in 1965 55 !Kung from other bands visited the Dobe and 34 Dobe left the region to go and live elsewhere, with kin or friends. During the dry season, the exploited zone around each watering place formed a circle of 9.5 kilometres radius on average — a distance which could be covered, going out and coming back, in a single day. During the rainy season, other watering places appeared, so that the zone exploited by the camps increased to a circle of 32 kilometres radius around the permanent watering place of the dry season. Individuals would often change camp. Within a band all the individuals were generally kin by descent or marriage, and they had kinship ties with members of other bands. But the bands were not in themselves kinship groups of the clan, lineage or section type.

Richard Lee concluded from his observations that these exploited zones 'were not really territories in the zoological sense of the term since they were not defended against outsiders'. He also asserted that the Bushmen knew nothing of aggressive conduct, war, inequality between the sexes and so on. All of these assertions were hotly contested by H. Heinz who based his own arguments upon his experience with another group of Bushmen, the !Ko, also from Botswana. According to him, each humid region was distributed among several bands who were partners in the use of one or several permanent watering places. These bands were no longer kinship groups, although their members were all more or less related. Several associated bands formed what Heinz calls a 'nexus', a network held together by intermarriage. Despite this, each band used to hunt on a portion of the territory common to the 'nexus' that was reserved exclusively for it and it used to set up camp a little distance from the others when they gathered near the same permanent watering place. Finally, each 'nexus' of bands was separated from other 'nexuses' by a stretch of desert, a no-man's-land which would rarely be crossed by individuals, and still more rarely by whole bands. Against Lee Heinz asserts that war used to break out between two nexuses if members of one had gone hunting on the other's territory without first asking their 'permission'. He also uses the testimony of G. Silberbauer on the !Gwi Bushmen and L. Marshall on the !Kung Nyaï-Nyaï to lend substance to his assertion that 'territories' do exist among the Bushmen, together with the aggressive conduct and armed action necessary to defend them. He emphasizes that the !Kung Dobe live in a region where resources are more plentiful than is the case for the other Bushmen groups — a factor which could well explain their lack of concern with protecting their resources.

It is worth enquiring whether the realities observed by Lee and Heinz were not distinct in the sense that they were not situated at the same level of social organization. It seems that the facility of reciprocal access to resources enjoyed by the members of the fourteen Dobe camps according to Lee, was a normal aspect of existence within a single nexus, and that the facility of leaving one band to go and live in another suggests that these bands together constituted what Heinz calls a 'nexus'. But what transpired between these !Kung and other groups of !Kung Bushmen? We do not know, although it may have been the same as Heinz records as happening between two 'nexuses' of !Ko bands — potential and sometimes real hostility. We therefore require more empirical data and more theoretical precision if we are to arrive at a conclusion. But it would seem that each local band enjoyed precedence in the appropriation of local resources, although this would not rule out considerable flexibility between the various local bands as regards reciprocal access to their resources.

According to Colin Turnbull, among the Mbuti Pygmies who live in the Equatorial forest of Zaïre, the space was divided up into distinct territories belonging to local bands each bearing the name of a river or a feature of the terrain, such as the Epulu band (named after the river Epulu) amongst whom Turnbull lived for several years. In contrast to Richard Lee's account of the Bushmen, the notion of territory here appears to be 'the sole concept by means of which a band may be defined' (Turnbull, p. 93). For a band is primarily a group of nuclear families sharing a common hunting territory (p. 27). One has the right to hunt in a band either because one was born on its territory and has kept one's rights in it (even if one no longer lives there) or because one has been accepted by the members of this band and incorporated into it through links of kinship or friendship. The band is therefore not a kinship group, even if almost all its members are related. The average surface of a territory forms a rectangle which, measured in distances covered on foot, could be reckoned as a day's march for the short side, which generally follows a path or a road through the forest, and as three to four day's march for the side which plunges deep into the forest, thus amounting to approximately 15 X 50 kilometres = 750 square kilometres in all. The band hunts with either net or bow and shifts camp within its territory from month to month once the game (a variety of antelope) is exhausted locally. Individuals change band frequently, either to adjust their numbers to the available resources or because they prefer to separate from families with which they have quarrelled. Thus bands and territories are fixed, individuals mobile. In the case of the net hunters, the local bands comprise from seven to thirty associated nuclear families (from 35 to 150 persons). Net hunting is not feasible with less than seven or more than thirty nets. According to Colin Turnbull (personal communication), there exists a no-man's-land in the middle of the forest which cannot be appropriated by any band. This exclusion is maintained by tacit agreement and justified by the idea that the god of the forest resides there. This unappropriated zone therefore functions for the benefit of all simultaneously, as a reserve in which stocks of wild game can be replenished. It is as if by means of this sacred and protected place, the Forest — a benevolent divinity — sends its children, the Pygmies, the game enabling them to live.

As we have seen, the tribal territory of the Australian Aborigines appears to have been divided up into particular zones in each of which a kinship group enjoyed prior rights of use handed down from generation to generation. Sometimes this precedence was absolute, so that other kinship groups were excluded from religious, ceremonial and symbolic practices by which each kinship group maintained its invisible relation with the spirits of its mythical or real ancestors, which still lived in certain sacred places within their territory. Sometimes, however, this precedence was relative, concerned with subsistence practices, and did not exclude other kinship groups. This is why the local bands are composite and traverse several territories whose actual ritual appropriation is fixed.

Furthermore, among the Australians rights pertain to kinship groups which combine to constitute local bands, whereas in the case of the Mbuti Pygmies and the Bushmen the local bands are groups of related individuals but not kinship groups. This forces us to direct our attention to the nature of the kinship relations which exist in these three societies, structured in a linear fashion in the case of the Australian hunters, but in a more undifferentiated fashion in the case of the Pygmies and the Bushmen

	Territories	Bands	Individual
Australians	fixed	mobile	mobile
Pygmies	fixed	fixed	mobile
!Ko Bushmen	fixed	fixed	mobile
!Kung Bushmen	mobile? fixed?	mobile	mobile

(as also in the case of the Tanzanian Hadza, the North American Washo and Shoshone, etc.).

To arrive at a more definite conclusion, it would be necessary systematically to develop the kind of typology of territorial forms and kinship relations among hunters that I have hinted at here.[10] This is not the place to conduct such an analysis, but the reader will already appreciate how risky it is to talk (as does Claude Meillassoux for example) of a 'cynegetic' mode of production.

2. Nomadic Shepherds

The fact that I have chosen to analyse pastoral nomadic societies *after* hunter-gatherer societies should not be taken to imply that I would endorse the idea that these two material modes of production and subsistence have necessarily succeeded each other in the course of history. However, it may be worth pausing to consider this idea, which was formulated as early as the fourth century BC by Dicaearchus and, much less clearly, by the poet Lucretius in the first century BC.[11] Ronald Meek has shown how the idea re-emerged in the seventeenth century under the impact of the Europeans' discovery of the North American Indians, but was still only sketched in by Locke whereas around 1750 in France and Scotland, it became an actual theory developed by jurists, philosophers and economists, amongst them the two most famous — Quesnay and Adam Smith.[12]

---

10. Since I wrote the present text, a further step has been taken in this direction by A. Testart, in his *Les sociétés de chasseurs-cueilleurs ou l'origine des inégalités*, Paris 1982.

11. Lucretius, *De Rerum Natura*, Book V. On this subject, see Arthur O. Lovejoy and George Boas, *Primitivism and Related Ideas in Antiquity*, New York 1965; Frederick J. Teggart, *The Idea of Progress*, Berkeley 1969.

12. Ronald Meek, *Social Science and the Ignoble Savage*, Cambridge 1976 (chapters 3 and 4 in particular). As regards France, Meek quotes explicit passages to this effect from the young Turgot's *Sur la géographie politique* (1751); Helvetius's *De l'Esprit* (1758); Goguet's *De l'origine des lois, des arts et des sciences* (1758); and Quesnay and Mirabeau's *La philosophie rurale* (1761). In Scotland Adam Smith had already presented an outline sketch of this idea in his course of lectures on moral philosophy at Glasgow. In 1757 Sir John Dalrymple formulated it explicitly in his *Essay towards a General Theory of Feudal Property in Great Britain*. In 1758, Lord Kames made it one of the central themes of his *Historical Law-Tracts*. In 1771, Adam Miller turned it into a genuine philosophy of history in *The Origin of Ranks*. Finally, Adam Smith developed this same idea in his *Treatise on the Wealth of Nations* (1776) where he describes the succession of four stages or modes of subsistence: 1. hunting; 2. stockbreeding; 3. agriculture; 4. the age of trade.

This theory of a succession of hunting, stockbreeding and agriculture was entertained throughout the nineteenth century, reiterated as much by Marx as by Spencer, by Morgan as by Tylor and received a tremendous impetus from triumphant evolutionism. It was not until 1896 that Hahn formulated the contrary hypothesis — that stockbreeding had probably first appeared in the Near East in sedentary communities already acquainted with agriculture. He held that *nomadic* stockbreeding had developed even later before spreading across the steppes of Asia and Africa which were less suited to agriculture.

Archaeological work in Iran, Iraq and Palestine has since served to confirm some of these views, although it has also shown that things were in fact much more complicated. While some hunter-gatherer societies seem to have domesticated cereals, goats and sheep simultaneously, others (in the valley of Jordan for example), which practised a selective hunting of herds of wild transhumant livestock with which they lived in a kind of permanent symbiosis, had proceeded directly to forms of domestication and stockbreeding independent of agriculture.[13]

Let me add that if the idea of a succession of necessary stages is nowadays obsolete, something still survives from the notion of a *mode* of subsistence, namely the idea that only certain forms of social life, thought and government are compatible with these various modes of subsistence. Marx retained this idea proceeding beyond Adam Smith from the notion of mode of subsistence to that of mode of production.

Pastoral stockbreeding is thus not a primitive system of exploitation of nature, a form superseded in the course of humanity's economic evolution. On the contrary, it has taken millennia to perfect the system and, right up until our own epoch, it has very often been adopted on the grounds that it is more effective and dynamic as a type of economy than many forms of agriculture. X. de Planhol has accumulated a large amount of information which suggests that it was only in the thirteenth century that the sedentary agricultural societies of Great Luristan adopted a nomadic pastoral system entailing summering and wintering, such as that of the Bassari or the Bakhtiari of Iran described by Frederick Barth and J.P. Digard, a pastoralism learnt from the Mongols who were then surrounding these mountainous regions. It was

---

13. See S. Bokony's synthesis, 'Development of Early Stock Raising in the Near East', *Nature* 264, November 1976, pp. 13-23.

only in the nineteenth century that the Regueibat of the Saharawi stopped being agriculturalists and sheep breeders and committed themselves to the large-scale breeding of dromedaries. Likewise, it was in the seventeenth century that the Rwala Bedouin who had shifted from Saudi Arabia to Libya and Iraq began to specialize in breeding dromedaries and in the caravan trade.

Comparing the territories of the Regueibat, the Rwala and the Bakhtiari, Pierre Bonte and J.P. Digard have drawn attention to the following differences.

The tribal territory of the Regueibat is vast and lacks any precise limits. In summer the domestic groups are dispersed as widely as possible, regrouping in winter around a central region, provided that the rains have been adequate. It may happen that in a ten-year period, a group does not camp twice in the same place, and the rights of use in pastures would seem simply to revert to the first arrivals (P. Bonte). This society is divided into lineages subdivided into six fractions, to which are added groups of clients and strangers; but it is still not very stratified.

Among the Rwala (see J. Chelhod), the territory is inalienable tribal property. Its limits are precise and it is divided into lots which correspond in number and size to the various clans. Within each lineage, each person can graze his herd wherever he wishes so long as he remains within the limits of the common lot. Each lineage is represented by a chief (*sheikh*) supported by a council, whose power can be put in question at any time.

Among the Bakhtiari, the land remains communal property in the sense that theoretically it cannot be either sold or exchanged. However, the chiefs have turned some fields into private domains upon which they practise agriculture for their own profit. The pastures are strictly divided temporally and spatially among the lineage groups so that 'such-and-such a pass or thoroughfare is reserved for such-and-such a group at such-and-such a time'. This strict discipline in the particular use of tribal resources is under the control of a central tribal power, a sort of miniature State in the hands of an aristocracy itself subject to the tribe's *khan* and local functionaries nominated by him. In striking contrast to the Regueibat's casual nomadism, the various fractions of the tribe and their herds are involved here in an almost invariable cycle of obligatory shifts in space and in time. Rather than a temporary right of use accorded to the first arrival, we are here concerned with a permanent right of use which expresses an unequal relation in power and wealth between the various segments of the society.

There thus emerges a range of variations and transformations in the forms of appropriation of nature among nomadic pastoralists, and this range ought to be systematically analysed. In all these societies there is apparently a duality in the forms of appropriation of nature. Pastures and watering places are generally the undivided property of a tribal community, whereas the herds are the property of much more limited groups, domestic groups organized on a kinship basis, but composed of several minimal segmentary units which constitute direct and very largely autonomous consumption and production units.

This being the case, we observe great variation within all of these societies, according to whether the kinship groups and local domestic groups do or do not have equivalent rights over common resources, pastures and watering places. Under certain conditions, which it ought in fact be possible to reconstruct, a clan within a tribe or a tribe within a confederation of tribes comes to control the other clans' or tribes' access to the common resources and to identify itself with their common interests through this control over the common conditions of existence. Within the tribes a hierarchy is thus established between aristocratic lineages and lineages of commoners which, in certain cases, may give rise to tribal States (Moors, Bakhtiari) and empires (Mongols).[14] Of course, these processes open the way to various forms of exploitation of man by man or accompany them. Thus among the Qashqaî — neighbours of the Bakhtiari — the chiefs ended up turning the services they rendered into a direct source of profit, since they demanded rent in livestock at the time of periodic redistribution of the pastures, which were now communal only in appearance. Likewise, we know that in the East African kingdom of Ankole, the king enjoyed exclusive ownership of all of the kingdom's livestock, just as the Pharaoh had done in ancient Egypt.

These various transformations, which tend towards a development of social inequalities within communal tribal forms of social organization, occur in two forms of appropriation of nature whose oppositions they accentuate: the 'particular', even private,

---

14. See Owen Lattimore, 'The Steppes of Mongolia and the Characteristics of Steppe Nomadism', in *Inner Asian Frontiers of China*, New York, 1951, pp. 53-102.

appropriation of livestock facilitates the development of inequalities between lineages, clans and tribes; whereas the 'common' appropriation of pastures and watering places limits and opposes such a development.

3. The Agriculturalists

For my discussion of agriculturists I shall consider the case of the Romanian village communities studied by H.H. Stahl. This author concludes a historical and anthropological analysis which combines observation of the last archaic Romanian communities with study of historical documents preserved since the early Middle Ages, by classifying the forms of these communities into four groups, which reflect the stages of a very unusual historical evolution. In the case of the most ancient communities which exploited the mountain forests with the help of extensive agropastoral techniques, it seems that within each community every family enjoyed equal access to all resources. Herds were moved and fields exchanges in the forest as and when their users, acting in concert, so wished. This procedure did not even include a rule for 'particular' appropriation of the soil, so that it somewhat resembles the way of life of the Regueibat shepherds. According to H.H. Stahl, this archaic model quickly yielded to communities which he terms 'genealogical'. Under pressure from a rise in population, and seeking to maintain *equality* of access to good land which is unequally distributed across the territory's surface, the communities divided it into two unequal parts. The larger part remained accessible to all for stockbreeding, gathering and so on, with no more supervision than had characterized the earlier system. But the land that was good for cultivation and the sites suitable for the planting of orchards were shared out equally among the families on the basis of their genealogical connections: each group of families descended from one and the same ancestor receives an equal share. The principle of equivalence was thus maintained.

However, owing to the uneven evolution of the various families' demography, some of them subsequently found themselves controlling a much larger area of land per member than others. Thus, the application of an egalitarian principle to the appropriation of the soil and its resources led over time and through various accidents to an unequal redistribution of the good land. However, these two types of community were still communities of 'free' men. Now, study of their historical evolution serves to show that gradually two successive forms of enserfment were instituted. In about the tenth century, certain communities in Wallachia gradually came under the control of an aristocracy of boyars and war chiefs (*voïvode*), with these boyars themselves living in familial communities and communally appropriating the tithes and corvées they levied from the peasant communities. Their sharing of these rents was modelled upon the distribution of good land among the families of a peasant community. Little by little, the growing demand for cereals connected with the growth of capitalism in the West led the boyars to appropriate the best agricultural lands for themselves and to oblige the peasants to produce wheat which they then exported. Increasingly the peasants lost their individual liberty, became 'bound is the soil' and the communal form of exploitation practised by the village communities was thus slowly turned into a quasi-feudal form. The boyar became an individual proprietor in communities which had lost almost every form of communal control over their lands. But this was not the result of a purely internal evolution; the development of commodity production and capitalism in the countries of Western Europe was necessary for such a transformation to occur.

A further example of what I have in mind is evident, yet again, in the case of the Incas. We know that when they conquered local village tribes or communities, the Inca expropriated their lands altogether so that they became his exclusive property. He would then divide the territory of each community into three parts: the first part would be reserved for his 'father', the Sun, the produce from it serving to maintain the priests and the cult; the second was intended for the Inca himself, i.e. for the State in its nonreligious activities; the third he graciously gave back to the local communities so that they might live, but on condition that they cultivated the other two parts of their former territory for the Incas. This was a transformation of an ancient model founded, not on exploitation, but on reciprocity. And John Murra has shown that even before the Incas' arrival each local community reserved part of its common lands for the maize cultivation or llama breeding required by the cult of their ancestors and gods, and another part for the needs of their chiefs (*curaca*) and for the poor, the old, orphans without resources, etc. It was on the basis of these forms of common property that the system of exploitation of local groups by the Inca State was developed. We are concerned here with a form of exploitation between 'communities' which is much more complex than that of the Romanian boyars. Once again we find that the extreme diversity of property forms in history arises from the fact that they express an evolution of relations not only with nature, but also between men. This therefore raises the question: can one discover any principles underlying this diversity in the forms of appropriating nature and these evolutionary processes?

Some Ideas on the Reasons for the Diversity of Forms of Property in Nature and for the Transformations They Undergo

So far I have done no more than sketch out a somewhat venturesome inventory of a number of property forms in territory and their resources, either natural or husbanded. I have deliberately reordered modes of subsistence and material modes of production around some of the major systems of exploitation of nature. A society's social mode of production is characterized by the social relations which determine the form (or forms) of access to resources and means of production, organize labour processes and determine the division and circulation of products of social labour. Of these three functions of the production relations, I have only considered some concrete forms of the first, although in the case of the Australian Aborigines I have pursued the argument somewhat further and suggested how the kinship relations could assume these three functions and thus serve as the framework and social armature for the abstract and concrete appropriation of nature.

This enquiry must be carried further. But it cannot be conducted by a single researcher, nor even by a small team, for nowadays anthropologists have at their disposal data (unfortunately somewhat uneven in quality) on nearly nine hundred societies, of which a few dozen are hunter-gatherer societies either on the point of disappearance or which disappeared during the last century; a hundred or so pastoral societies, many of which are now going over to agriculture or industry; and finally, several hundred agricultural societies. These figures should make it plain why I am cautious and sceptical about articles by certain anthropologists and philosophers of history which eagerly erect one or two specific cases into archetype such as the 'cynegetic mode of production', the 'pastoral mode of production', or even, in the case of Marshall Sahlins (who inflates his terms yet more), writing of 'the neolithic mode of production'. For to assert that one or several modes of production exist which are not so much cynegetic as peculiar to hunter-gatherer societies, one must first compare them in order to determine if their differences belong to one and the same group of possible transformations (which as things now stand, I do not believe). Note that these denominations — cynegetic, pastoral, etc., mode of production — tell us nothing about the social characteristics of relations of production, but instead place the emphasis upon techniques, upon the material modes of production and subsistence, upon relations with nature. That said, without waiting for all these comparisons to be made (a project which, if it were undertaken, might well require another two decades), we can already glimpse some of the reasons for the diversity of forms of property in nature, or at any rate, some of the directions in which we should set out in search of them.

A close relation will appear to exist between the forms through which the appropriation of nature by the individuals and groups comprising a particular society are defined and to a certain extent controlled, and the intellectual and material capacities this society possesses to act upon the surrounding nature, to master its processes, to transform it into material means of existence and to reproduce itself in determinate social relations and a determinate culture.

I do not propose to rehearse point by point the comparison between our three societies of hunter-gatherers — their techniques, the size of their units, the ecosystems in which they currently live, their recent or distant history, and so on. But I shall comment more abstractly on something common to all hunting societies: they depend for their livelihood upon the spontaneous reproduction of wild resources and they have little capacity to intervene in the various conditions underlying that reproduction. In doing this I shall necessarily give the impression that there exists an archetypal mode of production for all hunter-gatherer societies and that I am engaged in reconstructing it, therewith rendering myself vulnerable to my own criticism. This is not the case, however, for we know that a method which abstracts from the perceivable differences between these societies so as to emphasise their resemblances cannot, in principle, demonstrate whether they do or do not belong to one and the same group of social transformations.

The objective constraints which characterize all these societies (dependence upon resources which are wild, uncultivated but often protected by human beings who have little capacity, however, to intervene in the reproduction of the wild species, whether animal or vegetable) oblige the human groups involved to *divide* into local bands and to *scatter* in space so as to exploit resources when these are themselves spontaneously scattered in space (and time). The limited nature of the resources or questions, in quantity and quality and, above all, the fortuitous factors involved in their reproduction require cooperation and sharing within each local group, and oblige all the local bands to overcome their own separation and cooperate. The *communal* nature of the forms of appropriation of a territory and its resources would seem to be a response to these problems, with communal property guaranteeing all the members of a group (young, old, sick, healthy) access to the exploitable resources and a share in them. Yet these forms of appropriation common to a particular group are themselves defined in such a way that a wider cooperation between several groups, on a permanent or provisional basis, is always possible at times of drought, extreme cold, scarcity and so on.

The scattering of wild resources and the fortuitous factors involved in their reproduction may be held accountable for the overall *limits* to the size of the local bands (direct and everyday units of production and consumption), for the social *diversity* of their internal composition (a factor guaranteeing cooperation and security), for the *flexibility* of concrete labour processes, and for the *nomadism* of the way of life. The fact that the form of the territory's appropriation is a communal one and that (excluding neighbouring enemy tribes) in certain circumstances several groups may share resources, guarantees that the appropriation of nature is continuous and that there is a repeated distribution of its resources among all the individuals and groups forming a global society (tribe or ethnic group, and so on).

Furthermore, in contrast to territory, which is appropriated communally, tools and weapons are individual property, as are the products of hunting and gathering. The existence of *personal* rights over this or that fraction of the products of hunting, gathering or domestic handicraft work is also one of the conditions for the redistribution and circulation of such products within or between the local bands by the interplay of personal *gifts* and return-gifts. Of course this sharing via personal gifts is the origin of fluid networks of mutual obligation, but it is not the *sole* origin of mutual obligations, whether individual or collective. These also derive from the fact that, alongside or in addition to their direct cooperation in production (a cooperation which may not exist), the individuals and groups are bound by kinship relations, by mutual cooperation to reproduce life and ensure that groups have descendants and thus enjoy physical and political permanence.

It is at this point that differences arise which anthropologists are still unable to explain. Australian Aborigine kinship groups are closed in the sense that individuals belong by birth to a 'moiety' or a 'section', and must take a wife from another section, which in principle is always the same one. The Pygmies, by contrast, have an open and fluid kinship system which theoretically forbids the reproduction of the previous generations' marriage-relationships (so that one cannot reproduce one's father's or one's paternal grandfather's marriage-relationships). The Bushmen of South Africa have a system which is half-closed and half-open, since an individual cannot marry someone who bears the same name as one of his paternal and maternal ancestors, but can marry anyone else. Here one can recognize one of the principles of Crow-Omaha kinship systems, which are characteristic of certain agricultural societies in Africa, America and Asia. Do these three kinship systems belong to one and the same type, to one and the same group of transformations? It is possible, but so far to my knowledge at least, no one has sought to prove it.

Now, these differences in kinship relations have their effects upon the forms of appropriation of nature. They lead the Australians to delimit the territories of their 'ancestors' who, since mythical times, have metamorphosed into lakes, mountains, deserts, animals, etc. in and off which their descendants live. Within this abstract framework, secured by rigid relations (and a rigid theory) of descent, the material, ecological and technological constraints necessitating fluidity and cooperation in the concrete process of appropriating nature, find a response in the treatment of obligations between groups which are linked (through marriage) and also, necessarily, in the handling of descent relations. Aram Yengoyan has furthermore suggested that there could perhaps have been a close relation between the existence in the desert and sub-desert regions of Australia of living conditions more uncertain than elsewhere and the presence, in greater numbers than elsewhere, of complex kinship

systems, i.e. the subsection systems. He has formulated the hypothesis that the multiplication of these kinship groups creates more
complex networks of reciprocal obligations and exchanges and that
these are an 'adaptive' response to the often very uncertain material
conditions underlying their society's reproduction. This hypothesis
would seem to be a fruitful one but has not yet been proven.

Nothing of this kind exists among the Pygmies. The local
bands do seem, it is true, to settle around a central nucleus
consisting of a group of brothers living with some of their
descendants and relatives by marriage, but the kinship systems
does not generate true patrilineal lineages. Furthermore, as not
all the brothers live in the same band, because the sons may leave
their father to live with their parents-in-law, and so on, descent
relations do not possess the social weight they evidently have
among the Australian Aborigines. Ultimately, as Colin Turnbull
has shown, what is stable and fixed for the Pygmies is the bands'
territory, whereas their social composition may well have
changed entirely in the course of two or three generations.

This is as far as we have got. Nevertheless, a theoretical point
of real importance now seems to have been established. These
societies display elements in common which *cannot* be directly
accounted for by the constraints of the natural environment
which they exploit, since they exploit different ecosystems:
specialized, semi-arid ones (Australian Aborigines, Bushmen) or
generalized ones, such as the Equatorial forest (Pygmies). Thus it
appears that the common elements depend not so much upon
the natural environment as upon *the capacity* (or the incapacity) of
these societies *to act upon it in order to reproduce* the animal and
vegetable species off which they live. We are therefore concerned
not with an ecological determinism but with ecological determinations which only act upon societies when in combination
with the productive capacities these societies possess. So when we
speak of material 'constraints', we understand by this the
combined, hierarchized and simultaneous effects of natural and
cultural facts. Moreover, within this synthesis, what seems to
weigh more on these societies' functioning and evolution derives
from culture and productive capacities, rather than nature. Given
the same level of productive forces, different ecological data can
therefore pose similar problems, and similar problems can always
receive several different solutions. Yet as far as the organizational
forms of societies of hunters are concerned, these possible
responses are finite in number and this number is in fact small:

one can fix the territories without fixing the bands or one can fix both bands and territories, and so on; one can reproduce the same marriage-relationships and close the kinship groups or one can seek out new marriage-relationships in every generation and leave the kinship groups open, and so on. This shows the need to develop a method enabling us to reconstitute the systems of historically possible responses to 'sets' of specific constraints.

If we now direct our attention to nomadic pastoral societies, we shall obtain an even clearer insight into the role of the intellectual and material productive forces and the effect of their limitations in the genesis of the forms of appropriation of nature. Part of nature — a few animal species — has ceased to be wild and cannot be reproduced without human beings to guide the herds, look after the watering places, protect the animals against predators, care for them in cases of accident or illness, and so on. Grass and water, however, are still largely outside man's control, although he may affect these resources by regulating the frequency of his movements past a particular point and the number of animals which graze there, by burning the grass to revive the pasture, by sinking wells, and so on. But the reproduction of these resources essentially depends upon processes over which man has no control and whose effects are in part uncertain. Now in almost all nomadic pastoral societies, we note the existence of two forms of property which correspond to these unequal capacities for intervention in nature. The domesticated part of nature, livestock, is appropriated by small local communities which constitute direct, everyday units of production and consumption. Sometimes this form of appropriation leads to individual, if not 'private', property in part of the herd. The wild part of nature — grass, water, territory — is appropriated communally, but by the totality of the social groups forming a tribe or a confederation of tribes, and so on.

Once again we can see an internal link emerging between the productive capacities on the one hand, and the forms of appropriation of nature and social organization on the other. Like the hunters, societies of nomadic pastoralists are obliged to divide themselves into local production and consumption units which separately appropriate the resources common to all the groups. Here too kinship relations function as all or part of relations of production. Here too, for *all* the conditions of production to be reproduced, the use of communal resources *by particular groups* must be *socially* regulated. As we have seen, when the communal territory is united, one habitual response is to establish a rule whereby particular groups and their herds pass over the same spaces in a definite succession. Each group therefore *cooperates* with the whole *by abstaining* from being present at the same time as others on a given meadow or around a particular watering place. As in the case of the hunters, we are faced here with a form of cooperation which is positive but indirect, since it does not imply any personal cooperation with other groups in the daily process of concrete appropriation of nature. Conversely, when it is a question of protecting their common interests, religious sacrifices, marriages, war and so on, all the local groups are led to cooperate directly and personally.

To my knowledge, Pierre Bonte was the first to establish a connection between these two forms of cooperation and property among pastoralists and the observation made by Marx in 1857 regarding the ancient Germans' communal organization and mode of production. Marx speaks of a community 'in itself' when he describes their domestic groups, which are isolated in space and do not cooperate in everyday production, but which share the same language, history and customs. He speaks of a community 'for itself' when referring to the '*coming-together*' (*Vereinigung*) of these local groups, their assembling at the time of initiation ceremonies for the young, in time of war, and so on. The community would then exist not as a substantial unity (*Einheit*), but as a union (*Einigung*) resting upon an agreement (see the *Grundrisse*, pp. 483-4). Marx's observations provide food for thought, but we should not lose sight of the fact that they apply to societies combining stockbreeding and agriculture within which the domestic groups have, up to a certain point, become private owners or permanent users of a portion of the tribal territory which has been turned into cultivated fields. At the level of agricultural production, insofar as the cultivated lands have gone out of its direct control, the supra-local tribal community would seem to have only a very insignificant economic role to play.

On the other hand, among nomadic pastoralists membership of a supra-local community is a direct condition of production, not only inasmuch as the use of pastures and watering places in a general sense depends upon such membership, but above all insofar as use of a particular pasture at a particular time presupposes the tacit or explicit agreement of other groups which might want to utilize that pasture at the same time. It is therefore wrong to believe that just because groups do not cooperate *directly* in production, they do not cooperate at all. This would lead one to regard communal relations (kinship relations, age classes, and so on) as a set of superstructures existing alongside (?) or above (?) an economic infrastructure in which these relations play no part. This may perhaps be true of certain types of agriculture based upon private property in cultivated land, but not of the majority of nomadic pastoral societies.

This analysis should not lead us to lose sight of the essential feature, i.e. that there is a duality of forms of appropriation of nature, with the broadest communal forms serving to effect the appropriation of wild nature, and the narrowest ones, centred upon local domestic groups or even upon individuals, to effect the appropriation of domesticated nature. From this difference quite opposed social developments may arise, since forms of property in livestock favour an unequal accumulation as between the domestic groups — an inequality which the mere action of disease, ravaging the herds of some and sparing those of others, and of droughts drying up a well in one region but not in another, can produce, if not perpetuate.

As a counterweight to these factors inducing inequality, however, there is the fact that if they are to survive, all the groups must be ensured access to a fraction of the communal resources in water and pastureland, and this favours the maintenance of a degree of equality. Here too equality will have greater chances of being preserved the more the kinship relations presiding over the constitution and periodical reconstitution of the domestic groups require mutual aid and reciprocal solidarity. There is therefore a series of factors which favour preservation of the social *equivalence* of the local segments in pastoral societies and another series of factors with the opposite effect. Under what conditions does this social equivalence, which ensures equality of access to communal wild resources for local groups, disappear, and under what conditions do these resources cease to be genuinely communal? These are fundamental theoretical questions, to which I shall return below. But do these transformations begin from one and the same base? Are all pastoral societies variations on a single type of social organization corresponding to a common 'pastoral' mode of production? Insofar as pastoral production is organized in domestic production units, and thus within kinship relations, one can attempt to answer these questions by comparing these societies' kinship relations to see if they appear as variations of a single type. As things now stand, this remains unproven.

Admittedly, we find that almost all societies of nomadic stock-breeders — with the exception of the Tuareg — are patrilineal. Kinship relations assume the form of lineages which are united into clans and segment from generation to generation. Hypotheses can be advanced to explain the lineage-organized, segmentary and even patrilineal character of numerous pastoral societies (the role of men in stockbreeding, the capacity of an isolated domestic group to live off its herd, and so on). Yet there are two facts which raise problems to which once again Pierre Bonte has drawn our attention, although at the same time he agrees with J.-P. Digard and other researchers that it is no easy matter to find a satisfactory answer to them.[15] First, in some societies (East African pastoralists), lineage relations appear to have less importance than relations between generations or what is known as 'age class' organization (which concerns men in particular). Second, in societies where lineage organization is dominant, we find two different models with quite opposed logics: one model in which the lineage segments are exogamous (the Mongols and nomads of the Central Asian steppes, the Nuer of Africa), and another model in which the segments are endogamous (Rwala Bedouin, Tuareg). The most typical case is that of the Arab societies in which there exists preferential marriage with a patrilateral parallel cousin, one's father's brother's daughter.

Anthropology is not yet able to provide a satisfactory explanation for the conditions governing the emergence of generational systems, nor for the conditions governing the development of endogamous lineage systems. It is hardly satisfactory to assert that these are alternative structures, since it is not even known if these structures are responses to the same problems. Furthermore, as yet we have no satisfactory theoretical explanation for the process whereby different social segments cease to have equivalent access to communal resources — i.e. for the formation of classes and possibly the State in nomadic pastoral societies —

---

15. See *Cahiers du CERM* 109-110: *Etudes sur les sociétés pastorales nomades*, in particular Pierre Bonte, 'La "formule technique" due pastoralisme nomade', pp. 6-32, and Jean-Pierre Digard, 'Contraintes techniques de l'élevage sur l'organization des sociétés de pasteurs nomades', pp. 33-50; see also, by the same author, 'Histoire et anthropologie des sociétés nomades', *Annales ESC* 28th year (6), 1973, pp. 1423-1435 and 'De la nécessité et des inconvénients pour un Baxtyâri d'être Baxtyâri. Communauté, territoire et inégalité chex les pasteurs nomades d'Iran', in *Production pastorale et société. Actes du colloque international sur le pastoralisme nomade*, Paris 1-3 December 1976, Cambridge and Paris 1981, pp. 127-139.

even though Owen Lattimore's suggestions regarding the Mongols (see above, p. 101) did shed some light on the question.

I will now conclude these tentative observations on the relations between forms of property and societies' (material and intellectual) capacities for acting upon nature. Naturally, these capacities vary immensely from one pastoral society to another; to cite just two instances, the stockbreeding techniques of the Mongols are much more productive than those of the Masai of Tanzania.

I shall not now attempt to analyse agricultural societies which include manifold forms of communal property in the soil, and display a great variety of kinship relations and hierarchical social relations: castes, classes and the State. Depending on whether these caste or class, etc., relations are absent or present, kinship relations constitute either the general framework or simply a particular aspect of the conditions for abstract (property forms) and concrete (organization of production) appropriation of nature. Now, agricultural societies feature all known kinship relations: patrilineal systems; matrilineal systems in which the women transmit the titles and the rights in land; bilineal systems in which the women transmit the land and the men the political powers; or conversely, non-lineal systems (known as undifferentiated or cognatic) in which kin clusters are constituted — groups of relatives bound by the same ancestry beginning with a common ancestor (the old Scottish *clann* was probably a fluid group of this kind, whereas today the term 'clan' is used to refer to unilineal descent groups). I hope that I shall not be charged, as I sometimes have been, with saying that kinship relations invariably function in non-capitalist societies as relations of production! One must study each case in detail and seek to establish what social relations organize the process of production. But I hope that I shall not be asked, either, to believe in the existence of an agricultural mode of production or, even a lineage mode of production — although I would look with more favour on the latter expression, for it does at least refer to the social nature of the production relation.

In order to show how kinship can function in *several* different ways in the same society and thus mask *class* relations, I shall rehearse J.-P. Digard's analysis (1981) of the social organization of the Iranian Bakhtiari shepherds. This tribe, organized into a single huge segmented lineage system, numbers around five hundred thousand people, of whom half are now sedentary. The tribe (*il*) is divided into two sections (*buluk*), which are themselves subdivided into *bâb*, then into *tâyefa*, then into *tira*, into *owlâd* and into *xânewâda*:

> This very developed form of segmentation is supposed to corres-
> pond to a lineage organization of the patrilineal type, with prefer-
> ential marriage between paternal parallel cousins ... In fact it
> turns out to be practically impossible to obtain from Bakhtiari
> informants coherent genealogies exceeding the limits of the *tash* or,
> at best, of the *tira*; beyond this point, the genealogical trees reveal
> nothing more than a concern to express political alliances *a posteri-*
> *ori* in terms of descent.[16]

The *xânewâda*, the conjugal family, is the unit of individual appropriation of livestock and of consumption. The extended family, the *owlâd*, is the unit of direct cooperation in labour, and oversees the setting up of camps (from three to twelve tents). The *tira*, the lineage, represents the union of several related camps during the period of nomadism. At these levels of segmentation, kinship is the framework both for pasture use, for the organiza-tion of labour and for the consumption of products. Beyond them, the divisions into *tâyefa* and *bâb* constitute *political* relations dominated by aristocratic families or functionaries who receive their power from the tribe's chief, the *ilkhan*. One can see from this how classes and a State apparatus can be formed within a society which remains tribal (a notion denied by Morgan in 1877 but which had long been accepted by advocates of the Asiatic mode of production, Marx [1857] included), without thereby destroying the communal form of appropriation of nature or the society's general form, which retains the appearance of a huge set of kinship groups and relationships. Among the Mongols, for example, the distinction between aristocracy and commoners retains the form of relations between elders and juniors.

There is therefore a close relation between the forms of property in nature and the development of caste, class (and other such) relations.

We are not as yet in any position to present an accurate survey of the multiple evolution of property forms; this would require a long-term project involving numerous researchers. However, as

---

16. Jean-Pierre Digard, 'De la nécessité et des inconvénients pour un Baxtyâri d'être Baxtyâri ...', p. 29.

every property system combines different principles according to the diverse realities whose appropriation must be regulated (hunting territory, cultivable lands, tools, game, agricultural and pastoral products, rituals and so on), one can put forward the hypothesis that the development of new systems of exploitation of nature, of diverse forms of agriculture and stockbreeding, whether separated or combined, has increased the scope for social inequalities — which, in the case of hunter-gatherer groups, are restricted to control over products and rites (imaginary means of acting upon nature's reproduction) — so that they include control of the land and the means of production. Livestock is at once a means of subsistence, a means of production, an exchangeable good and sometimes a means of transport. For its part, in becoming agricultural, land becomes a means of production and may less readily 'circulate' among groups.

In the case of these societies, how do *hereditary* social hierarchies come to be formed? This is the main problem we have to resolve. I have nothing to offer here but what I *imagine* to be the mechanism that might gradually have led to the formation of these hereditary hierarchies. We must start from the fact that in hunter-gatherer societies — even the most egalitarian ones (the Pygmies of Zaïre, for example) — from time to time the local groups interrupt hunting and gathering for their immediate everyday reproduction, and hunt communally to celebrate religious ceremonies, rituals of death, initiation and so on, in short, to concern themselves with interests common to all the local groups. Very often this out-of-the-ordinary 'labour' is distinguished from the 'labour' which the members of a local group devote to their own reproduction, and to that of their group, by the fact that it is *directly* in the services of interests *common* to all the individuals and groups. In addition, it is more intense than normal labour, for it must provide the means for collective feasts, sacrifices and so on (consider the *elima* ritual for the puberty of the girls, and the *molimo* ritual for the death of an adult, among the Mbuti Pygmies).

We must therefore seek to identify the reasons and conditions which in numerous societies have led certain groups to identify with the interests common to all the groups, in such a way that the *additional* labour devoted to satisfying these common interests has gradually come to be devoted to celebrating and preserving in its difference this minority which enjoys a monopoly on the means (ritual or otherwise) of guaranteeing fertility, life and justice, etc., for all. The transformation which establishes new relations of production and develops with them consists in *additional labour of all for all* becoming *surplus labour of almost all for some.*

This transformation was effected within certain societies of hunter-gatherers and fishers who had adopted a sedentary existence on the shores of seas exceptionally rich in salmon, fish, molluscs and other marine resources, which they exploited with the help of complex techniques of capture and conservation. As examples, I will mention the well-known cases of Kwakiutl from the Northwest coast of America, and the Calusa of Florida who were rapidly decimated by French colonization. Pierre Bonte has shown that among the stockbreeders of East Africa, where an age-class system is dominant — a system which is still founded on the equivalence of individuals within the same age-classes but which allows serious inequalities between these age-classes (gerontocracy) — the development of social classes assumes the form of a development in the practice of prophecy. A social group, that of the prophet, secures a privileged and increasingly exclusive relation with the supernatural, and through this relation ends up enjoying ultimate control of the communal structure. Part of the livestock circulation, previously conducted to further the aims of social reproduction — sacrifices, in particular — is diverted to this group's advantage. It comes to occupy a place apart, something particularly obvious where marriages are concerned in that it receives a great number of women but makes *no return gift thereof.* Elsewhere, this evolution has culminated in forms of centralized State power, in the sacred monarchies of East Africa. Malinowski's studies of Melanesian chiefdoms in the Trobriand Islands and Firth's book on the Polynesian chiefdom of Tikopia have revealed an analogous monopolization by an aristocracy of the performance of fertility rituals, communication with ancestors and gods, management of common resources and appropriation of a large part (up to twenty per cent) of production, some of this wealth then being redistributed in the form of communal festivals and services. Violence undoubtedly plays a role in these processes, but less, it seems, than a certain consent on the part of the dominated to their own domination. This is one of the paradoxes in the formation (and future disappearance) of classes which has still to be explained.

To sum up, there everywhere appears to be an intimate link between the way in which nature is used and the way in which human beings themselves are used. However, whilst historians have given much thought to the path leading from ways of treating human beings to those of appropriating nature, researchers who have explored the opposite trajectory are still rare. One could of course mention Claude Lévi-Strauss, along with a number of anthropologists who have specialized in the study of indigenous representations of nature, including human nature. Joseph Needham and, above all, André G. Haudricourt belong to this last category, and we are indebted to them for synthetic approaches which have opened up for us immense vistas upon the differences that have contrasted Western and Chinese civilization since the Neolithic age.

> From the Neolithic age onwards, humankind is no longer simply a predator and a consumer with respect to the vegetable and animal world, for he *assists, protects* and *coexists over long periods of time* with the species which he has 'domesticated'. New relations of an 'amicable' type are established and they are in some ways reminiscent of those which human beings maintain among themselves within a group [...], but what I wish to draw your attention to is the fact that the diversity of the animal and vegetable world across the surface of the globe makes it impossible for there to be a qualitative identify of these 'amicable' relations in all civilizations.[17]

Comparing the agrarian systems of the Mediterranean West, which depend upon a complementarity between agriculture and stockbreeding, and Chinese horticulture, which has almost totally eliminated recourse to animals, Haudricourt showed that the respective models of power and of the treatment of human beings seem to harbour a parallel contrast. In the West, models of good government are formed in the image of relations with nature, and these always imply a direct, positive and brutal form of action: the shepherd leads his sheep with his crook in his hand; the farmer plants and harvests cereals such as barley and corn, which can be planted and harvested *en masse*; the navigator holds the rudder and steers the boat which the rowers propel forward. In ancient China, cattle and sheep quickly disappeared as an intensive agriculture akin to horticulture emerged: the main cereal — rice — was treated individually and with almost the same 'respectful friendship' as is displayed by the Melanesians

---

17. A.G. Haudricourt, 'Domestication des animaux, culture des plantes et traitement d'autrui', *L'Homme* II (1), January-March 1962, p. 40.

towards the tubers which they carefully plant and harvest one at a time. In either case, the principle is the same whether what is involved is a rice paddy or a ridged field. The aim is to produce a negative effect upon anything which can impede the plants' growth, and thus to have an *indirect* effect on them, in contrast to the various forms of positive and direct action aimed at by the western shepherd or cereal farmer. Haudricourt cites the 'Treatise on functionaries and treatise on the army' written in the seventh century AD, in which the ideal Chinese leader is described as one who intervenes *as little as possible* in the life of his subjects and allows the tranquility and prosperity of his people to increase. What a contrast this is with Aristotle, for whom 'there is no friendship or justice towards lifeless things, ... neither is there friendship towards a horse or an ox, nor to a slave *qua* slave.'[18]

But Aristotle wrote in the fourth century BC, whereas Solon had abolished debt slavery as early as the sixth century in Athens so that, in order to procure slaves, the Athenians were forced to buy them or to reduce other Greeks and, above all, barbarians to slavery. Much as in Black Africa in the eighteenth and nineteenth centuries, certain barbarian tribes undertook the task of providing the slave merchants with the merchandise they proceeded to sell in Chios or at other Greek markets.

Let us now take the path which leads from ways of dealing with human beings to ways of appropriating nature. For the historians, slavery only reached its height and assumed its harshest forms with the development in Greece (and later in Rome) of private property in the soil, of a property separated from the communal space (the *ager publicus*) but linked to the communal forms of appropriation of this space in that only a citizen could own a plot belonging to the City. Foreigners (the metics) were debarred from this right, as were slaves. This does not mean, however, that every citizen was a property-owner. Those who were not landowners had to follow a calling less 'noble' than agriculture, such as handicraft work or trade; but their living would then be dependent upon others. Only agriculture, or at any rate ownership of a sufficiently large plot of land guaranteed independence or 'autarky' — in other words, a superior social status as free man equal to the other citizens.

With the development of private property, slavery therefore

---

18. *Nicomachaean Ethics* VIII, 11.

gained momentum, in Rome going beyond the modest forms of familial exploitation known in Greece to become the chief means of production on huge estates which no longer produced just for local consumption but for the market and for money. It was the slave-commodity, himself a producer of commodities, who suffered the harshest forms of oppression and exploitation. Now, producing commodities in order to get rich is a new way of utilizing nature and exploiting its resources, with a view to satisfying not so much the limited needs of familial groups and local communities as the needs of social groups at the head of States which rule over empires. Separation of human beings from the means of production and of private property from communal property are two transformations in the relations of human beings among themselves and with nature which constitute the original pattern of the social inequalities and class structures of the West.

Things were much the same, as we have already seen (see above, p. 103), with the Incas. Each time they subjected a kingdom or a local tribe, they expropriated all its lands, only to return them, but with two parts amputated (one for the Sun and the clergy, the other for the Inca) which the defeated then had to cultivate as a matter of priority and with *corvée* labour. The separation of the community from part of its territory, from its means of existence, and the obligation to perform surplus labour are once again the two sides of humankind's exploitation by humankind (and of nature by humankind). These analyses converge with Marx's. In his treatment of the diverse forms of property in land and of extortion of surplus labour, he distinguishes between the 'Asiatic' form in which, the State being the exclusive owner of the soil, tax and ground rent are merged, and the feudal form, in which rent and tax are distinct. He then adds the following, which has much wider repercussions:

> It is in each case the direct relationship of the owners of the conditions of production to the immediate producers — a relationship whose particular form naturally corresponds always to a certain level of development of the type and manner of labour, and hence to its social productive power — in which we find the innermost secret, the hidden basis of the entire social edifice, and hence also the political form of the relationship of sovereignty and dependence, in short, the specific form of state in each case. This does not prevent the same economic basis ... from displaying endless variations innumerable different empirical circumstances ... and

these can only be understood by analysing these empirically given conditions.[19]

Here Marx formulates an analytical principle which is of general relevance, since alongside those cases in which the owner (collective or individual) and the producers are distinct and in a relation of sovereignty and dependence to each other, there are cases in which the producers are 'owners' of their means of production and conditions of existence (communal property, familial property, individual property, etc. in the means of production). Now, this principle, which Marx himself had generalized from the time of *The German Ideology* (1845) and *Pre-Capitalist Forms of Production* (1857), implies *two* hypotheses regarding the reasons for the diversity of the 'social edifices' which succeed each other in history — hypotheses which need to be proven in each case. According to the first, the innermost secret of the original logic of each social edifice will be revealed when one has uncovered the relations of production upon which they depend; according to the second, these relations of production themselves do not arise by chance, but correspond to a society's 'productive power', to its material and intellectual capacities for acting upon nature to make nature serve society's ends.

We are no longer concerned here with the eighteenth-century idea, fertile though it may have been, that for each mode of subsistence there exist corresponding forms of thought and government — that there is a global logic and an internal coherence to societies. With Marx we have moved on to an idea which is in some sense an extension of the earlier one, but which also transforms it by giving it much greater depth: the idea of a logic based upon the peculiar and contradictory dynamic of modes of production (which cannot be 'deduced' but are discovered via the analysis of empirical realities capable of great variation). The forefront of the analysis is thus no longer occupied by the relations of human beings with nature — their material modes of production and of subsistence, the diverse ways of exploiting nature's resources — but by the relations of human beings among themselves, their diverse ways of cooperating with or exploiting each other in the course of appropriating nature.

This is a contradictory dynamic of the material and social modes of production whose forms and rhythms would emerge, if

19. *Capital*, Volume 3, Harmondsworth 1981, pp. 927-8.

there were no external history to upset them, from transformations in the relations of human beings with each other in the appropriation of nature. The most spectacular dynamics arise out of the most pronounced forms of separation between property in nature (those who own and use it) and its concrete appropriation (those who 'produce', act directly and concretely upon it). Moreover, one must bear in mind that humankind's exploitation by humankind implies both the production and the destruction of wealth, if the latter is a condition for the reproduction of the production relations. I would remind the reader of the example of the Aztecs, who each year sacrificed up to ten thousand prisoners of war to their gods, or of ancient Egypt, with the construction of the pyramids and the tombs of the Pharaohs, the incarnations of Osiris. But need we choose such distant examples? The logic of the contemporary capitalist mode of production requires unceasing development of the productivity of social labour, lowering of its costs, and 'economizing', while at the same time engaging in an unchecked wastage of natural resources and of the producers' material and intellectual productive forces. Use of human beings and use of nature are linked, and there is no crisis in the use of nature which is not a crisis in humankind's way of life.

Anthropology and its materials only seem to distance us from the problems of our own society. In fact they never cease to return us to them, to their very heart, providing us with a standpoint from which we are better able to situate phenomena in space and in history, without falling prey to the illusory and improper generalizations of 'philosophies of history' which cannot help but be myopic vis-à-vis history, blind to their own nature and an obstacle to action. The present essay should be regarded as the first of a series of concrete analyses still to be made. Huge problems, such as size of territories, the productivity of systems of exploitation of nature and war, have remained in shadow. The time is past when a man like Hegel could read twenty-two thousand books before writing his *Encyclopedia of the Sciences of Nature* and take himself to be, as he declared in *The Science of Logic*, 'God before the creation of the world'.

This text is a modified and extended version of a talk entitled 'Territory and Property in Primitive Society', which was given to the international symposium organized by the Weiner-Reimers Stiftung at Bad-Homburg from 25 to 29 October 1977, on the theme 'Human Ethology: Claims and Limits of a New Discipline'. It was first published in *La Pensée* 198, April 1978, pp. 7-49.

Part Two
The Mental Part of Reality

3

The Mental Part of Reality

The journey of a thousand leagues starts with a single step. Lao-Tzu, *Tao-te-Ching*, Poem LXIV

Why begin with these fine words spoken by Lao-Tzu, the 'Old Man' as Etiemble calls him? It is not so much to impress people as to make clear how modest my ambitions are as I set out, in the wake of countless others, to write about ideologies, or, rather, about the ideological. In the first two chapters of this book, I have touched upon theoretical problems which I want now to tackle directly. I could not of course treat the representation of nature, or of its forms of appropriation, without identifying the place of thought in the production of social reality and its interpretations. Although I may return to some of the earlier examples in order to refine my presentation of them, I should like here to step out of the rut in which most analyses have been stuck, so as to continue on my way.

For something is wrong in the state of the human sciences where ideology is concerned. Caricaturing outrageously, we can say that there are two main contending theses in the age-old debate on the relations between ideas and social realities (or history):

Thesis 1. Ideas govern the world because they shape social realities in the first place and impel societies and their history in a certain direction during whole millennia. In support of this, people point to Islam, Hinduism, Christianity, Maoism — in other words, to all the great religions or political ideologies that seem to have shaped men in their image, to have been the living spring whence poured forth reality, and not its point of arrival, the expression in thought of realities born independently of, and unaided by it.

Thesis 2. A society cannot be reduced to the ideas its members develop about it. It exists independently of thought about realities, which are distinct from thought and of greater historical consequence, first among these being material realities and the social relations which organize them. In a word, in the order of social realities, infrastructural realities take precedence over superstructures and ideas. In any case, that latter are not just conjured up out of thin air: they must correspond to some determinate society and epoch, upon which they act in their turn. The gods of antiquity died with it. No doubt everyone will have recognized here views which are normally attributed to Marx.

To which upholders of the first thesis reply that the gods on Olympus were not born with the slave mode of production, and that Christianity, with its ideology of one God in three persons, dead upon the Holy Cross to save mankind, is still alive and well today — although not without experiencing a number of crises and metamorphoses — after two thousand years of history and three or four modes of production. Where, in these two cases, is the correspondence between infrastructure, superstructures and ideologies?

In fact, what is at issue is the existence and the nature of a logic in the functioning and evolution of societies. That such a logic does exist would seem to be an idea that is universally accepted, for experience denies that all social activities or relations have equally important consequences for the organization and reproduction of societies. Every society has something like an explicit hierarchy of different social activities. But does this explicit, conscious hierarchy — which is visible in the arrangement of institutions — really govern the reproduction of this society?

That is the crucial point of the argument. To the Marxists' primacy of the economic in all societies, non-Marxists answer with the primacy of kinship among the Australian Aborigines or the Nuer (Radcliffe-Brown, Evans-Pritchard), or that of religion (Louis Dumont) in the Indian caste system, or that of politics in fifth-century Athens (Karl Polanyi, Edouard Will). It should be noted that by asserting the primacy of kinship, religion or politics, these authors are not content merely to stress the primacy of systems of ideas, but are also asserting the primacy of ideas as embodied in institutions, and thus in social relations, social structures; in other words, they are asserting, against the Marxists, the primacy of what the latter call superstructures.

On closer inspection, there is every likelihood that this discussion will continue for a long time to come, but little chance of it progressing. For the two camps start from irreconcilable, irreducible theoretical assumptions, because their confrontation never occurs on the same level.

What, after all, are the non-Marxists really doing? Despite the fact that each of them answers the Marxists with a different primacy, depending upon the society to which he is referring, they all proceed in the same manner and from the same assumption: they refer to the existence of a visible social order, to the apparent domination in the social practice and consciousness of the members of any given society of activities that Marxists would call superstructural, in order to refute a hypothesis concerning the existence of a causal order which is not and cannot be immediately perceived by the individuals and groups of which the society is composed. They can agree that there is a certain measure of truth in the Marxist thesis, namely, that it corresponds to the logic of capitalist society, this being the only one in which the economic apparently dominates society's organization and working. After allowing for this particular case, however, the Marxist hypothesis is regarded as devoid of any explanatory value or scientific consequence. It could only be for other reasons — for partisan ones — that Marxists could so obstinately insist on taking an exception for the rule, and doggedly strive to fit all societies, and history, past or present, into it.

This argument, which apparently confines itself to facts, drawing all its strength and justification from them, rests upon a theoretical thesis that is assumed to have been proved, whereas in point of fact it has not been. The thesis is well-known, for it is the one upon which empiricism relies when it asserts that the visible order of things furnishes a self-evident demonstration of their reasons for being, that their order makes them intelligible. There would therefore be no point in hunting behind this visible order for some hidden order capable of refuting it or of subsuming it under a different explanation produced by science. It is, however, on the basis of this unproved thesis that empiricists refer to the domination of some social activity or other in a given society, as though this reference alone were sufficent to refute the Marxist thesis.

As for the Marxists, they start out from the opposite thesis: the appearance of facts does not reveal their essence. (They are not the only ones to hold this view, which is why they have been joined by Lévi-Strauss and the structuralists, who are also anti-empiricist in principle.) As a result, the Marxists are obliged not only to show that the fact of domination by a given superstructure in no way refutes the hypothesis of the primacy of infrastructures, but also to show how the primacy of infrastructures explains domination by a given superstructure. Is this not like asking them to square the circle? Marxists will not get out of it by attacking in self-defence, even if they can reply to the empiricists that the latter too need to provide an explanation for the domination of this or that superstructure, and without invoking the strength of an idea — for where does such an idea come from, whence does it derive the strength to impose itself, to shape humanity and society? These questions concern Marxists as much as they concern empiricists. They merely reformulate the problem of the nature, the role and the functions of ideas and ideologies in the working and evolution of societies.

Since we are aware both of what is at issue here, and of the fruitlessness of a debate about irreconcilable theses which can only result in a shouting match, why have we embarked upon this course by citing Lao-Tzu and the prospect of a thousand-league journey? If we have done so, it is in the conviction that a first step has been taken, one which consists in transforming the very terms of the debate, on the basis of two theoretical findings.

The first was established in the course of the two previous chapters, and may be formulated as follows: the distinction between infrastructure and superstructures is neither a distinction between levels or instances, nor a distinction between institutions — although it may present itself as such in certain cases. In its underlying principle, it is a distinction between *functions*. The notion of causality in the last analysis, of the primacy of infrastructures, refers to the existence of a hierachy of functions and not to one of institutions. A society has neither a top nor a bottom, and it is not a system of superimposed levels. It is a system of relations between human beings, relations that are hierarchized according to the nature of their functions, these functions determining the respective impact of each of their activities upon the society's reproduction.

The second, which we have not yet touched here, is that any social relation contains a mental element, an element of thought, of representations which are not merely the form that this relation assumes in our consciousness, but are part of its content. Do not confuse 'mental' with 'ideal' or 'imaginary'. Not all representations present pre-existing realities to the mind 'after-the-event' as it were (where these realities are conceived as having been born independently of and unaided by these representations). Ideas are not an instance separate from social relations; they are not merely appearances, nor are they deformed and deforming reflections in social consciousness. Rather, they are an integral part of social relations as soon as the latter begin to take shape, and they are one of the conditions for their formation. But, whilst there is an element of the mental everywhere, this in no way implies that everything that is (socially) real is mental.

Does this mean that all mental reality is ideological? Are there criteria for distinguishing between those ideas that are ideological and those that are not? Certainly not if we confine ourselves to dubbing as 'ideological' any representation of the world that is in the least organized. Ought we then to conform to another, more current usage and to term 'ideological' those illusory representations which men elaborate concerning themselves and the world, and which serve to legitimise an existing social order, and hence the forms of domination and exploitation of human beings by human beings that may be contained in this existing order?

This restrictive definition has the appearance of being Marxist. But is it really, and how does it tie in with the idea we have just put forward, namely, that any social relation necessarily contains an element of thought which is *not* necessarily either illusory or legitimizing, and which forms part of this relation from the moment of its formation?

In order to make progress in the resolution of these problems, we shall come back to these different points, and analyse the following problems in turn:

1) The nature of the distinction between infrastructure and superstructures;

2) The relations between economic determination and the domination of a given superstructure and the basis of this domination;

3) The mental part of reality and the distinction between the ideological and the non-ideological;

4) The paradigm (and the paradoxes) of the 'legitimacy' of the birth of classes and the State.

Finally, we shall conclude with a brief analysis of the relations between what can and cannot be thought, can and cannot be done in a given structural and historical context. In other words, this will be an analysis of the meaning of that mysterious expression, 'historical necessity'.

The Distinction Between Infrastructure and Superstructures

The first point which obscures everything that follows and condemns the adversaries to total mutual incomprehension from the outset, is the fact that both parties agree that the distinction between infrastructure and superstructures is a distinction between institutions and not between functions. First of all, however, what do we mean by infrastructure?

The infrastructure is the combination of the different material and social conditions which enable a society's members to produce and reproduce the material means of their social existence. These comprise:

1) The determinate ecological and geographical conditions within and from which a society extracts the material means enabling it to exist;

2) The productive forces, i.e. the material and intellectual means that members of this society utilize, after having invented, borrowed or inherited them, within the various labour processes through which they act upon nature for the purpose of extracting their means of existence, these means thereafter constituting a socialized part of nature;

3) The relations of production, that is, the relations between human beings — no matter what they may be — which fulfil the triple function of:

a determining the social form of access to resources and of control of means of production;

b distributing the labour power of the society's members among the different labour processes and organizing these different processes; and

c determining the social form of the circulation and distribution of the products of individual or collective labour.

For us, as for Marx, strictly speaking, the social relations of production alone constitute the economic structure of a society:

'Die Gesamtheit dieser Produktionsverhältnisse bildet die ökono-
mische Struktur der Gesellschaft' (Karl Marx, Introduction to
Contribution to the Critique of Political Economy). It is worth recalling,
however, that productive forces and production relations, though
distinct, never exist independently of each other but are always
combined, articulated in a particular way. The various specific
forms of these combinations constitute so many material and
social forms of production — or modes of production. Modes of
production cannot be reduced to different forms of the division of
labour. There is no such thing as an agricultural, pastoral or
handicraft mode of production. It is perfectly possible to practice
stockbreeding, agriculture and handicrafts within the framework
of the same relation of production, be they feudal, capitalist or
socialist. The specific characteristics of each of these productive
activities may entail particular forms of division of labour without
implying different forms of ownership of the means of production
and the product.

Let us take another look at these definitions for a moment.
They are formal, but they are not empty. Just as in reality one
finds only particular forms of production and particular products,
so general notions of production, relations of production and so
on are merely an abstract and convenient shorthand for aspects
that are common to all economic structures while characterizing
none in particular. These definitions are therefore both positive
yet general items of knowledge and also formal conditions for the
analysis of empirical realities which are always specific. They
enable us to seek, but by themselves they will not allow us to find.

Such as they are, however, these definitions entail consequences which are normally passed over in silence and which
contradict the usual ('Marxist') conception of relations between
infrastructure, superstructures and ideology.

Productive Forces

I shall start by examining the definition of productive forces:
material and intellectual means, and so on. In the first place,
material means are the human beings themselves, their own
bodies and physical capabilities. Then come the means inter-
posed by the human beings between themselves and nature in
order to act upon the latter. These means can be found ready-
made or else can be manufactured. However the use of both the

human body and the material means implies the application of a complex set of representations, ideas and idealities: represent-ations of the goal, the stages, and the effects of activities which we call labour but which rarely appear as such in a good many primitive or pre-capitalist societies. And these representations themselves connect up with rules governing the manufacture of tools, with bodily attitudes and, needless to say, at a deeper level, with indigenous conceptions of nature and humankind's relations with it.

We thus find *inside* all humankind's material activities upon nature a complex set of mental realities whose presence and intervention are essential if this activity is to occur at all.

Documenting these mental realities contained within the various material activities and differing from culture to culture and from epoch to epoch, is a vast and difficult undertaking, one in which historians and anthropologists have been long involved. Yet despite renewals due to ethnoscientists such as Conklin and historians of science and technology such as Gilles, Haudricourt, Leroi-Gourhan, Parrain and Joseph Needham, this remains a particularly neglected branch of the human sciences. To keep this discussion general, it seems to me that the different mental realities encountered within a given labour process can be classi-fied according to two main types, depending upon the functions that these representations fulfil.

On the one hand, there are representations and principles which, being interpretations of reality, have the effect of organiz-ing the forms taken by the different material activities (labour processes) and the phases through which they pass. I am thinking of taxonomies of plants, animals, soils, climatic phenomena, rules for the fabrication and utilization of tools, schemes of material action and symbolic conduct. On the other hand, there are repre-sentations which explain why this or that task must be reserved for men, women, young people, slaves, commoners, masters, aris-tocrats, the king etc. In other words, these are representations which legitimize the position and the status of individuals and groups in terms of the realities that are permitted them, imposed upon them and so on.

Of course, this distinction only exists for us, and is of purely analytic value. It is absurd to see Hesiod's *Works and Days* as a treatise on agronomy, as people often do, just because the peasant-poet includes a great deal of technical advice to his brother concerning harvest dates, soil selection, and so on. In fact

Hesiod wrote this religious and political poem right in the middle of an agricultural crisis in Greece in the seventh century BC. For him, the crisis was the result of man's excesses, which had driven the gods to return to heaven. Through his brother, he was advising all Greeks scrupulously to observe the rituals demanded by the cultivation of the fields. Practised thus, agriculture would become a source of merit, a school of virtue, and the gods would once more deign to communicate with humanity and shower their blessings upon it.

To appreciate the full import of this example, let us consider more closely the notion of labour in ancient Greece, and then take up two quite different cases, — ancient China and the Maenge of New Guinea.

As far as Greece is concerned, I shall rely upon Jean-Pierre Vernant's studies, for in my view his approach is exemplary.

There is no word in classical Greek for 'labour', 'work' in general, nor is there a verb to translate 'to work' in the general and modern sense of the term. The word *ponos* is used for all unpleasant activities, and the word *ergon* is employed to mean 'task' and may equally be applied to argricultural labours and to warlike activities. The verb *poiein* means 'to make' or to 'fabricate', while *pratein* means 'to do', in the sense of acting. Jean-Pierre Vernant has shown how, in the eighth century BC, the trades of blacksmith, potter and weaver were regarded in the same light as those of diviner, bard and doctor (one could find many similar instances in Africa). All of these activities are *technai*; they presuppose the use of occult procedures and a specialized knowledge, the fruit of a long apprenticeship, an initiation conducted outside of the *oikos* (the family group). They are directed towards all the members of the community, but, predominantly, to the most powerful and the richest among them, the aristocrats, for these latter like to surround themselves with craftsmen who produce luxury goods, or with musicians and singers who enhance their status. Agriculture, however, is not regarded as a *techne*, a trade. Each citizen can and must practise it. It does not require any secret apprenticeship, but above all a virtuous attitude towards man and a display of piety towards the gods. This is what Hesiod's poem taught. Together with war, agriculture is the lot of all free men. Its main quality is that it enables these free man to remain such since thanks to agriculture, they can cater for their own needs without depending upon others, whereas a craftsman depends for his livelihood upon his clients. In short, as in the case of war, agriculture is an activity which earns its practitioner merit, both in the City and in the eyes of the gods. Agriculture is not regarded as an action upon nature intended to transform it:

> 'Even if such a transformation were possible, it would be an impiety. Work on the land is a participation in an order both natural and divine that is superior to man. ... [It] establishes a personal contact between the farmer, on the one hand, and nature and the gods, on the other, rather than a commercial relationship between men.'[1]

Nor was the fabrication of an object considered in Antiquity as a labour of transformation of nature. Fabrication, *poiesis*, is a movement (*kinesis*) which aims at producing a form (*eidos*) in a material. This movement takes a form in the given individual whose mode of employment is a *techne*, a set of more or less secret procedures. Now, the form of an object is determined by the use to which it is put, and this use is in turn determined by a need. Only the user really knows what this need and this use are. The craftsman is therefore doubly subjected to the latter: he works for him and it is the user who possesses knowledge of the essence of the object which he has ordered to be made. As Aristotle observes, for a Greek the true cause of a fabricated object is not the craftsman, who seems to be nothing more than the motor of an activity. The true cause lies outside the object and outside the craftsman, in a form which is both the essence and the goal of the fabricated product, i.e. its formal and its final cause. The form and the science of the form are in the consumer's head and not the maker's. This means that, in Jean-Pierre Vernant's finely turned formula, '*socially, the Greek craftsman is not a producer.*'[2] The act of making is not a productive one. In this social and intellectual system, a man is not aware of 'acting' (*pratein, praxis*) when he makes things but rather when he uses them: 'Acting did not mean making objects or transforming nature. It meant influencing men, overcoming them, dominating them.'[3] The supreme form of *praxis* is politics, which is an activity performed by free men, members of their community, of a City which has produced them and which they reproduce.

In the last analysis, the only activity worthy of a free man is

---

1. J.-P. Vernant, *Myth and Thought among the Greeks*, London 1983, p. 254.
2. J.-P. Vernant, p. 263 (translation modified).
3. J.-P. Vernant, p. 295.

political activity, which implies leisure and separation from manual labour. It is interesting to recall that in Rome a citizen enjoyed *otium*, 'leisure', and that those who worked lived off *negotium* (*nec-otium*, 'deprived of leisure' — the origin of the French *négociant*).

However, from being a demiurge in the eighth century, the craftsman became a citizen of inferior status in the fifth century. This evolution in representations of the craftsman matches that of the City towards democracy, with the aristocracy losing a large part of its power, and with a partial and concomitant disappearance of the luxury handicrafts industry. Handicrafts therefore changed status in changing function and position in a new society. Agriculture itself, which had been celebrated in the earliest period of the City's history as the school of citizenship, gradually became an occupation almost unworthy of a free man — one a citizen could entrust to his slaves, doing no more himself than giving orders to the steward in charge of them. Thus, the simultaneous evolution of representations concerning agricultural and handicraft activities and of the status of those engaged in these activities expresses the progress of the ancient economy towards an ever more intense use of slaves and slave labour.

In 'Work and Ideology in Ancient China'[4] an analysis of the work of the philosopher Mencius, Michel Cartier has tried to reconstruct conceptions of work in ancient China. As in the case of the ancient Greeks, the peasants are soldiers, but they do not live in cities, and they are not citizens. The social hierarchy is divided into a class of governors, the *shih* — officials, administrators and judges — at whose head stands the sovereign, the Son of Heaven, who is both master of agriculture and war-lord. Below this class there is a class of peasant-soldiers (*nung*) who, through their manual labour, produce the kingdom's food and wealth. Lower still there are the craftsmen (*kung*). Finally, at the bottom of the ladder of free men, there is the most despised group — the merchants (*chang*).

In contrast to Western thought, the Chinese language employs the same term, *lao*, to designate both the activities of the gover-

---

4. In M. Cartier, ed., *Le travail et ses représentations*, Paris 1983. See also N. Loraux, '*Ponos*. Sur quelques difficultés de la peine comme nom du travail', in *Archeologia e Storia Antica* IV, Naples 1982, Istituto Universario Orientale; J. Maurin, '*Labor, opus, operae*. Représentations du travail dans la Rome antique', forthcoming; and '*Labor matronalis*, aspects du travail féminin à Rome', in *La femme dans les sociétés antiques*, Strasbourg 1983, pp. 139-55.

nors, who work with their thought, and those of the peasants, who labour with their hands to produce grain and to make war. All these activities are regarded as being tedious but as conferring merit upon those who perform them. The labours of craftsmen and merchants, on the other hand, because they only require skill and patience, create artificial realities conferring no merit upon their authors; the verb *ch'in* is used to refer to such people. It is worth noting that all feminine activities are *ch'in* activities.

In 'Energy and Virtue: Work and its Representations in New Britain',[5] Michel Panoff has shown how, when the Maenge horticulturalists want to refer to what we should call 'agricultural labour', they employ three verbs with different connotations: *lege*, which means to 'to regulate, to balance' relations; *kuma*, 'to expend energy', to mobilize it in a lasting manner; *vai*, to do what is necessary in order to attain a particular goal and, in a wider sense, a way of behaving, a body of custom. For a Maenge, to cultivate the earth is not to 'produce' or 'transform' nature, but to engage in an activity which is conceived as lying at the point of intersection between the three semantic fields described above. Now, the idea which dominates the encounter between these different significations is that to practise horticulture is to effect an exchange with one's ancestors and the gods; it is not a question of transforming matter but of maintaining, through this relation, a fundamental link with nature's invisible forces, which include the dead (who are still alive) and the gods (who are always powerful). Like the ancient Greeks or the Chinese peasants, the Maenge accumulate merit through their attention to the beauty, the arrangement, and even the fine smell of their gardens. They treat the quality of the harvest, as a measure of their 'virtue', and as a sanction employed by the ancestors and the gods to confer recognition on the aptitude of each to honour them and himself.

What, then, did the Maenge think when a colonial power forced them to build roads, or to go and 'work' for money in coconut or rubber plantations owned by the Whites who had invaded their island? Given their representations of traditional agricultural activity, could they be conscious of being 'exploited' in their new productive activity, and in the social form (wage labour) assumed by this work?

Thus, right at the heart of the most material area of societies' infrastructure, at the very heart of the productive forces available

---

5. *L'Homme* XVII (2-3), 1977, pp. 7-22.

to them for acting upon nature, we come across a mental element (knowledge or abstract representations of all kinds, with their extensions in the form of know-how which is also a system of bodily techniques). This mental *element constitutes a kind of armature, the internal organizing plan behind their activation.* But productive forces are only activated within the framework of determinate social relations, which impose a determinate form of division of labour by attaching a specific value to a specific task and by linking that task to a specific social category (men/women, older/younger people, masters/slaves and so on). These bonds, these links also contain a mental element consisting of representations which legitimize the values attached to different social activities.

But these representations do not only exist in the mind. They are also ideas that are expressed in a language. This is one of the essential conditions of learning techniques and of their transmission and thus of the conservation of the productive forces. These representations must be communicated from generation to generation via language and body language. So we are going to have to count among the productive forces not only the idealities which we have enumerated, but also the means — linguistic or otherwise — required to express them socially and to transmit them within a given society and 'culture'.

This analysis thus leads us to conclude that thought and language necessarily belong to the productive forces. The distinction between infrastructure, superstructures and ideology is therefore not a distinction between material and non-material reality. It is a distinction between functions. Finally, if thought is present at the heart of the most material aspect of social activities, *a fortiori* there can be no social relation which does not contain within it an element of thought, a mental part. Seen thus, thought ceases to be a level separate from other levels. By demonstrating its ubiquity in social reality, we can put paid to the notion of level or instance.

Relations of Production

Professional economists, and with them the general public, spontaneously represent the economic structure of every society in the image of the form that takes in our own — as a body of institutions distinct from other social relations, political, familial, religious, etc.

In the capitalist mode of production, the production process takes place inside 'firms', social units distinct from the family, churches, parties or racial communities. This is the case neither in pre-capitalist nor non-capitalist societies. On this point, Marx (if not Marxists) was the first to condemn the temptation to apply our own particular view of the economy to all societies. A century later, after Max Weber, we find the same position in the writings of Karl Polanyi and the 'substantivist' tendency in economic anthropology.

Historians and anthropologists have noted that when one attempts to isolate the economic structure in pre-capitalist societies, one is obliged to examine those social relations which Marxists class as superstructures. To illustrate these different possibilities, I shall select three examples from among the many which history and anthropology offer.

Most ancient Australian Aborigine societies, which lived off hunting, gathering and sometimes fishing, were divided into kinship groups which exchanged wives, these wives circulating, from generation to generation, in the same directions (division into moieties, sections or sub-sections practising a restricted or generalized form of exchange). These social divisions not only regulated marriage and descent, which is the explicit and universal function of kinship relations. They also served as a framework for the exercise of power and for ritual practices designed to act upon the conditions of reproduction of the universe and society, upon the sun, the moon, the rain, and so on. Political and ritual powers and *authority* were in the hands of the old men who were masters of the initiation rites, married to several wives and representative of the different kinship groups composing each tribe.

As we have demonstrated in chapter 2, however, these kinship relations also served as a social framework for the appropriation of each tribes's territory and of its natural resources. This worked in two ways, one abstract and the other concrete, which distinctly yet complementarily employed the two indissociable aspects of kinship — descent and alliance. On the one hand, each kinship group inherited from its ancestors (real or mythical) 'rights' to the use of certain portions of territory. On the other, while these rights were common to all members of each kinship group, they were not exclusive; in certain circumstances, other groups, those in particular connected by marriage were allowed access to territory and resources. In practice, the 'concrete' appropriation of these resources occurred within the framework of local bands roaming over different portions of the tribal territory. These, not the sections, were the units of direct, everyday production and consumption. These bands consisted of a small number of families and individuals belonging to several sections but centred on a patrilineal and patrilocal core of families belonging to the section of whose territory the natural resources were normally exploited. The band took advantage of the presence of relatives by marriage in its midst to exploit the resources of several patches of territory when circumstances demanded it.

Relations of kinship (descent and marriage) thus served as a framework for the abstract (property) and concrete (labour-process) appropriation of nature. These relations, combined with relations between the sexes and between generations formed the social framework for the various material production processes, functioning: 1) as a social condition of the abstract appropriation of nature and its resources; 2) as the basis of the social organization and cooperation of individuals and groups in the various concrete processes of material exploitation of resources (hunting, gathering, fishing); and 3) as the framework for their distribution. Thus, kinship relations in these societies assumed the three functions which define relations of production. They therefore constituted the economic structure, they were the locus and the form of the economy, in these societies.

If we now turn to Oppenheim's work on ancient Mesopotamia, we find an entirely different situation, not unlike that existing in the Inca empire. In Assur, most of the land was regarded as the property of the god Assur. In the centre of the city stood the temple, dwelling-place of the god and his priests. The economy functioned as a vast centralized system within which the local communities and individuals were subject to the authority of the temple and the priests, to whom they were obliged to consign a portion of their labour and their products. Here religious relations form the framework for the appropriation of resources while at the same time constituting the society's economic structure, its social relations of production.

Finally, in my last example — fifth-century Athens — it is the political relations which constitute, from within, the relations of production. One became a citizen by birth, because one's father was an Athenian and because one therefore belonged to a *politeia*, a community of free men who collectively formed a *polis*, a City-State. To be a citizen was also to have an exclusive right — but one which was not necessarily realized — to own a portion of the city's territory. Citizenship thus nearly always entailed being both a free man and a landowner who did or did not personally cultivate his farm, depending upon whether he owned slaves. Ownership of land entitled the citizen to participate in the magistracy and in all political responsibilities, and to bear arms and fulfil the duty to defend the sacred soil of the fatherland. Finally, only citizens could enjoy the protection of the city's gods and officiate at their worship. A citizen who was not a landowner had no access to any of the magistracies or priesthoods, but neither was he exempt — as the non-citizen was — from every responsibility. Clearly, here the political aspect (the fact of belonging to a *polis*) far exceeds what we now understand by a person's having political rights.

Foreign freemen residing in the City and doing business there (metics, in other words) were prohibited from owning land (except in the case of rarely accorded exemptions, from the fourth century on), from acceding to the magistracies, from entering temples and places of worship of the City's gods. Nor were they entitled to serve in the civic corps of hoplites. This gave rise to an initial division of labour, since they were confined to such activities as handicrafts, trade, banking — these being considered unworthy of citizens, even though the latter could also engage in these activities when they had no land to cultivate.

Freemen, whether citizens or metics, could have themselves replaced in all their economic activities (even banking) by slaves. Under these circumstances, slaves could grow rich and purchase their freedom or even own slaves themselves.

Slavery existed long before the advent of the City-State. It had existed in the form of domestic slavery, but underwent a change of function and began to weigh ever more heavily upon the evolution of ancient society when it came to be associated with the development of commodity production and became an essential factor in the accumulation of wealth and the creation of inequalities among citizens. Slavery became the most dynamic and most contradictory characteristic of the Greek economic system in the fifth century BC. In order to grasp the system's originality, one must avoid jumping to the conclusion that it was the forms of division of labour that engendered the forms of property in the means of production and products. The reverse was true. It was because personal membership of a *polis* functioned simultaneously as a social condition of land-appropriation that all those activities which we regard as economic were distributed along a hierarchy of personal relations and statuses and thus enjoyed greater or lesser social value in comparison with the highest status, that of the full citizen.

In passing, it should be noted that in ancient societies, as in a good many primitive ones, by the very nature of the production relations the primary aim of production is not the accumulation of wealth but the preservation of the status of individuals or groups within the community, the preservation of their relations with the rest of the community and hence the reproduction of the community itself. Let us compare these situations, in which membership or non-membership of a community serves as the point of departure for economic relations, with the situation which arose in China after the socialist revolution. In socialist China the workers, the peasants, and working people as a whole, are considered to be the common owners of the land, the means of production and products. There too economic relations are simultaneously political relations. But in this case the community constituting the social 'nation' is the point of arrival and not the point of departure for the economic relations existing within it. However this new type of fusion between what we call the political and the economic bears no resemblance in principle to that of the ancient Greeks since, theoretically, its continued existence and development do not entail domination by a minority of free 'citizens' over the remainder of society, who are enslaved. But for socialist development to occur without exploitation or without constantly recreating hierarchies, one needs, in addition to political and cultural revolutions, a tremendous increase in the material means that can be made available to each through the mediation of all.

After this analysis in which we have seen kinship relations, religious relations and political relations respectively forming the economic structure of society, we reach the same conclusion as in our analysis of the productive forces: the distinction between relations of production and superstructures is, in its underlying principle, a distinction between functions and not between institutions. We have clearly seen this in all three cases, particularly in that of the Australian Aborigines. In each of them the distinction was one based on functions within the same social relations, the same institutions. In some societies, including our own, there are distinct institutions corresponding to these distinct functions. But this is an exception rather than the rule — an exception that has enabled Western thought to perceive with greater clarity the role of material activities and economic relations in social evolution, that is, the material and social relations which men enter into in their active appropriation of nature. We have now demonstrated what was simply asserted in the first chapter: that in the course of history, relations of production (or the 'economic') do not occupy the same sites and consequently do not assume the same forms; their mode of development is not the same and they therefore do not have identical effects upon the reproduction of societies.

The first theoretical question that needs to be answered in constructing a comparative scientific analysis of socio-economic systems, social forms and modes of production, concerns the reasons and the conditions which have caused the production relations to shift from one focus to another in the course of history. Needless to say, neither an individual, nor even a single discipline, could conduct such an analysis. Furthermore, it no longer corresponds to what we understand by economic history and economic anthropology. It is already hard enough to isolate and define a society's economic structure, and it is a measure of the greatness of Malinowski, Firth, Audrey Richards, Gluckman and many others that they managed to do this for the societies they studied. But it is far more difficult to answer the following question: why is it that in a good many primitive and peasant societies kinship relations between groups and individuals serve simultaneously as social conditions of the production of their material means of existing socially (not of surviving but of accomplishing all those things that are naturally demanded from a member of society)?

I shall not attempt an answer here. I shall merely say that as a Marxist I shall seek some of the major reasons for this among the constraints imposed by the level of the productive forces available to these societies, and especially in the fact that living labour power counts for more in these societies than accumulated labour power (in the form of tools or developed resources — means that are external to humankind yet which extend and enhance its action upon nature). The reader should bear in mind something indicated in the very first pages of this book: that the means of production among hunter-gatherers, agriculturists and primitive stockbreeders alike are essentially constituted by the human being himself (or herself), to which are then added a few relatively easily made tools. Now in all of these societies, human beings reproduce themselves within the framework of kinship relations.

Kinship relations may therefore have functioned as the main framework for production processes because they were the focus for the reproduction of the human being's principal means of production, i.e., himself or herself. But this would draw us into a discussion of the theory of male domination and the 'exchange' of women, and a 'Marxist' analysis of the incest taboo. I do not propose to tackle this large issue in the present book.[6]

To return to the main theme of this chapter. Have I not just played into the hands of those who reject Marxism? They are inevitably going to jump to the conclusion that with the exception of capitalist societies, the economic has not played a determinant role in history. It was always something else which 'dominated'. Am I then hoist with my own petard? Is it possible to identify determination with dominance and to infer the non-determination of the infrastructure from the dominance of a super-structure?

The Problem of the Foundations of the Dominance of Non-Economic Structures

Let me begin by making one point clear. The dominance of a given social activity and its corresponding institutions within a society cannot be deduced or hypothesized. It is something one observes. In the first place, it is evident to the members of the society in question. They can observe it concretely around them, in the configuration of their institutions, in their social relations; they may think it and experience it as such; in a word, they recognize it both in and outside themselves, in their individual practice and in the general practice of the other members of their society. They are thus able to point to it as such to outsiders who question them about their customs. This is why Herodotus was able to write in his *Historiai* that 'the Egyptians are an excessively religious people', and why Aristotle, a Macedonian lured to Athens by the glory of that city, placed at the head of his treatise on *Politics* these remarks characterizing the Greeks as human beings *par excellence*: 'The human being is naturally a political animal, a being destined to live in a city, and when, by nature and not through the effect of some circumstance or other, does

---

6. See above, chapter 1, p. 59.

not belong to a city, is a creature either inferior to or superior to the human being.'[7]

At the beginning of this century, enquiring into the nature of Australian Aborigine society, Radcliffe-Brown was struck by the dominance of kinship relations among them: 'Wherever the Australian native goes all the persons he meets are his relatives by the working of the kinship system. These are further classified for him by the section system.' It is clear today that this division into sections applied not only to humans but to the entire universe, that the sun, the moon, the rain, sperm, lightning, kangaroos, etc, were also supposed to 'belong' to one or another of the sections which allocated men for the purpose performing rites.[8]

However, I should not like to give the impression that it is always as easy as this to identify the dominant 'superstructure' in a social formation. Often enough, the form of dominance is blurred and scarcely discernible. To give but one example, historians still find it difficult to measure the importance of Christianity in the functioning of medieval society. Did it not become the dominant institution and ideology in feudal society when, at the turn of the tenth century, the church was still the premier landowner in Europe and the theory of the three orders had just achieved its most complete formulation, sanctioning the domination of the *oratores* and the *bellatores* (those who prayed and those who fought) over those who worked, placing human beings who were in the service of God — priests — at the summit of the human order? However, Christianity, unlike religion in ancient Assur, was not the direct framework for the control and exploitation of men and land. In this sense it did not control the reproduction of society as a whole. This took the form of an immense hierarchy of relations of personal dependence which subordinated lords to each other and peasants to lords; the substructure, the matrix of this hierarchy, was the seigniorial institution in all its forms — domestic service, agrarian tenure or the obligation of the *banalité*.

It was within this framework and on this basis that the lords spiritual and temporal were able to deduct from their peasants' labour the means for glorifying God, certainly, but also for

---

7. Aristotle, *Politics* 1253a9.

8. Some elements of this theory were spelt out in my *La Production des Grands Hommes*, Paris 1982. See also C.G. Brandenstein, 'The Meaning of Section and Section Names', *Oceania* XVI (1), September 1970, pp. 39-49.

making war and glorifying themselves. The dominant institution, that of relations, was born before the peasants and barbarians had been completely evangelized, before Europe had become Christendom. It arose from the efforts of a warrior aristocracy slowly organizing the forms of its domination after the close of the age of the great invasions, at the end of the sixth century AD; this lay aristocracy was to remain the dominant element in the new dominant class. It is in relation to the growing dominance of this institution that we ought to seek to measure and explain Christianity's dominance over people's minds and over society, and not the other way round.[9] I shall not pursue this analysis but rather my initial examples, since they are simpler and should allow us to clarify things a little. How are we to account for the dominance of kinship, politics or religion, and how are we to explain changes in dominance over the course of time?

We can begin by rejecting the argument which begins by 'explaining' that social relations dominate a society's functioning because they fulfil several functions, and which then goes on to 'explain' that they assume several functions because they dominate society's functioning! This is a manifestly tautological argument. Considerably more interesting is the argument put forward by some which starts from thought and the ideas that may govern it to account for the dominance of social relations founded upon kinship, religion, etc. It should be pointed out here that we are not concerned with ideas which dominate a society's thinking temporarily and then 'go out of fashion'. What concerns us are ideas that are in some way 'embodied' in durable social structures or whose appearance seems to entail a deep, enduring alteration in the social relations between human beings and of human beings with nature.

Yet it is easy to show that one cannot take ideas alone as one's starting-point in accounting for the content and relative strength of ideas. Unless one assumes that ideas arise in a wholly arbitrary way in thought or (what amounts to the same thing) are introduced into thought from the outside (by forces external to humankind and for reasons peculiar to these forces); unless, again, one assumes that the whole power of an idea depends merely upon the circumstance that the majority if not all the members of a society in which it is dominant believe it to be 'true', then one element in the reasons for its content and its

9. George Duby, *Guerriers et Paysans, VII*-XII* siècles*, Paris 1973.

power to dominate exists independently of thought and in the very nature of the social relations between human beings and between human beings and nature. For to say that an idea is 'true' means saying that this idea has the capacity to explain the order or disorder reigning in society and the cosmos. And it entails claiming that this explanation facilitates effective action upon the problems connected with the maintenance of this order or with the abolition of this disorder. Proofs of the veracity of an idea can never be reduced merely to a question of thought. This idea must correspond to something outside of or beyond thought in social and cosmic reality. Ideas never contain in themselves all the reasons for their influence and their historical role. Thought alone can never produce these reasons, for this influence never derives simply from what they *are*, but from what they *do*, or better still, from what they *get done* in society, on it or on the world outside it.

This is why any analysis that commences by isolating thought from the other components of social reality (the mental from the non-mental) and then attempts to deduce the latter from the former (the idealist approach), or the former from the latter (the vulgar materialist approach), will, by virtue of its underlying principle, inevitably box itself into a corner. Of course, one may commence with thought alone in order to analyse the dominance of social relations (just as one may set out from the material aspects of these social relations). But one ought not to do so since, if ideas dominate as much because of what they do and get done as because of what they are, then the emergent causal relation is one of a hierarchy of functions, co-existing and presupposing each other, rather than a relation founded on linear causality and a logical and chronological priority between a cause and effects external to it. But to say that there is a functional relationship between an idea and its dominance is not reducible to saying that kinship relations and ideology dominate many primitive and peasant societies because the problems of descent and marriage-relationship have more impact there than elsewhere; or that political relations and ideas dominated in Athens because problems of personal status and power were more acute there than elsewhere. In each case one would still have to explain what it was that made these particular problems more important than elsewhere.

To return to our three examples. In these societies, kinship governs descent and marriage-relationships as it does in every society, and yet is not dominant in all of them. Religion organizes their relations with the supernatural, just as it does everywhere else, and yet is not dominant in all of them. We may therefore logically and legitimately advance the idea that the explicit, universal functions of kinship — the social regulation of the reproduction of life via the regulation of marriage and descent — do not suffice to explain its dominance in cases where it is dominant. The same goes for the 'political' and for religion. We thus need something *more*, a function which is *not* present in all cases of the functioning of kinship, politics or religion, but which is present in *each* case where these particular social relations and the corresponding ideas dominate the functioning of society.

We know what this function is: in each case, the dominant relations function simultaneously as social relations of production, as the society's structure, and as a framework for the material appropriation of nature. I therefore propose to render this observation more general by offering the following hypothesis:

For a social activity — and with it the ideas and institutions that correspond to and organize it — to play a dominant role in a society's functioning and evolution (and hence in the thought and actions of the individuals and groups who compose this society), it is not enough for it to fulfil several functions; in addition to its explicit ends and functions, it must of necessity directly fulfil the function of a relation of production.

Of course it takes more than three cases to verify a hypothesis (and one needs to be sure that these three cases do in fact verify it). Let us provisionally accept it as a hypothesis and turn straight away to the theoretical consequence which it entails.

1) In itself this hypothesis says nothing about the nature of the social relations that may function as production relations. It contains no prior judgement, ethnocentric or otherwise, as to what the economic 'ought' to be.

2) In itself this hypothesis says nothing about the specific reasons and conditions which cause relations of production to shift in locus and form in the course of history. It merely contains a general indication to the effect that there is a close relationship between the topology and morphology relations of production and the level of the productive forces.

3) This hypothesis does tell us something about the reasons for the unequal influence of certain relations upon societies' functioning and reproduction. This influence depends less upon what they are than upon what they do. It amounts to the claim that, of

all the social relations making up a society, those which, among their other functions, determine access to resources and to the means of production and constitute the social form of appropriation of nature have greater influence than others upon that society's functioning and transformations. It therefore presupposes the existence of a hierarchy among the functions that must be fulfilled by social relations in order for a society to exist as such and to reproduce itself. Social relations have a more or less determinant role depending upon the functions which they fulfil, and the relations that are 'determinant in the last analysis' are always those which function as relations of production: because they function as relations of production they dominate the society's reproduction and, together with these relations, dominate the representations which organize them and express them.

This brings us back by another route to Marx's hypothesis concerning the determinate role in the last analysis of economic structures and the material conditions of social existence. It is clear to me that this notion of determination in the last analysis should not be taken to imply the existence of a hierarchy of levels or instances, nor even of institutions, which would be the same everywhere. What it refers to is the existence of hierarchy of functions which in every case bestow more influence upon those social relations that serve as direct supports to the production processes.

It thus becomes impossible to attempt to counter Marx by invoking the fact of the dominance of kinship (Radcliffe-Brown), or politics (Edouard Will) or religion (Louis Dumont), since each of these examples serves to confirm his hypothesis — one designed to facilitate research and not a law from which reality could be mechanically deduced.

I am perfectly aware that my approach to Marxism is not the one normally encountered among Marxists, who, like Althusser, still represent relations of production as separate from kinship, religion, politics and, in ethnocentric fashion, project this characteristic of the capitalist mode of producing and organizing society onto all societies. They are led to conceive of causality in the last analysis as the effect of a dual action of the infrastructure upon the superstructures, as the selection of one of the superstructures which is them elevated to a dominant position (Balibar, Terray). But as I have pointed out this assumes that relations of production and superstructures are invariably distinct institutions and it takes our own society, which is an exception, as the rule.

Let me emphasize yet again that it was in fact this exception which, for the first time, enabled humanity to arrive at a clearer understanding of the role of the economic and the material conditions of production (the nature and efficacy of the productive forces) in the historical formation and transformation of societies. This was Marx's real 'epistemological break'. The new and unique character of the capitalist mode of production enabled him to discern other forces in history than those hitherto apparent to the actors themselves; or more precisely, it enabled him to see these forces, which had always been evident, in a different way. For, in Antiquity, there were no invisible classes 'hidden' behind the visible estates into which the Athenian population was distributed in a fashion comprehensible to all — citizens, metics, slaves, freedmen, etc.

A class that managed to remain concealed not only from the Greeks themselves but also from all non-Marxist historians would in any case be something of a paradox. The problem is one of interpreting social reality and its internal logic.

Does this mean that all the interpretations given by the Greeks of the reasons for the dominance of the political in their society and for the domination enjoyed by citizens over the rest of society were mere illusion, and that they were living in an ideological, i.e. imaginary relation (Althusser) with themselves? But illusion for whom? For the Greeks or for us? And how would this illusion have arisen? Because someone deceived them, because they deceived themselves, or because they wanted to deceive others? All these are the kind of questions that usually crop up as soon as one attempts to distinguish ideological from non-ideological ideas. Does acquisition of another view of the reasons for the dominance of superstructure and the ideas that organize them help us to see things any more clearly?

The Mental Part of (Social) Reality and the Distinction Between the Ideological and the Non-Ideological

In analysing the most material aspect of social realities — the productive forces available to a society for the purpose of acting upon surrounding nature — we observed that they contained two closely interwoven components: a material element (tools,

human beings themselves) and a mental element (representations of nature, rules governing the manufacture and use of
tools, and so on). These representations are indispensable to the
production and utilization of these material means. And this
utilization takes the form of connected sequences of action which
constitute what we call the labour process.

We have also seen, in the case of Hesiod, that a labour process
often involves symbolic acts through which one acts not upon
visible nature, as is done with tools, but on the invisible forces
which control nature's reproduction and are thought to be
capable of granting or refusing man his wishes: a good harvest,
good hunting and so on. This symbolic element in the labour
process constitutes a social reality every bit as real as material
actions upon nature; but its purpose, its raisons d' être and its
internal organization constitute a set of mental realities arising
from thought that interprets the world's hidden order and organizes action on the forces controlling it. The performance of these
rituals often involves material means (sacred objects, clay for
body-painting, etc), but these have no meaning or efficacy
outside the interpretative system of the social order which selects
them.

Next, when we analysed the significance of the absence of a
term to designate 'labour' in ancient Greece, and the representations connected with the practice of agriculture, handicrafts and
commerce in ancient Athens, we saw the emergence of another
type of mental reality — namely, representations which attach a
positive or negative value to an individual or group depending
upon the material and/or symbolic task it accomplishes, conferring upon it a status within the social hierarchy. And these representations are only meaningful within a system of ideas and
values that defines and legitimises the distribution of all those
tasks essential to a society's reproduction among men and
women, older and younger people, masters and slaves, aristocrats
and commoners, priests and laymen, etc. This value system is an
effect produced in the division of labour by the relations of
production. Finally, in analysing the example of the Australian
Aborigines, we saw that their kinship relations are simultaneously relations of production, and we detected a series of
rules governing the 'abstract' appropriation of nature, which are
transmitted from generation to generation through relations of
descent. Here these mental realities defined and legitimized
individuals' and groups' concrete access to the material resources

and supernatural realities which constituted their territory.

We could go on with this analysis, but we should simply continue to observe the emergence — in the midst of the manifold facets of social life — of mental realities which are distinguishable by the functions they fulfil, and which appear not as the effects of social relations in thought, but as one of the internal components of these relations and as *a necessary condition of their formation (as well as of their reproduction)*.

No kinship system can either exist or reproduce itself without making use of mental realities well-known to anthropologists — rules of descent, marriage, residence, kinship terminology, a body of principles defining and legitimizing the personal rights and duties attaching to these relations and delimiting what is meant socially by being a relative as opposed to a non-relative (friend or enemy) or a foreigner. Far from existing independently of these mental realities, kinship relations constantly presuppose them. Of course kinship relations cannot be reduced to this mental element since they are also a set of personal relations of dependence or obligation, material or otherwise, reciprocal or non-reciprocal. Thus they are not only what they are in thought (mentally) but also what they get done (concretely).

This is even more obvious in the case of religious activities. The fact that the Pharaoh was considered to be a god, the temporary incarnation and permanent resurrection of Horus, son of Osiris, lord of the earth and of the lives of his subjects, was a representation and a mental reality which both legitimized his power and served as the principle underlying the organization of his realm, the division of tasks and material and spiritual obligations, and the labour performed by the peasants for the glory of the gods, the Pharaoh and all those who received power and wealth from him.

In short, there is an element of the mental in all (social) reality; which does not mean that everything in reality is mental. Ideas are not an instance separated from social relations, offering them afresh, after the event, as it were, to thought. The mental is thought in all its functions, present and active in all man's activities, and something which only exists in society. The mental cannot be opposed to the material for thinking involves setting matter — the brain — in motion; an idea is a reality, but an impalpable one. The mental then, is what thought does, and its diversity corresponds to that of thought's own functions. What are the functions of thought and its representations?

The first function of representations (which I shall call $f1$) is to make realities which are external or internal to humankind — including thought itself — present in thought. These realities can be material and/or intellectual, visible and/or invisible, concrete and/or imaginary, and so on.

But presenting a reality to thought always involves thought in interpreting this reality. This is the second function of representations ($f2$). Interpreting means defining the nature, origin and functioning of a reality present to thought. There can be no such thing as a representation which is not simultaneously an interpretation and that does not presuppose the existence of a system of representations, that is, a set of representations governed by a specific logic and coherence, whatever these may be. These interpretations only exist through and in thought. The moment they represent an invisible world or being, this invisible world starts to exist socially — even if it corresponds to nothing tangible in the reality represented.

The third function of these representations-interpretations ($f3$) is to enable thought to organize the relations human beings sustain between themselves and with nature: thought serves them as a kind of internal framework and as an abstract end. It then exists in the form of rules of conduct, principles of action, permission or proscription, and so on.

Finally, as regards their fourth function ($f4$), representations of reality are interpretations which either legitimise or undermine relations between human beings and between human beings and nature.

In my view, these are the four main functions of thought — functions which, whether separately or conjointly, are assumed by the various mental realities dealt with in my examples. These functions are present to differing degrees in all social activities and they combine with other functions of social relations that cannot be reduced to ideas: producing and controlling the material means of existence, ensuring the unity and permanence of human groups despite inevitable contradictions (of interest, of power) and, through them, acting upon the visible and invisible order of the world, and so on. These functions cannot be fulfilled without thought, but are not reducible to acts of thought. Nor can thought simply deduce them from itself. They are not born of thought alone; their roots lie rather in the fact that men belong to a social species which, from the pre-human evolution of nature, has inherited the capacity to act upon its material and social conditions of existence, in order to transform them. Thought exercises the brain's possibilities: it does not create them.

Now representing, interpreting, organizing and legitimizing are all different ways of producing *meaning*. All thought's functions therefore conspire to produce meaning and, on the basis of meanings produced, to organize and recognize relations between human beings and between human beings and nature. But at the same time, nature and the human being — as a being capable of living in and producing society — are realities which precede the meaning with which thought can endow them and do not depend upon this meaning for their existence.

Does this analysis enable us to distinguish, among mental realities, those that are ideological from those that are not? Is there a formal or functional criterion that would enable us to discriminate between them? I asserted at the beginning of this chapter that we should have to answer these questions in the negative so long as we confine ourselves to labelling ideological any and every system of representations, even relatively unorganized ones. Is it conceivable that there could be representations which have no links with any others, even if only by way of contrast, and live in a 'free' state, like particles wandering in the interstellar void?

We thus need a rather more restrictive definition of ideology. The most usual one looks like a Marxist definition, and may be formulated as follows: 'ideological' refers to those illusory representations that men have of themselves and the world, and which serve to legitimize an existing social order born independently of these representations, thus leading to acceptance of the forms of domination and oppression of some human beings by others on which this order depends.

What happens to this definition when we set it against our analysis of the four functions of thought and against the fact that all social relations contain a mental element which organizes them from the inside and is one of the very conditions of their formation? Are we to consider representations that legitimize social relations as ideological ($f1 + f2 + f4$), and those that organize them as non-ideological ($f1 + f2 + f3$)? If the answer is yes, taking into account the fact that legitimation has to be based upon illusory interpretations, we should have to distinguish within $f2$ between illusory interpretations ($f2$) and non-illusory interpretations ($f2^{non-i}$). This yields the following formula:

Non-ideological mental	Ideological mental
$f1 + f2^{non-i} + f3$	$f1 + f2^i + f4$

Seen thus, to some extent religious representations become paradigmatic of all the illusory representations which man had developed, does develop and will develop always different, concerning himself and the world in which he lives.

However, not all the representations man has evolved of himself and the world when fishing, hunting, farming, and so on, and which help him to organize these activities, are illusory — even from a European point of view. They contain an immense treasure-house of both supposedly and genuinely true knowledge constituting a veritable 'science of the concrete', as Lévi-Strauss put it when speaking of the 'savage mind'. But for whom, then, is what is illusory in them illusory? Not for those who believe in it, but for those who either do not or no longer believe in it. Hence they are illusory for us, for example, we who are capable of countering them with other representations of the world that strike us as better verified, more true, if not as the only true ones. By definition, a myth is only a myth for those who do not believe in it, and the first to believe in myths are those who invent them, in other words who think them out and formulate them as fundamental 'truths' which they imagine to have been inspired in them by supernatural beings such as gods, ancestors and so on. So it is only to others that ideological representations appear as such, i.e. as mistaken representations that are not recognized as such. We may thus straight away reject the narrow eighteenth-century notion that religion is just a pack of lies invented by the priests — who never believed a word of it — in order to deceive the ignorant people and subject it to their domination (see Condorcet).

Not that I would deny that there have been, and will be in the future, a good many priests or ideologues who do not believe or have ceased to believe in the ideas they profess. Nor do I deny that lies have always been one of the means employed by the dominant to preserve their domination. And, in addition to declared lies, there are also lies by omission, silences, bits left out in discourse — all of which are highly revealing. The problem, then, is not merely to account for the fact that outside observers of a society, whether contemporary or not, may not share the beliefs held to be true by that society and consider them false, but how to account for the fact that in a given society at a given epoch ideas held to be true by the majority of this society's members are considered false by various minorities. Whence do these contradictions spring? Can they be reduced to opposing views on the same things, or do they express opposing interests, contradictions that exceed the bounds of thought and lie within the very functioning of social relations among human beings in this society and with the nature surrounding them? In Athens, Aristotle was undoubtedly expressing the dominant opinion when he stated that barbarians were 'naturally' born 'to be slaves'; but he was opposed by certain Sophists such as Antiphon, who declared that by nature human beings were identical in all respects, and that one was not destined from birth to be either free man or slave. This critique of slavery did not, therefore, amount to a difference of ideas. Its foundations lay in the very contradictions inherent in slave relations of production, although in Antiquity the vast majority of free men never seriously imagined for a moment that their society could exist without slavery.

We thus come back to the conclusions reached in our analysis of the foundations of the dominance of social relations. No single formal criterion exists which is sufficient to distinguish ideas that are ideological from those that are not. And the fact that certain ideas seem truer than others in a given society stems not only from their abstract veracity but also from their relationship with the various social activities, hierarchized according to the nature of their functions, amongst them being the function of production relation. This relation is such that ideas seem all the truer for legitimizing existing social relations and the inequalities they contain. Is this the ultimate criterion distinguishing ideological from non-ideological ideas? Are ideas that reflect and protect the existing social order ideological because of this function? Once again, this is a biased and partial approach to the question, since it neglects the representations which regard this order as illegitimate and which legitimize a return to a previous order or else the advent of a future order. It also entails forgetting all those Utopias which from the outset are thought of as 'realities that have never existed and will never exist anywhere (U-topia), but which make it possible to erect a "principle of hope" against the existing order'[10]. Here again, what distinguishes these represent-

---

10. See Ernst Bloch, *The Principle of Hope*, Oxford 1986.

ations is not only a difference in the content of the ideas, but a different relationship with the existing social order, a relationship of the contradictions entailed by this order's functioning.

Consequently, when we look at ideologies in all their diversity, we cannot possibly say that they are nothing but illusions developed after the event, as it were, to legitimize concrete social relations supposedly existent prior to and independently of them. It is when they do not appear to the exploited as illusions or as instruments of their exploitation that they contribute effectively to persuading these people to accept their exploitation. So, ideas have to be considered fundamentally 'true' by the majority of a society's members — by both dominant and dominated groups — for them to become dominant themselves. And how can they be if, objectively, they contradict the interests of the dominated? Only an enquiry into the basic elements and foundations of all power to dominate and oppress will enable us to find an answer to this question.

Paradigm and Paradoxes of the 'Legitimacy' of the Birth of Dominant Classes and the State

The power to dominate is composed of two indissolubly linked elements: violence and consent. My analysis leads me ineluctably to the assertion that, of the two components of power, the strongest is not the violence of the dominant but the consent of the dominated to their domination. For the installation and maintenance in power of part of society (the male sex, an estate, a caste or a class), repression is less effective than adherence, and physical or psychological violence counts for less than intellectual conviction which brings with it the acquiescence, the acceptance if not the cooperation, of the dominated.

I hope that I shall be neither misinterpreted nor made the object of accusations in bad faith. I shall set aside for a moment cases of domination directly imposed by violence either real (war) or potential (the threat of force). Such cases involve situations of forced consent which are nothing more than unstable compromises between unequal forces. I shall come back to this later. Here I am interested rather in those forms of consent which are somehow spontaneous, such as the belief in the Pharaoh's divinity in ancient Egypt or even the acceptance by the majority of women, in almost all societies, of masculine authority, which moreover varies from the mildest forms, involving quasi-equality, to the most extreme oppression. There is of course a great gulf between passive acceptance and active consent. And an apparently spontaneous active consent is itself never wholly spontaneous, since it derives from an education, a culture, a formation of men and women capable of reproducing their society. Furthermore, consent, even when passive, is never shared by all the individuals and groups in a society and, when it is active, it is rarely free from reservations or contradictions. Every society — even the most egalitarian primitive societies — contains both common and private interests which, day in day out, either come into opposition or are reconciled. If this were not the case, there would never have been any history.

This is not the crucial point, however. The crucial point is that violence and consent are not, fundamentally, mutually exclusive. No domination, particularly if it stems from the brutal force involved in war and conquest, can endure if it does not rest uon some combination of these two factors. The proportions will of course vary according to circumstances and the level of resistance encountered, but even the least contested and most accepted form of domination will always contain the implicit threat of recourse to violence if consent weakens or gives way to refusal, even to resistance. There is no domination without violence, even if this is only distantly threatened. It is therefore pointless imagining a form of lasting domination resting solely upon violence or upon total consent. If such extreme cases exist, they can only apply to transitory, indeed ephemeral, states of historical evolution.

The above observations, presented here in order to avoid any misunderstandings, leave us with only one way of explaining how dominated individuals and groups can 'spontaneously' consent to their own domination: the latter must appear as a *service* rendered them by the dominant, whose power henceforth seems so legitimate that the dominated feel it to be their duty to serve those who are serving them. The dominant and the dominated must therefore *share* the same representations if the strongest component in the power of the former over the latter is to emerge, i.e. consent resting upon the recognition of the benefits, the legitimacy and the necessity of this power. Suppose we consider two societies with which we have already become familiar in the course of this book: the So and the Incas.

The So, who are settled on the slopes of the Kadam and

Moroto mountains in Uganda, live off sorghum, livestock and a little hunting; but their situation is a precarious one. Their agriculture is threatened by periodic droughts or by various diseases which attack their plants. Their livestock is regularly stolen by the Karimojong shepherds who live on the plain. Slash-and-burn has driven back the forest so that game has almost entirely disappeared. The So are about five thousand in number, and are divided into scattered patrilineal clans. It is a society in which the men dominate the women and seniors dominate juniors. But among the seniors, each of whom represents his line-age and clan, there exists a small minority of some fifty men who dominate all the rest of this society. These are the initiated men (*kenisan*) who have the power to communicate with the ancestors (*emet*) and to obtain from them all the good things of life, such as peace, health, good harvest and so on. The ancestors themselves communicate with Belgen, a remote god. When a person dies, his soul (*buku*) becomes an *emet*; the lineage elders memorize the names of their *emets* but only the *kenisan* can address them by their names and speak to them face to face. If someone who was not initiated dared to do such a thing, he would immediately be struck down by madness, begin to eat his own excrement, start to behave like an animal and die. This threat, which hangs over the whole So population, surrounds the person and acts of the *kenisan*, who perform their rituals in a sacred place near the house of the god Belgen and hidden from the public, with a penumbra of violence.

What functions do these initiated elders fulfil? One of their tasks is to bury the more important of the dead, both men and women, and to guarantee that each soul attains the state of being an *emet*. They also intervene whenever society is threatened, whether by severe drought, epidemics, external enemies or inter-nal conflicts. When the latter are involved, the *kenisan* set up a kind of court of justice which, after consulting the ancestors, names the guilty parties. Their power in witchcraft is such as to strike fear into the hearts of their enemies, the Karimojong who regularly raid their territory. When drought, insects, worms or mildew devastate their harvest, they perform ceremonies to make the rain come or to bless the sorghum. A goat is sacrified to the *emets*, a portion of the meat is laid upon their altar and the rest is consumed by the *kenisan*. The rain ritual and the site where it is performed belong to certain clans, only one of which has the power to make the rain fall for the *whole* tribe, in which case the *kenisans* of the clan in question perform the ritual by themselves.

These few men base their power on the fact that they enjoy privileged access to the ancestors and to the god Belgen, who have it in their power to reproduce the life of plants, animals and men, to ensure the rule of prosperity, justice and peace, and to vanquish enemies and every adversity. In some sense they therefore have a monopoly of action over the conditions (which are imaginary in our eyes) of the society's reproduction. By wielding their powers and sacrificing to the ancestors, they serve the general interest and are identified in the eyes of the living and the dead with interests common to all members of the society — men, women, seniors, juniors, those who are well off and those who are not. They personify their society, they embody it. In exchange for their services, they enjoy the highest prestige, authority and a number of material benefits.

I shall not linger too long over my other example, the Incas, for the works of J. Mason, J. Murra, J. Earls, Zuidema and others have made us more familiar with it. The Incas worshipped the dead and their ancestors, some of whom lay in a mummified form in tombs upon which they would offer them in sacrifice llamas, maize beer, fabrics and so on. The Earth-Mother, the Sun, the Moon and a host of divinities, infernal or celestial, were venerated on the consecrated altars, the *huacas*. The ancestors, like the gods, owned land and herds which provided the maize and the animals for the sacrifices, and which as a matter of priority, were cultivated and tended by the members of the various local communities. With the development of the Inca Empire, the Inca himself appeared as a living god, son of the Sun, and therefore as master of the conditions governing the reproduction of life, of the whole universe and of each of the peoples and individuals subject to him. In the garden of the temple of the Sun, as offerings to the gods, many copies in gold were kept of all the useful plants and animals of Tawantinsuyu, the Empire of the Four Quarters, foremost among them ears of maize and figures of llamas and shepherds. In another garden, the Inca and his closest relatives themselves sowed, watered, tended and harvested the maize used at the great festivals of the sun-god. When the Inca was gravely ill, human sacrifices were offered to the sun so that it would not stop lighting the world. A large part of the peasant population subject to the Inca's power believed in his divinity, his mastery of the conditions of the universe's reproduction and his generosity.

While the services rendered by the Inca seem to us to be

imaginary and the labour *corvées* performed in the Inca's fields or in the building of roads, temples, towns and granaries in contrast to be only too real, this serves at least to demonstrate, on the one hand that this 'imaginary' was not regarded by the Indians as 'unreal' or opposed to the real, and that it was therefore not illusory; and on the other, that the Inca and his kin's monopoly on the imaginary conditions of the reproduction of life had very early become a fundamental condition of their right to appropriate part of the soil and the labour of the village communities. The belief in the supernatural powers of certain aristocratic lineages — a belief very widespread among the Indian populations long before the appearance of the Inca Empire — not only made it possible to legitimize relations of production which had arisen without this belief (when the Incas forced all the conquered peoples to honour the Sun in addition to their own gods). It was also one of the conditions for the appearance of an oppressive power which made religion not a reflection of but component in the internal framework of the production relations.

The Inca required of his subjects that they work his fields, and the Sun's, wearing festive clothes, singing and playing music. He then made them serve up a meal, with maize beer, as every Indian did when his neighbours helped him to cultivate a field or to build a house. But the maize which the Inca gave to the Indians was part of the same crop which they had cultivated in fields he had taken from them in return for their safety. However, as John Murra emphasizes very forcefully, the crucial point is that the Inca always organized his exactions in the terminology and forms of traditional Andean reciprocity.

This leads me to formulate the following hypothesis: *for relations of domination and exploitation to be formed and reproduced in a lasting fashion, they must be presented as an exchange, and as exchange of services.* It is this that establishes that active or passive consent of those who are dominated. I shall also advance a further hypothesis: among the factors which, in the course of history, have effected the internal differentiation of social statuses and the formation of hierarchies founded upon divisions into estates, castes and classes, *the fact that the services rendered by the dominant have been predominantly concerned with the invisible forces controlling the reproduction of the universe has always been crucial.* For the terms of the balance which is established between the services exchanged, those rendered by the dominant seem all the more fundamental for being the more imaginary, whereas those rendered by the dominated seem all the more trivial for being the more material, since they only concern the universally visible conditions needed for the society's reproduction.

Debt is the usual formula for the bonds of dependence and exploitation which link the dominated to the dominant. And with regard to the Inca or the Pharaoh, whose life-force animates all beings in nature, the debt contracted by each of their subjects is nothing other than their very existence. Nothing would seem to be sufficient to settle a debt of this kind — neither the offer of their labour, nor that of their goods, nor their personal fidelity and devotion, nor even the sacrifice of life itself — since the debt is reborn in each generation. The stronger the imaginary component, the more potent are the powers of the dominant over the invisible, and the more derisory seem the services rendered by the dominated, since their relation assumes the form of an unequal exchange that is more advantageous to the dominated than to the dominant. In extreme cases, the burden borne by the exploited must have seemed to them like a benefit and the power wielded by the dominant must have been experienced by the latter as if it were a burden. And we know that some African kings were put to death when they grew old or fell ill, because their weakness threatened their kingdoms with bad harvests, epidemics or other catastrophes.

No domination, even when born of violence, can last if it does not assume the form of an exchange of services. Thus, as Jacques Soustelle has shown concerning the Aztecs, victory in battle gave them rights of life and death over the vanquished, but in most cases they offered the latter the chance to redeem their lives. A kind of contract was then drawn up between victors and vanquished, which fixed the amount of tribute the latter henceforth had to pay to the former, together with the reciprocal obligations the two peoples had to fulfil. A kind of consensus was established replacing the original violence, which was there after kept in reserve, and constituted a mechanism which organized and legalized — without altogether legitimizing — the exploitation of the one people by the other. Much the same occurred with the Babylonians, the Medes, the Mongols and so on.

Another, still more striking example is provided by the ceremonies held for the enthronement of a new king among the Mossi of Yatênga. The Mossi are descended from horsemen who came from Ghana and who, towards the middle of the fifteenth century, conquered the Volta basin. They subdued the autochthonous agricultural populations, who were called 'sons of the soil' or 'people of the soil' and who did not relinquish any of their ritual powers over the soil. Upon the death of a Mossi king, a new king was chosen from among the sovereign's sons solely by the Mossi, the descendants of the conquerors. Then the new king, alone and poorly dressed, set out on a long enthronement journey (*ringu*) which after fifty days brought him back to the gate of his capital. Dressed all in white, on horseback, he made a triumphal entry worthy of a king. This journey took him from autochthonous village to autochthonous village, where the masters of the soil lived. These masters taught him one by one the taboos affecting his kingly function, after having made him, alone of all the Mossi, and all 'foreigners', participate in rituals addressed to the ancestors of the subject populations and to the soil. As Michel Izard, has shown in his remarkable study: 'The new king of the foreigners presents himself alone, humbly, before the representatives of the country's earliest inhabitants to ask them to accept his authority, to give him the legitimacy which alone will confer the land upon him, and he offers or promises them presents. A game begins between the king and the sons of the soil; the new king is humiliated, he is kept waiting ... he is mocked, and nothing is done either to feed or to lodge him.'[11] By then allowing him a place in their rituals, the priests and chiefs of the autochthonous lineages, which have been subjected since the conquest to the Mossi power, have their ancestors and the soil recognize the king as one of their own people: they give his power a legitimacy which the original conquest prevented him from fully possessing. And this recognition obliges them from then on to give part of their labour and of the soil's to the king. But at the same time, their power has been, of course, once more recognized by the king of those who conquered them in former times.

This journey, which began in solitude, concludes with a full expression of the king's royal function. A monarchy which originated in armed violence is transformed into a sacred and legitimate institution. Only the king, through his own person, unifies the community of the conquerors and that of the conquered. He alone personifies the unity and the opposition of the two communities. He represents the entire society on a higher level, and he is a State all by himself. His person becomes sacred and

---

11. M. Izard, 'Le royaume du Yatênga', in R. Cresswell, ed., *Eléments d'ethnologie*, Paris 1975, I. p. 234.

precious — hence the taboos which apply to him and every person who approaches him. (Likewise in Peru, no one — no matter his rank — could approach the Inca without removing his shoes and without bearing a load upon his shoulder as a symbol of submission. No one was supposed to look the Inca full in the face.)

In the Mossi example we once again observe violence being transformed into reciprocal exchange, political and economic power legitimizing themselves and seeking to win consent by actions upon the invisible forces which control the reproduction of life. Once again we find that the dominant social relations are those which function as relations of production, controlling land, persons and products, and that the dominant ideas are those linked to the nature and reproduction of these dominant relations.

Finally, I shall present an example which is closer to us and even more paradoxical — Graeco-Roman slavery — for which I shall use the searching analyses of J. Maurin. Separated by force from their communities of origin (and sometimes sold by these same communities), slaves belong wholly to their masters who, may, if they wish, have them put to death for no reason at all. A slave had no rights in the ancient City. He did not exist or, at any rate, to no greater degree than an animal did; he could not marry or establish kinship relations; his children did no belong to him. He was subject to the domination and violence not only of his master but of all other citizens as well. Appearances notwithstanding, slavery never exists in relation to a single master and Man Friday could never have become Robinson's slave. Although it arises out of violence, the master/slave relation can never permanently depend upon physical constraint. Within the *familia*, the slave is treated as a child, *puer servus*, but is quite different from the son of a citizen (*puer filius*) who is emancipated at the age of sixteen and and becomes a citizen (*vir*) fit to bear arms and to start a family — in other words, to produce citizens. The only hope for a slave, virtually as a child, is that his master may one day free him, in a ceremony which is a copy of the *liberalia*, when a young citizen is presented to the City and to the gods of the Forum by his father. Accordingly, violence must be attenuated and a fictive kinship established, the slave is to cooperate with his master in his own exploitation, and if the master is to extract from him all the service and labour he expects. The Pseudo-Aristotle put this very well: 'We may apportion to our slaves (1) work, (2) chastisement, and (3) food. . . . To set the prize of freedom before him is both just and expedient; since having a prize to work for, and a time defined for its attainment, he will put his heart into his labours. We should, moreover, take hostages (for our slaves' fidelity) by allowing them to beget children . . . .'[12]

This text bears out the present analysis, for it shows quite clearly how violence and contract conjoin to enable the functioning and reproduction of slave relations of production. Punishment (violence) is not sufficient. The promise of liberty must be added if a slave is to be goaded into giving his consent, identifying his own interest with his master's and thus cooperating in his own enslavement. It is therefore clearly impossible to separate representations which legitimize from those which organize, and to contrast them as ideological and non-ideological, since one cannot organize enduring oppressive power without giving it the form of an exchange — in other words, without in a way legitimizing it by turning it into a reciprocal commitment between the dominant and the dominated. A commitment of this sort — legitimation as a social force — restricts recourse to brute force, and physical violence, whether it be the oppressive violence of the dominant or the rebellious violence of the dominated. But this social force is added to violence at the same time as being opposed to it, and it helps to keep the confrontation between dominant and dominated in forms and proportions which are compatible with the enduring reproduction of the domination of some by others.

Very special conditions are therefore necessary for the dominated to become aware of the illegitimate nature of the domination which they endure for their consent to be exhausted, and for the idea to arise of turning to violence not to contain, as before, but rather to abolish the domination which weighs upon them. They must also have some idea of what to replace it with, and of how to give effect to this idea in the real world. Thus a number of other (non-intellectual) conditions must be satisfied if their attempts to overcome their dominated situation are to be brought to a successful conclusion.

---

12. Translated in Aristotle, *The Metaphysics, The Oeconomica and The Magna Moralia* (2 vols., London 1935), vol. II, pp. 337, 339.

Do 'Historical Necessities' Exist?

The analyses presented above may perhaps shed some light upon the process which, some ten thousand years ago, impelled humanity to set out upon the path of social differentiation and the birth of estates, castes, classes and the State, and upon the reasons which enable us, though only now, to envisage the gradual abolition of class relations as feasible rather than Utopian.

Suppose we reconsider the example of Athens. There the range of the thinkable and the feasible was determined by the fact that political relations functioned as production relations, and dominated the thought and the action of the members of the whole society, whether free men or slaves. Thus, the very nature of the relations of production prevented the contradictions between free men and slaves from appearing directly at the political level. As a consequence, it was almost unthinkable for the slaves to achieve a political awareness of their own problems and to wage directly political struggles to terminate their servitude. And even when the slaves rose *en masse*, as occurred in Rome under the Republic, they did not want radically to abolish the institution of slavery but rather to turn it back upon their masters, in a 'kingdom of the sun' such as Spartacus imagined.

The contradictions which occupied the forefront of the historical stage were those opposing the free men to each other — the rich to the poor, and the landowners to the merchants. However, as large-scale use of slaves developed, the social system accumulated fundamental contradictions which weakened it in the long term and finally caused it to stagnate. Many other factors had to intervene, however — amongst them the Barbarian invasion — before slave relations yielded to other forms of domination. What can be thought therefore far outstrips what can be done; but what can be done does not outstrip the nature of the production relations and the production forces existing in a society. This is what historical necessity means. As for our own time, it is only within the functioning of capitalist relations of production that the idea of one day abolishing all forms of domination (class, caste, sexual, etc.) has been born and has gained in strength. And it is the contradictory development of these relations which creates the material, political and intellectual conditions for their abolition.

But while it may today seem both possible and legitimate for caste, class and other such relations to disappear, was it not just as legitimate and necessary, historically speaking, for them to appear in the first place? My analysis has, I believe, shed some light on the most ancient formative processes of stable hierarchies of statuses and powers, no longer between the sexes and the generations — as was the case in the nomadic hunter-gatherer societies — but between social groups sustaining kinship relations with each other in the same global social unit. From archaeology we learn that such hierarchies began with the sedentarization of certain goups of hunter-gatherers, but that they only expanded and diversified with the development of agriculture and stockbreeding. The need to exert ritual and material control over an ever more domesticated nature (without which man can not reproduce himself but which is itself less and less able to reproduce itself without man) and the material possibilities offered by the new productive capacities for differentiating and opposing the interests and wealth of individuals and groups gave rise to hierarchies which could appear to be to everyone's advantage, and to differences which served the general interest and consequently appeared legitimate.

It must therefore have been the case that not all the services provided by those who were dominant were purely imaginary or illusory. Otherwise the movement which engendered estates, castes, classes and the State, when that emerged in certain class societies (for we ought not to forget that class societies without a State have existed and do exist — e.g. the Tuareg) would not have forged ahead.

The power that was claimed over the invisible world must also have had to give proof of its reality and truth in the visible one; and if their power was presented as a contract involving reciprocal commitments, the dominant must have had to keep their promises. Yet we are confronted here by symbolic powers and representations and we know that anything, or almost anything, can symbolize these powers, and furnish proof of their truth. Did not the annual rising of the Nile, by flooding the land, bring life and prove that the Pharaoh was indeed a god — and a beneficent one at that, for was it not he who, by performing the rites, had caused the waters to flow back into the parched river bed? Furthermore, when disorder, misery or famine struck, that happened either because the Pharaoh had not been informed or because he was a usurper.

However, not everything in this power and this representation of the Pharaoh god was symbolic. Had not the establishment of the monarchy and the unification of the Upper and Lower Kingdoms been necessary for men to succeed in diverting the course of the Nile and regulating the flow which each year brought nourishing alluvial soils, the fertile 'black' earth surrounded by the 'red' earth of the desert? Was the Inca not prepared to open his granaries to the needy and, in cases of catastrophe, to all and sundry? Had he not undertaken to build a huge number of terraces, thus reclaiming the uncultivated mountain slopes for maize? Admittedly, maize was the crop used in libations to the gods and in ritual ceremonies; furthermore, it was easy to store and transport to the towns and the palace, where it would meet the needs of the Inca, the administration and the army. But not all the maize that was produced was there solely for the Inca and the dominant class.

More than religion was therefore required for religion to dominate peoples' minds and their social life. Several supplementary conditions had to be met for it to become the form assumed by sovereignty:[13] it had to become the form of the production relations and one of their internal components. Yet this does not only apply to religion, for representations do not exist only as that which interiorizes in the individual relations born without it:[14] *social relations are always born simultaneously outside and inside thought.* Thus, as I shall try to demonstrate in the next chapter, *thought is always born contemporaneously with social reality.* It cannot see more clearly than the reality which it sees and which makes it see. And I shall close this chapter with the following remark by Marc Augé, from his analysis of the development of prophecy among the Alladin, the Avikam and the Ébrié of the Ivory Coast, at the mercy of the vicissitudes of the price of cocoa and the transformation of their country into a capitalist nation inheriting much of its identity from colonial Africa: 'The price of cocoa: a reflection in the cave. A double life too, if not a triple one, is that of the Ébrié fisherman who contemplates in the waters of the lagoon the blurred image of the towers of Abidjan.'[15]

---

13. See G. Dumézil, *Les dieux souverains des Indo-Européens*, Paris 1977.
14. Pierre Bourdieu, *Outline of a Theory of Practice*, Cambridge 1977.
15. Marc Augé, *Théorie du pouvoir et idéologie*, Paris 1978, p. xxiii.

A long time will be needed before misfortune and good fortune cease to be the work of dead gods who do not wish to die and have never stopped feeding off the flesh and the thought of living men — off their and our relations.

A shortened version of this text appeared with the same title in *L'Homme* XVIII (3-4), 1978, pp. 155-88 and as 'The Ideal in the Real' in *Culture, Ideology and Politics*, edited by Raphael Samuel and Gareth Stedman Jones, London 1983, pp. 12-38.

4

The Role of Thought in the Production of Social Relations

Every social relation, as we have just seen, exists both in thought and outside of it, and the part which is in thought therefore belongs to thought and is a mental reality. But if it belongs to thought, what form does this belonging assume? If it is mental, in what sense is it so?

The mental part of a social relation consists, first of all, in the set of representations, principles and rules which must be 'acted upon' to engender that relation *between* the individuals and groups which constitute a society needed to make it into a concrete mode of organization of their social life. Let me give an example. One cannot imagine individuals marrying each other without knowing what marriage is, or whilst being unaware of the kind of marriage rules operative in their society, or without being acquainted with the consequences that their marriage will have for their descendants, in other words, without being acquainted with the rules of descent. One can therefore see that the mental part of every kinship relation is first of all the set of marriage and descent rules which individuals and groups must act upon in order to produce this order of relations between them. Of course, marriage and descent are not the only components of kinship relations. To them one must add rules of residence, rules concerning the inheritance of land, of status and so on. But this is not the place to debate these issues.

What has just been established with regard to kinship could likewise be demonstrated for any kind of social relation.

I will therefore advance the proposition that the mental part of every social relation is first of all the set of representations, principles and rules which must be *consciously* acted upon in order to generate such a relation in social practice, both individual and collective.

But the individuals and groups who constitute the society in which this social relation is one of the modes of organization, always apprehend, live, and think it as more or less legitimate, or even illegitimate. This being so, the mental part of a social relation also consists of the values, both positive and negative, which are associated with this relation, and of the rules and ideal principles which enable it to be generated. By 'values' I mean here both principles and judgements, and representations charged with a force of attraction or repulsion.

These two mental constituents of social relations are therefore linked to the fact that the latter are only produced and reproduced through the combination and articulation of two types of practice, individual *and* collective. Within the first type, a social relation exists as a means to attain certain ends — e.g. initiation rituals, which are held to be a necessary means allowing new generations to gain access to the secret knowledge of their elders and to share occult powers with them. The second type posits (or refuses to posit) this social relation as a reality-worth-reproducing, as the obligatory means of organizing part of the relations of human beings with each other and with nature, and therefore as a relation which is exclusive of other relations — as a Norm, an End.

None of this implies that the mental part of social reality can be reduced to its conscious part. I deliberately used the term 'thought', and it goes without saying that for me thought considerably exceeds consciousness (and language). Thought is a set of mechanisms which more often than not function without one being aware of them. Fundamentally, we know that thought depends upon a complex fragment of living matter — the brain — which has the capacity (amongst other things) of apprehending relations of equivalence and non-equivalence between 'objects', relations, and relations of relations, and which can elaborate or construct organized sets of representations of these objects, relations, and relations of relations — representations which are themselves present in consciousness, and act in and upon it. We also know that this capacity to apprehend relations of equivalence is not produced by contemporary history, by the contexts in which and the problems upon which it operates. We inherit it and, if we wanted to trace its genesis, we should have to refer back to a history which preceded humanity by a long way: the history of nature before the coming of humanity's, even if the latter, through interactions with surrounding nature, subsequently played a part itself in the evolution of the human brain.

In reminding ourselves that thought is more than consciousness, however we should not forget that it is the *conscious* mental part of our social relations which serves as the main support for children in their apprenticeship to these social relations, in the process of the social formation of individuals — a process which cannot, of course, be reduced to the conscious transmission and 'interiorization' of the rules governing the production of these relations and the social, moral, affective and other values which are associated with them. In spite of what certain sociologists and psychologists still maintain, the social formation of individuals cannot be reduced to the child's interiorization of external norms of behaviour which then increasingly become all but unquestioned habits. Even for the child, the social relations into which it is born never exist entirely outside its own self. This is also the reason why more than an evolution of thought in and upon itself is necessary for social relations to lose their appearance of legitimacy and for thought in this process to come to be opposed to itself.

But it is also through and in thought that a historically specific social reality contains other societies and other social relations as possibilities, either imagined and desired, or else rejected. Even if there exists within a society only one kinship system or organization of production that is activated and produced each day, this system or organization never really exists alone. It always co-exists, on the mental plane, with one or two other systems, which are both possible and known but which thought and social practice (necessarily the thought and social practice of historically determinate individuals and social groups) reject and exclude or, conversely, more or less successfully strive to bring into the world. Indeed, 'around' each social relation there exists a series, more or less numerous and more or less elaborated in thought, of other social relations which are in relations of logical transformation with it and exist only mentally. These ideal relations present themselves, for example, either as the inverted image of the 'real' relation or as one of its possible deformations in one or other of its aspects.

Thus, in a matrilineal society where it is the norm for a man to transmit his goods to his sister's son, people are not unaware of the fact the one *could* do otherwise and transmit them to one's own son. In certain circumstances this idea, which ordinarily is excluded, is excluded no longer. It becomes a temptation to which one man will yield, then another, then another; in this respect they find themselves at odds with the overall logic of their kinship system, to which they continue to adhere in other respects. In the long run, this practice can profoundly subvert the system, which gradually gives way to a patrilineal system or to a mixed formula, with land passing from father to son, whereas political power continues to be transmitted from uncle to uterine nephew.

In many societies, there are also representations which describe a distant or vanished world where things happen in the opposite manner to how they proceed in their own world. Thus, in societies where there is heavy masculine domination, one encounters myths describing a time, long since past, in which women dominated men. Of course, far from being an apologia for the power of women or an objective trace of past epoch, these myths are a further instrument of masculine domination, since they invariably display the disorders and calamities occasioned by women's exercise of power. In order to put things right, the men had had to seize power from them and henceforth wield it themselves to the satisfaction of all, whilst striving to prevent any reversion to those ancient aberrations.[1]

Thus, every real and realized social relation coexists in thought, and through it, with other possible social relations. These are finite in number and always preserve some mark of the concrete social relations from which they are distinguished and to which they are sometimes even opposed on a mental plane.

It would, however, be an error to oppose what is real to what is possible, since the latter is part of what is real. Indeed, a social relation cannot begin to exist 'really' or be transformed without there arising contemporaneously other possible social forms which, far from being inert in thought, 'work' continually therein, and thereby act in and on it.

We have already seen one example of this working of the possible within the real when we cited a father's temptation in matri-

---

1. I have analysed one of these myths in *La Production des Grands Hommes.*

lineal societies to transmit his inheritance to his own son instead of to his uterine nephew, his sole legitimate heir. But there is a yet more simple and more universal example. This is the idea — present in all societies — that an individual (whom in this case we shall suppose to be masculine) could commit incest with his mother or with his daughter: an idea that is everywhere present and everywhere forbidden.

In fact, as Lévi-Strauss has shown, the practice of incest would subvert any kinship system; such a system can therefore only exist if this possible is forbidden, and the idea of it censured and repressed. The actual production and reproduction of kinship relations depends upon the negation of incest, which demonstrates the truth of Spinoza's assertion that every determination is a negation. Now, all social relations may be regarded in the same way. They can only be reproduced if individuals and groups permanently act upon themselves and upon their relations with others, to prohibit, repress and exclude other possible ways of doing things, and other possible forms of societal organization which are present in social consciousness, but which appear as a threat to the society's reproduction.

Of course in history the threat of a potential reality is insufficient to induce a society's transformation. This possibility must become the goal of a fraction of that society, of individuals and groups who act in order to realize it, who transform this thought into a collective force which acts in and upon the society and makes it move in another direction. At any rate this is true if we confine ourselves to the endogenous aspects of a society's development; but that would be to exclude those cases, (in fact more numerous) where one society is subjected to another which imposes its own forms of organization upon it. Of the potentialities contained in social reality, one must therefore distinguish between those which sustain its existence on condition that they are never actually acted upon (for instance, the possibility of incest), and those which, without posing an immediate threat to its existence, already refer thought and action to paths that are to be pursued in order to transform it and substitute another social order. In fact, the conditions of existence cannot be transformed into new social relations, or into new forms of old relations, without an interpretative working of these new conditions by thought — an interpretation which endows them with meaning and which is accompanied by a labour of organization of society that endows them with an institutional form and structure.

One should also bear in mind that in many societies there exist not one but several forms of social production, and not one but several kinship systems, and that one of these forms generally dominates the others. Thus, in the Middle Ages wage labour existed as a form of the utilization of others' labour power, but one that was occasional and of minor importance. Something over and above intellectual efforts and transformations as required for this form of work organization to become the dominant, reigning one in our own societies. But this could not have happened *without* some effort of thought consciously to elaborate this type of production relation and gradually cause it to effect a transformation of the conditions and aims of production.

Let us note in passing that it was not capitalism which invented wage labour, still less the use of money for profit, and even less private property. Before capitalism these social relations were engendered on several occasions in history and in a number of societies. Their dissimilar geneses do not therefore constitute a genealogy of the capitalist system, which on the contrary arose out of the increasingly frequent combination from the beginning of the sixteenth century of these distinct relations with distinct geneses. But this combination did not take place like the blind encounter of several ships each travelling from a point of its own through the mists of history.[2] History is not merely the product of involuntary embeddings and destructions. It is born from the effects of two types of rationality, the intentional and the unintentional. But the unintentional cannot be reduced to the involuntary consequences of human actions; it refers to a domain which is larger than men's actions. It is the domain constituted by the actual properties of social relations, by their capacities for reproduction within certain limits — properties and limits whose ultimate sources do not lie in thought. The unintentional is therefore not a reality which can be said either to precede or to follow after history: it is in fact history itself, born of the actions of men, but including everything that lies beyond their intentions and endeavours.

The difficulties which emerge once one seeks to grasp the relations existing between social structures and their historical context, and when one attempts to analyse the part played by

---

2. I am developing an analysis of the processes of transition between economic and social systems in another book, which I am working on now.

thought in the transformation of these contexts and structures are patent. For analysis must take into account the various gaps which exist between a structure and its setting: the fact that this structure may have arisen several different times and in different historical contexts; the fact that it coexists with other structures born before or after it, and which it dominates or is dominated by; the fact that it may itself be surrounded by a nimbus of possible forms, of ideal social relations — some of which are realizable, though others not (being perhaps purely imaginary or Utopian), and some of which, therefore, may begin to exist where circumstances allow. A theory of such 'circumstances' has therefore to be developed.

Societies always appear to us to be in an unstable, variably firm or precarious relation with their own conditions of reproduction. It is this which causes them to shift, to undergo movement and, most often, to end up disappearing and being erased from human memory. Those societies that have managed, before disappearing, to bequeath us their history, or to survive in other forms up until the present day, have become the concern of our profession — whether we are historians or anthropologists — and the domain of all the human sciences.

Part Three
Critical But Non-Polemical
Considerations

5

Karl Polanyi and the 'Shifting Place' of the Economy in Societies

'In effect, sociological problems within the sphere of the economy have been defined by economists, and one result is that today we are largely ignorant of economies other than our own. And, lacking a sociology of the market, we understand even that only partially.' — Terence K. Hopkins

The question posed by the collective work *Trade and Market in the Early Empires*, produced by a group of researchers associated with Karl Polanyi, is clearly expressed by the above statement taken from that book. We need to know if the theories developed since the beginning of the nineteenth century to explain the functioning of the industrial and market-centred capitalist economy provide historians and anthropologists with the concepts and methods they need in order to account for the original logics underlying the functioning and evolution of the multiple forms of economic and social organization which they study. The majority of these have disappeared forever or are condemned to disappear owing to the overwhelming effects of erosion, mutation or destruction entailed by the domination — nowadays over most of the world — of the same capitalist system and — over the rest of the world — of the 'socialist' system.

Polanyi and his associates answered in the negative. Yet neither the answer not the question were original for, a century before, in 1859, the *Contribution to the Critique of Political Economy* had appeared. In it Marx had not simply disputed the possibility of 'generalizing' the theorems of political economy to pre-capitalist modes of production. He had also denied that contemporary political economy could account for the deeper logic of the capitalist mode of production, for the hidden nature of its crucial motor: profit and the social conditions for its accumulation — capital's exploitation of wage labourers.

If we are to understand both the reasons which impelled Karl Polanyi to criticize the economic thought of his own era and the limitations of his critique — which, in the last analysis, does not question the validity of such economic theories vis-à-vis the capitalist market economy — it may be worth recalling, with the help of an article by S.C. Humphreys, a few of the more significant moments in his life and work. Born in 1886 in Budapest, Polanyi belonged to the radical fraction of the Hungarian bourgeoisie which, ever more fiercely contesting the economic and political domination of the Magyar landed aristocracy, proved incapable of engaging in political action. Polanyi studied law and political economy. For the German and central European intelligentsia of this period, sociology and Marxism were theories which, although denied official status in the universities, could be employed to analyse urgent economic and political problems. From 1922, while the Soviet revolution was only just beginning to move towards a planned development of the economy and eminent liberal economists (Heinrich von Hayek, Michael Polanyi, Gaétan Pirou and a number of others) were denying that it had the slightest chance of surviving (let alone of making progress), Karl Polanyi sought to demonstrate the 'social and moral' superiority of a planned socialist economy, guided by 'social demand', over the market economy and free enterprise system in promoting the economic and social development of the backward countries of Central Europe.

In 1933 Polanyi fled from fascism and anti-semitism and emigrated to England, just as the capitalist countries were emerging from the Great Depression. He went on to teach economic history and attempted to arrive at satisfying explanations for the causes of fascism, the economic crisis and then for the world war. He felt very close to British socialism in those years and, during the war, sympathized with some of its more utopian currents which engaged in drafting reconstruction programmes for post-war society. In 1944 he published in the United States, under the title *The Great Transformation*, his conclusions regarding the rise and fall of liberal capitalism, which seemed to him to be daily retreating before the growing role of the State. Once again

Polanyi affirmed his belief in the superiority of a planned economy, informed by a humanist socialism, for this would enable society once again to dominate the economy instead of being dominated by it (as had been the case since the nineteenth century with the market economy).

For Polanyi, the economy being organized entirely on the basis of the market was radically separate from other social institutions and, through establishing itself as separate, forced the rest of society to function in submission to its laws. It was at this point — at the juncture between scientific analysis and utopia — that there appeared in a minor key the first references to primitive societies and to the works of a number of anthropologists, such as Thurnwald, Malinowski and Radcliffe-Brown. In these societies, he argued, the economy does not exist as a separate entity; it is 'embedded' in other institutions, such as kinship or religion. Moreover — and here Polanyi subscribes to a romantic notion of the primitive — these societies hardly know competition or social conflicts. They are 'integrated'.

In 1947 Polanyi was appointed Professor of General Economic History at Columbia University in New York[1] and, in a violent pamphlet directed against our 'obsolete market mentality', he reiterated the arguments he had advanced in *The Great Transformation*. He decided upon a programme of research into the origins of economic institutions and distancing himself ever further from the problems of contemporary economies, whether capitalist or socialist, he turned his attention to anthropology and ancient history. A group gradually formed around him, including anthropologists, historians of Antiquity, sociologists and economists, and he steered their research in three separate directions: the critique of economic theory; the construction of a typology of economic systems; and the origin and history of economic institutions, with particular attention to regulated trade, the free market, the various uses of money, and so on. In 1957 the results of these enquires were published as a book, *Trade and Market in the Early Empires*.

After 1957 Polanyi devoted himself to the study of the economic and social history of Dahomey for which, from 1949 onwards, he had begun to assemble the relevant ethnographic

---

1. Polanyi actually lived in Canada, near Toronto, because his wife, who had been a member of the Hungarian Communist Party from 1919 to 1922, was never given permission to live in the United States.

and historical materials. A monograph, *Dahomey and the Slave Trade*, which was all but finished at his death, was published posthumously by Dalton. During this same period, however, he returned to the problems of a planned economy and helped to found the journal *Co-Existence*. Together with Paul Medow, a disciple who was an economist and a mathematician, Polanyi tried to initiate a dialogue with economists from the socialist countries and a debate on socialist humanism. He died in 1964.

For Polanyi, the point was 'not to reject economic analysis, but to set its historical and institutional limitations [and to] transcend these limitations in a general theory of economic organization,'[2] There is nothing ambiguous about this formulation. By 'economic analysis' Polanyi means the entire corpus of economic theories taught in the universities — with the exception of Marxism, which seemed to him to lead to an erroneous conception of value and prices. Thus he does not question the scientific status of this theoretical corpus which, broadly speaking, coincides with the neo-marginalism of the period. What he does deny is the notion that these theories can be applied outside the particular institutional and historical context of economies with a generalized market. For Polanyi, it would therefore be pointless and absurd to employ such theories to interpret the functioning of pre-market economies, or even the market mechanisms present in societies whose economy basically depends upon non-market mechanisms. Since contemporary economic theories have no general historical scope, they cannot constitute the basis for a general theory of economic institutions. Such a theory would have to be a comparative one, and a comparative theory is obliged to take its materials and its models from history and anthropology. Nevertheless, Polanyi does not accord exactly equal status to these two disciplines, for he holds that in the last analysis it is up to anthropology to provide history with the models it requires if it is to account for the original functioning and subsequent development of ancient institutions. Thus not only does anthropology supply history with its key models but, in the last analysis, anthropology and economic history are destined to be fused into a new discipline which is still to be created — economic anthropology which will be called upon to provide both a general theory of the economy and a comparative history of humanity's economic institutions.

---

2. K. Polanyi, *Trade and Market* ..., pp. 234-5.

We can readily grasp the complex network of ideas and schools of thought with which Polanyi and his associates must have come into direct conflict. Discussions, even disputes, flared up on all sides and, in journals and books, have continued until the present day. Although the main contenders are not yet prepared to lay down their arms, many onlookers regard such battles as outmoded or as leading nowhere. Polanyi's polemic was obviously first and foremost at economists who claimed to have defined the universal principles of economic rationality and laid the foundations for a general theory of the economic. But this also implicated all those sociologists, anthropologists and historians who had taken the economists at their word and shared their 'ethnocentric myopia'.

Naturally the guiltiest were the anthropologists — such as C.S. Coon, R. Firth, D.M. Goodfellow, G. Wagner and M.J. Herskovits — who had begun to develop an economic anthropology upon the basis of the economists' formalist postulates. In Karl Polanyi's eyes, they were all the guiltier for having strayed from the right path, the one which starts with a substantive definition of the economy because this had been shown to them as early as 1921 by Bronislaw Malinowski, the teacher of them all.

Polanyi therefore pitted the conceptual inheritance of one of the founding fathers of modern anthropology, the fieldworker *par excellence*, against his natural heirs who — in this respect — had grown deaf to his teachings. But the project of comparing economic systems also ran counter to the approach of a host of 'culturalist' historians and anthropologists, such as Sombart or Linton, for whom the unique character of each culture rendered every attempt to compare them absurd and pointless. However, Polanyi found himself to be in agreement with all those, whether culturalist or not, who rejected the hypothesis of a necessary evolution of social institutions. Such institutions undoubtedly have a history but it is one which expresses neither the laws nor the stages of a necessary evolution. And since Marxism, which was often presented at this time in the vulgar form of an interpretation of humankind's history in five ineluctable stages, could barely be distinguished from evolutionism, Polanyi had a further reason for rejecting it as well.

Yet his liveliest and most developed critique, occupying the whole of one chapter and half of two others, was directed against Talcott Parsons and, through him, against his master Max Weber. When the latter, who was much older than Polanyi (he had been born twenty-two years before him), died in 1920, he left unfinished a huge work devoted to the very same theme as Polanyi's own researches — *Wirtschaft und Gesellschaft (Economy and Society)* — whose most important sections were translated and annotated for the American public by Talcott Parsons himself. Now in 1953, when Polanyi (who had just retired) decided to continue with his research into the conditions for a 'general theory of economic organization', Talcott Parsons gave the Marshall Lectures, dedicated to the memory of Alfred Marshall and Max Weber. In them he presented the outlines of a 'general economic sociology', deeming it applicable to all economies, market or non-market. This was the very same objective as Polanyi and his team were pursuing, but for Parsons this was merely one aspect of the development of a much more ambitous work, his *General Theory of Action*, a book which appeared in 1954 and was to dominate American empirical sociology for two decades. Moreover in 1956 (the year before Polanyi's *Trade and Markets in the Early Empires* appeared), Parsons, in collaboration with Neil J. Smelser, published a reworked version of his Marshall Lectures as *Economy and Society* — the very same title as Weber had used. Meanwhile, Parsons had sent the manuscript of this work to Polanyi, who did not respond in person. Instead K. Hopkins and Harry W. Pearson wrote a reply which was courteous but uncompromising.

They began by emphasizing the points of agreement between the two approaches. Analysis should not start out from individuals but from societies considered as totalities. A society's economy therefore always functions within an overall structural context. The universal function of the economy is to provide society with the means to attain its objectives, whilst at the same time adapting itself to the context of an external environment. Now, since numerous organizational levels of society can 'participate' in the performance of this function, no institution or concrete social unit can be purely and simply economic, but must always be a 'multifunctional' reality. Yet for Parsons and Smelser all global societies 'tend to be differentiated into sub-systems with specialized functions'. For Polanyi, on the contrary, the fact that the economy may exist in the form of a separate institution with a specialized function, is a historical exception and should not be interpreted as an expression of the tendency of every global society to become differentiated.

This is not the crucial point at issue, however. Parsons had always been more concerned than Weber to oppose the 'institutionalist' appoach, whether adopted by the Germans or by the Americans, and Thorstein Veblen in particular, on the grounds that it deprived the economic aspect of social action of its 'theoretical specificity' and dismissed the theories of the neo-marginalist economists. Parsons, on the other hand, used Pareto and the postulates of the formalist economists as the starting-point for every analysis of economic realities. The reader will doubtless be familiar with these theories, which feature in the opening pages of every introductory textbook of political economy in the Western world, and have received their best-known formulation from Lionel Robbins. Economic activity is defined as a response to the scarcity of means available to satisfy our needs. Rational economic activity is that which seeks to 'combine as well as possible scarce means in order to attain alternative ends'. The market appears here as the economic institution *par excellence*, since it provides the most favourable social context for the exercise of rational economic activity. The formalist arguments of the economists thus turn out to be both an apology for the market economy and an ethnocentric prejudice in favour of their own economic system, declared to be if not only one then at any rate the most rational one.

Hopkins shows that Talcott Parson's general theory of the economy is by its very premises lacking in any generality, since it shares the ethnocentric prejudice which implicitly takes the market to be the prototype for all rational economic institutions. By the same token the generality of the famous 'general theory of action' is annulled, and all the more easily because 'rational' commodity exchange had been used by Parsons as an implicit paradigm for all social relations of exchange. Finally — and still more damagingly — Hopkins shows that Parsons' whole theory presupposes that society be regarded as an 'agent', which amounts to an unscientific conception of both society and sociology. All in all, Parsons had simply replaced the 'irrelevant' categories of the economists with 'empty' sociological categories, and the whole work was nothing more than 'a series of metaphorical constructions, as mistaken in their underlying principle as in their conclusions.'[3] So much for the abstract and ethnocentric empiricism of Talcott Parsons.

What then does Polanyi have to offer? He too advocates an

---

3. T. Hopkins, *Trade and Market* . . ., p. 239.

empiricist position, but from the outset he seeks to jettison every ethnocentric *a priori* regarding the sites occupied, the forms assumed and the effects produced by the economy within the many different kinds of society which have existed in history. This empiricism is therefore established on the basis of a critique, certainly limited but nevertheless real, of some of the ideological presuppositions of liberal economists, of their apologetics in favour of the market economy and of their complete failure to appreciate the narrowness of the field in which their own doctrine could be applied. This critique does not strike at the content of the liberal economists' theories, but only at their blindness and their employment of these theories outside their proper sphere — the generalized market economy. Nevertheless, Polanyi does advance an explicit critique of the system itself, the market economy, but always on a moral and political plane, as when he denounces the fact that within this system, instead of the economy being subordinated to human beings it is human beings who are subordinated to the economy. However, he does not go as far as the young Marx did when in 1844, having just read — as a philosopher — the classical economists, he denounced not merely the ill effects of the market but those of private property as well.

Where did Polanyi's critical empiricism lead him next? From the start what was required was a general definition of the economy which could subsume all its possible forms in advance and which was untainted by any prejudice concerning the potential forms. This definition would also have to designate not so much and formal principles governing the behaviour of individuals, but rather a specific function of certain relations. He therefore proposed the following 'substantive' definition of the economy: our 'interchange with his natural and social environment in so far as this results in supplying him with the means of material want satisfaction.'[4]

It is not hard to see that this definition accords with spontaneous and commonsense definition of the economy, and with the more developed general notions placed by the classical economists at the beginning of their books, and which Marx had reproduced and analysed in his 'Introduction' to the *Contribution to the Critique of Political Economy*. Economic activity is a process, that is (as Polanyi takes some pains to emphasize) a set of 'movements'

---

4. K. Polanyi, *Trade and Market . . . .* p. 243.

of production, circulation and appropriation of material goods. But this process only has 'unity and stability' because it is 'institutionalized', because it functions by means of institutions, that is, the general social relations of men in a given society.

We are therefore concerned here with general — 'abstract' — empirical concepts, which sum up a certain number of characteristics common to a set of concrete realities. These concepts are neither empty nor useless. If I may borrow the terms that Marx applies to the concepts of 'production', 'consumption' and even 'labour', these concepts are 'rational abstractions' which 'save us repetition'. In reality, we all know that 'if there is no production in general then there is also no general production', that the abstract concepts 'do not correspond to any real historical stage of production':

> Labour seems quite a simple category. The conception of labour in this general form — as labour as such — is also immeasurably old. Nevertheless, when it is economically conceived in this simplicity, 'labour' is as modern a category as are the relations which create this simple abstraction ... This example of labour shows strikingly how even the most abstract categories, despite their validity — precisely because of their abstractness — for all epochs, are nevertheless, in the specific character of this abstraction, themselves likewise a product of historic relations, and possess their full validity only for and within these relations.[5]

Marx is therefore not guilty of the 'ethnocentric myopia and blind eclecticism' of which Polanyi had accused the liberal economists. Not only does he too rule out the projection onto all societies of capitalist relations and the categories which, for good or ill, express them. He also recommends the greatest caution in employing more general and apparently ideologically more neutral concepts, such as labour. This is also the case with the categories of money, exchange, capital, and so on.

For Polanyi, as for Marx, an economic process only has 'genuine reality' in a specific, concrete or, to use his own term, 'institutionalized' social form. In this form a process is inscribed in a 'context of social structures' which in some way constitutes the 'semantics' of its forms and functions, and which ensures its 'unity and stability'. Taking his argument a little further, Polanyi notes that 'depending upon the time and the place', the

---

5. K. Marx, *Grundrisse*, Harmondsworth 1973, pp. 103-05.

economic process can 'be set and enmeshed' in the most diverse
institutions, in kinship, politics or religion, and thus in institutions which are not simply 'economic'. He insists upon the fact
that 'the inclusion of the noneconomic is vital. For religion or
government may be as important for the structure and functioning of the economy as monetary institutions or availability of tools
and machines themselves that lighten the toil of labour'[6]. The task
of a new kind of economic anthropology, which should conjoin
economic theory and economic history, is indeed 'The study of
the shifting place occupied by the economy in society, which is
... no other than the study of the manner in which the economic
process is instituted at different times and places.'[7]

Finding answers to this crucial problem involves something
quite different from the construction of an additional discipline,
economic anthropology, even if this were to be invested with the
privilege of supplying historians with the key models they require
in order to think their materials. But before we broach this
decisive debate, I want quickly to reconsider the notion of
whether or not an economy is 'embedded and enmeshed' in
other social institutions.

The idea was not new. Evans-Pritchard had revived it in 1940
in his monograph on the Nuer, showing how in that society
kinship relations functioned as a kind of 'general institution',
since they regulated not only relations of descent and alliance but
also economic and political life. But if we wish to retrace the path
back from Marcel Mauss to F. Tönnies, from L.H. Morgan to
H.S. Maine, from Marx to Hegel, the idea would certainly take
us back to the eighteenth century and, if Polanyi is to be believed,
as far as Aristotle. Of course it is not a question of putting everything on the same level and forgetting what separates Tönnies'
distinction between *Gemeinschaft* (community) and *Gesellschaft*
(society) from Maine's famous formula according to which 'the
movement of the progressive societies has hitherto been a movement *from Status to Contract*.'[8] Moreover, Maine's thought should
not be equated with Morgan's, and still less with that of Marx.

But beneath the diversity of such formulae and perspective
there lies a datum of experience which, by dint of being emphasized in connexion with so many ancient and exotic societies, has

---

6. K. Polanyi, *Trade and market* ..., p. 250.
7. Ibid.
8. H.S. Maine, *Ancient Law*, 1861, chapter 5.

come to seem almost banal: the difficulty of discovering economic institutions which are separate and distinct from other institutions. Hereafter the interpretations diverge. For some, the various forms of economy, whether' embedded' or 'disembedded', correspond to necessary and successive stages in humanity's economic evolution. For others, and indeed for Polanyi himself (to go by certain passages), this diversity is only an accidental consequence of the history of societies. There is therefore no need to search for the mechanisms, still less for the 'laws', governing the transition from one form to another or from one place to another. We should limit ourselves to making as complete an inventory as possible, and to discovering the effects that such-and-such a 'place' occupied by the economy in society, such-and-such an 'embedding' in such-and-such a 'structural context', determine in relation to its functional principles and mechanisms.

Thus, at no point does Polanyi really ask himself just why it is that the economy occupies a particular position in a given society, and why it functions, 'embedded' or not, within kinship or political or religious relations. Admittedly, in order to explain how the modern economy has gradually become 'disembedded' from the rest of society and begun to function as a quasi-autonomous institution dominating our society, he mentions the fact that 'labour power had been transformed into a free commodity that one could buy on the market'. But he says nothing further about this complex problem regarding the conditions for the appearance of modern capitalism in agriculture and above all in industry — a problem which the classical economist christened with a formula which has remained famous: primitive accumulation of capital. Yet here Polanyi had moved on to the same ground as Marx, for whom 'what is characteristic is not that the commodity labour-power can be bought, but the fact that labour-power appears as a commodity'.[9]

However, the notion of 'embeddedness' itself gives rise to problems which deserve further discussion. For one cannot conceive of any form of economy being compatible with any form of kinship, religion or government, and *vice versa*. In their preface the authors themselves certainly seem to have doubted whether this could have been the case, and on at least one occasion pose the problem quite clearly:

---

9. K. Marx, *Capital*, Volume 2, London 1978, p. 114.

In the Western world, where this institution [the free market] had come to emerge and to blossom into extreme elaboration in a Manchester-School England of the 19th century, *was it historical accident alone* that a 'free enterprise', a free and equal democracy, an 'open' class system, a free choice of religious and associational membership, and a free choice of mates in a small ego-reckoned family structure, should all have historically *coincided?*[10]

Unfortunately, claiming that their researches 'had not enabled them to adopt a position on such vast problems in history and sociology', they provide the reader with no answer to this question.

If there really do exist relations of reciprocal compatibility between particular forms of economy and certain other types of social relations, we must try to work out what the basis for this is. In my view, it can only lie in the actual properties of these social relations. Being properties of relations, these properties exist independently of the mode of representation which the individuals living within these relations may have. This in no sense means that the relations themselves do not evolve under the impact of men's conscious action. But although modes of consciousness may cause social relations to evolve, they do not in any way change their immanent properties. It is these properties which are the *unintentional cause*, the source of the *effects* which each type of social relation can have upon the *internal* organization of the other social relations, which are combined within one and the same social system. And it is the *complex network of the reciprocal effects of their properties* that articulates, in a specific and more or less stable fashion, the social structures within a social system, which receives its unity and a relative stability — historically provisional stability — from this articulation.[11]

Consequently, once one sets oneself the task of building a comparative theory of the shifting 'place' of the economy in society, one is duty bound to pose the question — even if one does not have the time to answer it — of the 'role' of economic relations, of their 'effects' upon societies' functioning and evolution. The fundamental problem is then to know up to what point and through what mechanisms the economic relations — the relations of human beings with each other in the production and

---

10. K. Polanyi, *Trade and Market* ..., p. ix (my emphasis).
11. See above, chapter 1.

redistribution of their material conditions of existence — determine the functioning of this evolution. By the same token we have to consider the problem of the specific weight of each type of social relations upon the reproduction of the systems to which they belong, upon the reproduction of different 'ways of life'. Of course this entails something quite other than history or economic anthropology. But I would emphasize that it is only through studying a system's history that one can determine the specific role and relative importance of each social structure and each level of this system in the maintenance of its unity and stability. It will readily be acknowledged that not all forms of social practice have the same importance for the reproduction, maintenance or transformation, even the disappearance, of a social system. Their unequal importance depends upon their functions, not only the explicit ones, but also their function and weight in the production/reproduction of the society as *such* — as an organic totality. Consequently, the attempt to discover the social relations which determine, not singlehandedly but more than others, the reproduction of social systems — their functioning as well as their evolution — is something quite different from instituting an economic anthropology, or indeed any other discipline which would be added to the abstract, fetishistic and every often arbitrary partitions dividing the human sciences.

It is, then, a question of knowing whether what determines the reproduction of a social system in the last analysis should or should not be identified with whatever visibly dominates its functioning. Is it the case that the social relations and institutions which occupy the foremost place in the practice and consciousness of the individuals and groups comprising a society determine in the last analysis the reproduction of that society? Those who hold that the essence of things is not to be wholly identified with their appearance will quite legitimately ask whether the visible hierarchy of institutions and the unequal importance they assume in the eyes of individuals should be identified with their invisible weight upon historical evolution. Of course, this weight is not entirely hidden from the consciousness of historical agents, whether individuals or groups. In periods of profound crisis, mutations and transition from one socio-economic system to another, social consciousness and practice has to confront the question of the weight and importance of institutions in the reproduction of societies. This same question should be the special concern of the human sciences.[12]

However, seeking to assess the weight of the various social practices and social supports in the reproduction of societies is not to search for some reality hidden behind these relations and practices. For there is nothing behind them. The problem is not to see something else, but to view the same things in another way.

Now, for Polanyi this question has no meaning, his rationale being precisely that there is nothing hidden behind the institutions. Once one has drawn up an inventory of the societies studied by anthropologists and historians, discovering the institution which dominates each of them will suffice to identify the place occupied by the economy and the role it plays, and thereby understand the specific forms that it must assume on account of the dominance of that institution. Then, by comparing the various principles which have been isolated and identified, one will be in a position to establish a typology of the different 'models' of economic systems encountered.

Polanyi proceeded to devote himself to this task, analysing the works of a number of anthropologists, in particular those of Thurnwald and Malinowski on Melanesian societies, the works of historians on ancient Greece and those of Assyriologists. He concluded that there exist three general principles for the functioning of these various systems, three possible 'models' 'for their integration as systems': the principles of reciprocity, redistribution and exchange. Polanyi stresses that this list is not an exhaustive one and T.K. Hopkins likewise insists that it is provisional. These principles (or models of integration) have given rise to such diverse interpretations and critiques that it is hard to define precisely what they are.

The best way of obtaining a closer understanding of their true nature is to start from the thesis that in pre-capitalist societies, the economic process is 'embedded' within various institutions and that as a consequence, its various aspects and moments are dispersed among these institutions. In order for this process really to exist and perform its function ('supplying ... the means of materal want satisfaction'), all these aspects and moments must be *integrated* into a single mechanism which guarantees its continuity and stability. The unifying mechanisms are thus a response to a functional necessity; they can be one of several different types, depending upon whether the principles which regulate

---

12. See above, chapter 3.

them are those of reciprocity, redistribution or exchange: 'Reciprocity denotes movements between correlative points of symmetrical groupings; redistribution designates appropriational movements towards a centre and out of it again; exchange refers here to vice-versa movements taking place as between 'hands' under a market system.'[13] For Polanyi, however, it is not fortuitous if one or other of these principles or models of integration is operative or, above all, dominant. They are both the expression and the direct consequence of the presence, in the background, of 'determinate institutional supports' — in other words, of determinate social relations. These principles undoubtedly regulate the intentional forms of individual behaviour (interpersonal relations) but they are not 'the simple aggregate of diverse forms of individual behaviour'. They express the presence of social structures and their functional logic. To understand such principles, one must therefore commence not with individuals but with given social structures and social relations:

> The significant fact is that mere aggregates of the personal behaviours ... do not by themselves produce such structures. Reciprocity behaviour between individuals integrates the economy only if symmetrically organized structures, such as a symmetrical system of kinship groups, are given. But a kinship system never arises as the result of mere reciprocating behaviour on the personal level. Similarly, in regard to redistribution. It presupposes the presence of an allocative centre in the community.[14]

The limitations of Polanyi's approach become apparent here. Although this does not undermine the value of his analyses — which at any rate represent a necessary stage — he does not seek to account for the presence within determinate society of a particular social structure, for example a symmetrical system of kinship groups, such as a segmentary lineage system. Nor does he set out to discover the reasons why the process of production of material means is 'lodged' within these kinship relations. He restricts himself to searching for the particular effect of this 'embeddedness' upon the economy's mechanism; here the effect consists in mechanisms of reciprocity between individuals and social groups, and in the domination of the reciprocity principle over all the other principles. Morever Polanyi notes that the

---

13. K. Polanyi, *Trade and Market* . . ., p. 250.
14. Ibid., p. 251.

presence of a reciprocity menchanism is not only linked to the presence of a symmetrical system of kinship groups but, more generally, to the existence of 'symmetrically ordered social groups' which may be of a religious, military or political nature, and which may or may not constitute voluntary associations, and so on.

Polanyi therefore concludes that the principle of reciprocity is the dominant principle underlying the mechanism whereby the economic process is integrated whenever 'symmetrically ordered' social relations, whatever they may be, dominate social organization. And he quite rightly insists that the dominance of a principle does not mean that other principles are absent or excluded. In those societies in which reciprocity dominates, mechanisms of redistribution and exchange also exist; it is simply that they 'do not integrate' the whole of the economic process but remain subordinated to and articulated with the principle dominating that whole, while playing the primary role at certain levels of social organization and in certain activities. For example, while the mechanisms of reciprocity will prevail in a society dominated by segmentary kinship relations, mechanisms of redistribution might well dominate within the actual kinship groups and commodity exchange regulate part of these groups' relations with neighbouring societies. Contrariwise, in archaic empires of the 'redistributive type', such as ancient Egypt or Peru, the mechanisms and principle of redistribution integrate the whole of the economy and play the dominant role inside the local groups and may even, in the form of 'gift and counter-gift', regulate 'trade with the exterior'. In certain modern industrial states, of which 'the Soviet Union is an extreme instance', commodity exchange plays only a minor role, whereas the principle of redistribution again assumes the greatest importance: 'Redistribution [therefore] exists for numerous different reasons and at all levels of civilization'.

For its part, commodity exchange came to dominate the economic process in the West 'in so far as land and food were mobilized through exchange, and labour was turned into a commodity free to be purchased on the market'.[15] This is something that has only occurred quite recently, at a specifiable time. Previously, other forms of 'trade' between communities existed, sometimes alongside commodity exchange. This trade did not

---

15. Ibid., p. 256.

pass through a 'market-place' but through a trading port. It tended to be an 'affair of State', 'trade administered' by the State, which organized long distance expeditions to procure indispensable raw materials, or entrusted them to merchant castes. What the merchants stood to gain from such enterprises took less the form of direct monetary profits from the 'prices' of the commodities than of a social status or a *rente* derived from a function granted by the king. Of course, the operative rates, the 'prices', were themselves fixed through agreements between the various States and had nothing in common with the kinds of prices which are 'created' on a 'free market' through fluctuations in supply and demand.

Money performed different functions in different contexts. It is only within the framework of the modern market economy that it has become 'an all-purpose money', one enabling its owner to acquire all the factors of production: land, labour, and instruments of labour. Within this framework, the three functions of money (means of payment, standard and measure of value, instrument of exchange) operate jointly and are unified. But in other forms of exchange and trade, any one of these three functions, or two of them together, may exist on their own. The assumption that these three functions appeared at the same time and characterize every form of money from the beginning is unjustified. We are now in a position to understand to what extent, in Polanyi's view, the economists — together with those historians and anthropologists who follow their lead — obscure the facts when they project onto every form of exchange and money the concepts which serve to analyse the modern forms of the 'free and price-creating' market and its monetary forms. We are also able to understand why it is that they meet with failure when they seek to theorize the non-market mechanism of reciprocity and redistribution in terms of the mechanisms and principles which regulate generalized commodity exchange.

The above will, I hope, serve as a summary — albeit a brief one — and 'reconstruction' of Polanyi's corpus of theoretical ideas concerning the diversity of economic systems encountered in history and the nature of the basic principles underlying their functioning. However Polanyi never stopped at abstract analysis but to the end of his life sought to confront concrete, empirical materials. In *Trade and Market in the Early Empires*, he used his theoretical results to analyse two problems in ancient history.

On the one hand, Polanyi tried to interpret the 'marketless' trade of the Babylonian State at the time of Hammurabi. On the other, he attempted, as so many others (Marx and Schumpeter among them) have done before, to interpret Aristotle's text on exchange and money. Similar efforts to interpret various ancient or exotic forms of trade and money — in the ancient East, among the Maya and the Aztecs in the sixteenth century, in India or in the kingdom of Dahomey in the eighteenth century, or among the Berber tribes of the Maghreb at the end of the nineteenth century — have been made on the basis of concepts originally advanced by Polanyi by a number of the historians, anthropologists and economists who collaborated with him over a period of years in his enquiry into the history of economic institutions. The studies by Anne Chapman, Rosemary Arnold, Harry Pearson, Robert Revere, Francisco Benet, Walter Neale and Leo Oppenheim are all of interest, but those by Pearson and Neale are, in my view at any rate, particulary noteworthy.

In his chapter on the mechanisms of reciprocity and redistribution within Indian villages, Walter Neale demonstrated that the caste system exceeds the framework of the village and can only be understood in terms of the larger framework within which the Hindu kingdoms operated. The redistribution of agricultural products among the castes of agriculturists and the other castes therefore expresses the general and reciprocal dependence of them all in a hierarchy of statuses dominated by the Brahmins and the king. Here Neale anticipates one of the most remarkable of Louis Dumont's analyses in his *Homo Hierarchicus*.[16] But at the same time, and probably without being aware of it, Neale touches upon the same problem Marx had analysed a century earlier, namely, the nature of landed property and rent in India. Like Maine a few years later, in 1853 Marx had taken a position in the lengthy debate involving the great British colonial administrators of the eighteenth century on the question of who in India owned the land and ought to pay land tax to the State, which had passed into the control of the colonial power. Marx concluded that the modern categories of capitalist ground rent or of land tax could not be properly applied to the rent in kind which the castes of agriculturalists paid to the Brahmin castes and to the king, because this levy involved an elision between tax and ground rent.

The first chapter of *Trade and Market in the Early Empires* by

---

16. Louis Dumont, *Homo Hierarchicus*, translated by Mark Sainsbury, London 1980.

Harry Pearson refers to another famous debate, this time involving the historians of ancient Greece, which had opposed 'primitivists' to 'modernists'. Pearson summarizes, and expresses his agreement with, the analyses and conclusions of a remarkable synthesis by Édouard Will — 'Three quarters of a century of research into the ancient economy' — which appeared in 1954 in *Annales ESC*, and which I shall consider in greater detail below. In another from 1954, which appeared in the *Revue historique*, Édouard Will brought out 'The ethical aspect of the Greek origins of money'. Polanyi was unaware of this article, but his own analysis converges with that of Édouard Will.

If we are to do justice to Polanyi's theoretical endeavour, and if we are to assess the epistemological scope of his concepts, we need to dwell on what he wrote about Aristotle. Another eminent specialist in Greek economic history, Moses I. Finley, did just this in 1970, in 'Aristotle and Economic Analysis' where he drew up a kind of balance-sheet of Polanyi's theses. According to the latter, Aristotle was witness to the birth of a trade based on markets, and this 'embryo' gave him a presentiment of what the fully grown specimen would be. Secondly, Aristotle was unaware of the part played by the mechanism of supply and demand in price formation because it had developed in the third century through international trade. Finally, the economy was not, generally speaking, quantified in Aristotle's time.

Finley has shown, however, that in the fourth century trade based on markets was no longer just emerging, and that Aristotle's contemporaries were not unaware of it. Furthermore, quantification was not absent from the economic domain, for in the *Politics* (1258 b 39) Aristotle refers to calculations contained in the agronomic treatises by Chares of Paros and Apollodorus of Lemnos. Elements of calculation may also be found in the treatises on botany by Theophrastus, who was a pupil of Aristotle. Nor is this an error of detail concerning only Aristotle. Polanyi is clearly unaware of the works by Roman agronomists, from Varo to the treatise of the 'Sasserna', and from Cato to Columella and Posidonius, which are very much concerned with defining the appropriate size for an agricultural slave-based enterprise (an average-sized property or a latifundium), the number of slaves to employ, their ethnic origin and its effects upon their docility as workers, their capacity to learn and perform well without engaging in sabotage or taking flight, and the choice of kinds of cultivation to be adopted in this framework.

Similarly, one could mention works by thirteenth-century English agronomists. In each case, concern to run things well is present, together with concern to exploit the labour of others effectively. Polanyi never breathed a word about these texts, or about the social contradictions which they imply. There may be a fundamental reason for this silence.

Polanyi holds, in my view wrongly, that only the modern, generalized market economy renders eonomic 'calculation' both possible in a formal sense and necessary in a practical sense. In fact, it seems to me, there exists in all societies an empirical knowledge — which is often very advanced — of society's productive capacities, together with rules for a measured use of these resources so as to ensure their reproduction, and with it the reproduction of social life. This is something that Richard Lee has demonstrated with regard to a population of hunter-gatherers living in the Kalahari desert, the Bushmen. The same is true of the slash-and-burn horticulturalists of Melanesia (R.A Rappaport) or of the nomadic pastoralists of Asia or East Africa (O. Lattimore, N. Dyson-Hudson, P. Gulliver). The employment of genuine mathematical calculation becomes necesssary when it serves the purposes of a class-State in its exploitation of the peasant masses, as in the case in the theocratic States of ancient Mesopotamia or ancient Mexico. Fo these reasons, part of Polanyi's dispute with the 'formalists' seems to me to be ill-founded and to have a merely illusory content, inspired by a kind of 'socialist' humanism which leads Polanyi to deceive himself as to nature of pre-capitalist non-market economic systems.

But in spite of these factual errors regarding ancient Greece, or the more fundamental ones concerning the supposed absence of economic calculation in pre-capitalist societies, Polanyi's text on Aristotle is nevertheless of real interest. Its great merit consists first of all in having commenced from the actual context of the passage which Aristotle devoted to exchanges and money. In the *Nicomachean Ethics* (Book V), the subject treated is justice, which Aristotle divides into two different levels: universal justice and particular justice. These are then subdivided into two kinds, distributive justice (*dianemêtikos*) and corrective justice (*diorthôticos*). Distributive justice is concerned with the redistribution within the City and by the community of citizens of the goods, honours and other possessions of the community. It must be in proportion to the 'value' of the person and depend therefore upon the rules of geometrical, not arithmetical, equality.

Corrective justice, by contrast, corrects injustices which have been committed in direct, private transactions (*synallagmata*) between free men. Aristotle therefore does not discuss 'just or unjust' prices but fraud and breach of contract. He insists that exchanges between free men should be based upon reciprocity (*antipeponthôs*), a relation corresponding to the feelings of mutual friendship (*philia*) which ought properly to reign in a political community (*koinônia*) or in any voluntary association. 'Honest reciprocity' fixes equivalences between the labour of an architect and that of a shoemaker which have nothing in common with the 'prices' that would be established in a 'free market'. In the *Nicomachaean Ethics*, Aristotle was not concerned to found a theory of prices, and still less was he interested in a theory of the 'just price' of the kind that medieval theologians were to develop.

Likewise, Polanyi was practically the first person to have seen that the notion of chrematistics in the *Politics* refers to *two things* at once: on the one hand, the art of administering a domestic or 'economic' unit (an *oikos*); on the other hand, the art of acquiring *chremata*, things that are useful for one's existence (money included) — or 'chrematistic'. What Aristotle condemns is not chrematistics in its first, generic sense but in its second and more particular sense — the art of accumulating money *beyond* the needs of the maintenance of the *oikos* and the *polis* in *autarkeia*, through subjection of free men or the City to wills which are alien to the *oikos* or the *polis*. What Aristotle condemns is not the existence of trade or money, but the existence of trade for trade's sake and the pursuit of monetary profits 'to the detriment of others'. Marx had interpreted this text from the *Politics* in much the same way as Polanyi, but the context of the passage from the *Nicomachaean Ethics* had eluded him. For both Marx and Polanyi however what characterized the Greek economy was the fact that the land, the basis of an agricultural civilization, lay almost wholly outside the market. For all their money, the metics and traders could not buy it. Polanyi brings out three crucial aspects of Aristotle's sociology — community, autarky and justice — and he rightly shows that the *modern* concept of 'economy' could be not thought by the Greeks because with them, the elements of the economy were to be found dispersed among distinct social relations, political and religious.

Finley is in complete agreement with Polanyi here, recalling that a host of texts prove that the Greeks had a 'substantive' approach to economic facts. Indeed, they knew full well that the material means of their existence depended upon what we call agriculture, the mines, trade and money; that there were several 'institutionalized' way of procuring these material means; that their own ways were socially more complex than the barbarians' and their technologies superior to those of the barbarians and of their own ancestors. Finley also praises the acuteness of Polanyi's commentary, contrasting it with Schumpeter's judgement of Aristotle, in whose texts he saw nothing more than 'decorous, pedestrian, slightly mediocre and more than slightly pompous common sense'.

The simultaneous publication of these works by authors who were unaware of each other's work and concerned with domains of historical or anthropological scholarship ordinarily quite self-enclosed and, above all, the immense bibliographies appended to these articles, referring readers to works and disputes more than a century old, make it quite plain that the concern not to project modern ideas and realities onto ancient or exotic realities was a constant epistemological necessity, a permanent critical condition if the human sciences — even at the most empirical level — were to be developed. Polanyi's critical empiricism is not a novelty, nor is his distinction between three models of integration of the economy (reciprocity, redistribution, exchange), between the different types of trade or again between different functions of money. Polanyi was mistaken in crediting Thurnwald, and Malinowski in particular, with being the first, prior to himself, to provide a clear formulation of these three principles and to assert that they are encountered whenever symmetrical or hierarchical forms of social organization are discovered. This is a fairly routine observation, since these concepts are merely *descriptive* ones concerning *formal* aspects of certain social relations — empirical concepts which summarize in an abstract and useful fashion some common features pertaining to the *form* of social relations which in actuality are profoundly different.

Only a structuralist or a Marxist approach is explicitly concerned with searching, beneath the diversity of resemblances or differences, for an underlying order, the invisible logic of the objective properties of social relations and their laws of transformation. Polanyi's great merit — and likewise his shortcoming — is to have made explicit and clearly codified in a coherent corpus empirical, descriptive concepts which had been very widely employed by historians and anthropologists. But he was condemned in advance to being unable to do more than describe the shifting place of the economy in various societies, without ever really being able to pose the theoretical problem of its effect upon the functioning and evolution of societies, and therefore of its role in history. It is this problem that I shall to try to pose afresh before concluding this chapter.

Polanyi would have been the first to accept that the three 'principles of integration' of the various historical economic systems are 'formal principles', and that these concepts merely serve to describe mechanisms pertaining to totally different economic systems which only resemble each other in their form:

> Redistribution occurs for many reasons, on all civilizational levels, from the primitive hunting tribe to the vast storage systems of ancient Egypt, Sumeria, Babylonia or Peru ... Redistribution may also apply to a group smaller than society ... The best known instances are the Central African *Kraal*, the Hebrew patriarchal household, the Greek estate of Aristotle's time, the Roman *familia*, the medieval manor, or the typically large peasant household before the general marketing of grain.[17]

It is not hard to see that the concept of 'redistribution' describes features which are apparently common to totally dissimilar modes of production and historical realities. Polanyi uses it as a basis for arguments which attack evolutionism and Marxism, the latter being reduced by him to the 'historically quite misguided [theory] of stages of slavery, serfdom and proletariat', in other words to the Stalinist vulgarization of the thought of Marx and Engels: ' ... forms of integration do not represent 'stages' of development. No sequence in time is implied. Several subordinate forms may be present alongside the dominant one, which may itself recur after a temporary eclipse.'[18]

I certainly do not propose to challenge Polanyi on this point. The 'forms of integration' which he describes and classifies merely identify 'features common to the form' of concrete historical realities which are in fact so different that it would be absurd to interpret their presence or absence as the necessary effect of a regular succession of 'stages of development'. But one cannot stop here. One may, in opposition to Polanyi, interpret, not the presence or absence, but rather the dominance or subordination of these forms, and therefore the presence of a specific hierarchy

---

17. K. Polanyi, *Trade and Market* ..., p. 254.
18. Ibid., p. 256.

of these forms, as the effect of a stage attained by the evolution of humanity's forms of economic and social organization. Marshall Sahlins, Elman Service, Eric Wolf, Morton Fried, and all the American neo-evolutionists who came under Polanyi's influence when he taught at Columbia University, have attempted precisely this. For them, the evolution of society has entailed a succession of ever more differentiated forms of social organization — from primitive *bands* of hunter-gatherers, chiefless *tribes and chiefdoms* to *States* and the first class societies. The dominance of kinship relations in the bands and the chiefless tribes would account for the dominance of reciprocity, while the dominance of the politico-religious dimension in chiefdoms and States would be accompanied by the dominance of redistributive mechanisms. Commodity exchange would first appear in segmentary tribal organizations, but it would then fall into the background in chiefdoms and States to cede first place to redistribution, only to re-emerge later, in a different context, with a different content and form. Polanyi himself says much the same: 'Tribal societies practice reciprocity and redistribution while archaic societies [that is, the State societies of Antiquity] are predominantly redistributive, though to some extent they may allow room for exchange'[19]; 'Price-making markets, which alone are constitutive of a market system, were to all accounts non-existent before the first millennium of Antiquity, and then only to be eclipsed by other forms of integration.'[20]

Polanyi thus could not help noticing, in an empirical way, a certain statistical regularity in the *dominance* of such and such a form of integration of the economy in a given epoch in humanity's history, in a given form of economic and social organization. But he did not want to go any further. Yet he could have done if he had analysed more closely what he meant by the generic term 'form of integration'. For in fact this term served to confuse *two* distinct realities, namely, the social relations of production and the social forms of circulation of the product of the production process.

These two aspects of reality *are not* on the same plane.[21] In *every* economic system, there exists a relation of compatibility and subordination between the relations of production and the forms of

19. Ibid.,
20. Ibid., p. 257.
21. See above, chapter 3.

circulation of material products. The production relations determine the respective number, form and importance of the forms of
circulation of the social product existing within each socio-
economic system. And in practice Polanyi recognizes this when
he explains at length that:

> Dominance of a form of integration is here identified with the
> degree to which it comprises land and labour in society. So-called
> savage society is characterized by the integration of land and
> labour into the economy by way of the ties of kinship. In feudal
> society the ties of fealty determine the fate of land and the labour
> that goes with it. In the floodwater empires the land was largely
> distributed and sometimes redistributed by temple or palace, and
> so was labour, at least in its dependent form.'[22]

One cannot therefore accuse Polanyi, as Pierre-Philippe Rey
and Georges Dupré have done in the name of Marxism, of adopting the perspective of 'bourgeois' economists who prioritize forms
of circulation over relations of production. Polanyi would
certainly have accepted the idea that the forms, the importance
and the mode of development of the market could not be the
same when the relations of production were slave, 'Asiatic',
feudal or capitalist. But what he absolutely could not bring
himself to accept was 'the historically untenable theory ...
according to which the character of the economy was set by the
status of labour. ... The integration of the land into the economy
should be regarded as hardly less vital.'[23] This is an odd sort of
criticism, directed against imaginary Marx who himself never
reduced the relations of production to the status of the workforce
within the process of production: for him instead they define the
entire body of social relations which facilitate appropriation of all
the factors of production, and first and foremost the land and its
resources. I will not dwell upon this point here, since I have
already sought to demonstrate it at length above.

This is why Polanyi restricts himself to fighting the liberal
economists, not for the content of their arguments but for their
blind and ethnocentric eclecticism and their absurd claim to
apply such arguments to systems other than the 'generalized
market' one (as he prefers to call the industrial capitalist system).
The basis of his position — which, in the last analysis, belongs to

22. K. Polanyi, *Trade and Market ...*, p. 255.
23. Ibid., p. 256.

the same theoretical field as that of the liberal economists — is rejection of Marx's value theory and of the theory of capitalist profit or of seigniorial ground rent as so many forms of extraction of 'surplus labour' from the direct producers by one or several social classes controlling access to and use of the means of production.

To explain the internal mechanisms of the 'generalized market' economy, which Polanyi recognized as having an exceptional position, both at the abstract level of the theoretical representations of the economy which we construct and on the plane of concrete historical reality, since it is the system which has dominated the world for nearly two centuries, Polanyi nevertheless needed a theory of price formation, of profits, of the accumulation of capital and so on. Yet the one he epouses is the most banal and empirical there is. For him the value of a commodity is simply its price, which is 'created' on the market through the mechanism of supply and demand. Wages, rents and profits are regarded as 'revenues' from the different factors of production — labour, land and capital. This helps to account for Pearson's chapter, 'The economy has no surplus: critique of a theory of development', which lumps together the classical economists, Marx and the 'Marxist' archaeologist Gordon Childe. He suggests that the labour theory of value, an unscientific theory elaborated by the classical economists, was transformed by Marx into an ideology for combatting man's exploitation by man, an ideology which derived from moral denunciation and not from scientific critique:

> For those who were morally opposed to the distribution of wealth under capitalism, however, the classical surplus dilemma was too obvious a tool to miss. It was left for Karl Marx to turn the contradictions of 'this very Eden of the rights of man' into a theory of exploitation ... As soon as economic theory recognized, in the second half of the 19th century, that a commodity is worth what it will fetch on the market, the logical, if not the moral problem of surplus ceased to plague economic theory.[24]

This is how the question of Marx and the theoretical implications of *Capital* is settled by Pearson. It is easy enough to point to any number of somewhat caricatural misconceptions in his reading of Marx, whereas he seems to have found it less difficult — or

---

24. Ibid., p. 333.

perhaps was more scrupulous in his attempts — to understand Karl Bücher and Edward Meyer's theses on the ancient Greek economy. For example, Marx did not 'revive' the classical labour theory of value. He radically reworked it by showing that labour in itself has no value: 'price of labour' is just as irrational as a 'yellow logarithm'.[25]

Only labour power has a value, which is measured, like any other commodity's by the labour time socially necessary for its production — in other words, for the production of the material means required for its formation and maintenance. When he works, when he expends his labour power in the service of the capitalist, the worker creates not only the equivalent of the value represented by his wage, but also some surplus value, for which he is not paid. This *unpaid* labour, this additional value, constitutes the origin and essence of surplus-value. The capitalist-worker relation is therefore one of exploitation of man by man, a form of exploitation which wage-payment *conceals*.

Indeed, in practice, in the eyes of both capitalists and workers everything happens *as if* the wage paid is paid for *all* the labour provided by the worker (bonuses, overtime and so on are added to the wage). The wage, whether it is reckoned in terms of time or in terms of piecework, therefore endows unpaid labour with the appearance of paid labour and, conversely, it necessarily makes profit appear as the product of capital. Profit is only one form and one fraction of surplus-value, of the additional value created 'a form in which its origin and the secret of its existence are veiled and obliterated'.[26] Thus each social class seems to draw from the production and circulation of commodities a revenue to which it has a *right*. The economic categories of wages profit, interest on capital and rent therefore express the visible relations of everyday economic practice and, as such, have a pragmatic utility but no scientific value. Furthermore, the circulation of commodities *does not create* value but realizes it, and through this circulation the surplus-value created in the process of production is distributed among the different varieties of capitalists (industrial, financial, landowning) and assumes the forms of business profits, interest or ground rent. Everything happens as if capital, labour and land were *autonomous* sources of value added together and combined in order to produce the value of commodities. In this relation the

---

25. K. Marx, *Capital*, Volume 3, p. 957.
26. Ibid., p. 139.

appearance of the economic production relations conceals and contradicts their essence:

> The finished configuration of economic relations, as these are visible on the surface, in their actual existence, and therefore also in the notions with which the bearers and agents of these relations seek to gain an understanding of them, is very different from the configuration of their inner core, which is essential but concealed, and the concept corresponding to it. It is in fact the very reverse and antithesis of this.'[27]

But Marx's analysis has a much wider scope then this, for it shows that the relation of capital to labour is only *one of several* historical forms of the exploitation of man by man, a *specific* form in as much as it depends entirely upon a mechanism for the creation and accumulation of exchange-value:

> Capital did not invent surplus-labour. Wherever a part of society possesses the monopoly of the means of production, the worker, free or unfree, must add to the labour-time necessary for his own maintenance an extra quantity of labour-time in order to produce the means of subsistence for the owner of the means of production, whether this proprietor be the Athenian καλος κάγαθός, an Etruscan theocrat, a *civis Romanus*, a Norman baron, an American slave-owner, a Wallachian Boyar, a modern landlord or a capitalist. It is, however, clear that in any economic formation of society, where the use-value rather than the exchange-value of the product predominates, surplus-labour will be restricted by a more or less confined set of needs, and that no boundless thirst for surplus-labour will arise from the character of the production itself. Hence in antiquity over-work becomes frightful only when the aim is to obtain exchange-value in its independent monetary shape, i.e. in the production of gold and silver.[28]

It is now clear how opposed Karl Polanyi's approach is to that of Marx. For the former, there exist visible resemblances on the one hand and visible differences on the other, and he takes his argument no further. For the latter, to do scientific work is 'to reduce the visible and merely apparent movement to the actual inner movement',[29] and to find the common basis of the resemblances and differences. Polanyi did not speak about the contradic-

---

27. Ibid., p. 311.
28. K. Marx, *Capital*, Volume I, Harmondsworth 1976, pp. 344-45.
29. *Capital*, volume 3, p. 428.

tions, the conflicts and the struggles which the form of exploitation contained in economic relations presuppose and entail. And yet Hopkins, in *Trade and Market in the Early Empires*, reminds us that the notion of integration leaves the presence and operation of contradictions in shadow and serves 'as an inadvertent apologia for exploitation'.[30]. This is something that Polanyi certainly did not intend. He was a socialist, but his humanist socialism was above all a moral and philosophical attitude which he did not think could be based upon developments in the human sciences and history.

Actually, what mattered to me in Polanyi's work some twenty or so years ago — and what to my mind still matters — is the fact of his having insisted so emphatically, and with so many arguments, upon the 'shifting place of the economy' in societies and in history. This emphasis encourages us, just as Marx had done, to seek the reasons and the conditions which historically have produced the shift in sites, forms and effects of this function indispensable to every society and which, for brevity's sake, I shall call 'relations-of-production'.

It is in order to account for another fact which Polanyi, like so many before him, also very much emphasized — the dominance in a given society of kinship relations or religious relations or political relations — that I shall advance as a working hypothesis the idea that social relations, whatever they are, only play the dominant role in the reproduction of societies when they fulfil, in addition to their explicit functions, the function of relations of production.

But we are then faced with a further question: under what circumstances do they assume this function? In the light of the above hypotheses, I shall devote the next chapter to the material and analyses concerning fifth-century Athens which Edouard Will, who has as deep a knowledge of the ancient economy as anyone, has published.

---

30. T. Hopkins, *Trade and Market* ..., p. 288.

This text is a revised version of the introduction I wrote for the French edition of *Trade and Market in the Early Empires. Economies in History and Theory*, New York 1957, a collective work edited by Karl Polanyi and Conrad Arensberg, which appeared in French as *Les systèmes économiques dans l'histoire et dans la théorie*, Paris 1975.

6

Politics as a Relation of Production. A Dialogue with Edouard Will

> The truth is that we cannot include as citizens all those that the city needs in order to exist.
>
> Aristotle, *The Politics* III, v, 2.

Throughout this book I have sought, in various ways, to advance the hypothesis — to my mind a fundamental one — that social relations dominate the overall functioning of a society and organize its long-term reproduction *if — and only if — they function at the same time as relations of production, if they constitute the social armature of that society's material base.* This is only a hypothesis and not an act of faith. In order to verify it, we must analyze or reconstruct (when we have no alternative) *the conditions and reasons* which lead social relations primarily concerned with the organization of kinship relations or political relations between men to assume in addition the function of relations of production, to organize socially the conditions of material existence of the members of a society, in short, its infrastructure. We are therefore treating as a problem what empiricists take for a fact. To resolve it, we believe we have taken a step forward by proposing to treat infrastructure and superstructures as *distinct and hierarchized functions* which may or may not be embodied in distinct institutions. This said, there can be no *a priori* answer to these questions. It is for the anthropologist and the historian to pose and answer them, and to seek to construct an analysis of societies which is simultaneously an analysis of their history.

Without this preamble, what follows might at best have

seemed odd, at worst unsuited to an anthropologist. For while it is now fairly common for historians to use anthropology to clarify the data of ancient or medieval history (a development in which we should take some pride — examples are the works of Moses Finley, Marcel Detienne, J.-P. Vernant and S.C. Humphreys in ancient history and Jacques Le Goff and Georges Duby in medieval history), it is fairly unusual for an anthropologist to do the contrary and use history to advance his thought. Furthermore, why choose ancient Greece and 'classical' Athens, a difficult example — since we at once know too much and too little about them — and dangerous to handle, since they have been exalted in Western culture for centuries as the paradigm of civilization and therefore continue to fuel some of the ethnocentric prejudices which haunt the consciousness of European anthropologists?

I have chosen 'classical' Athens principally because it provides an example of a society where politics seems to function *from within* as relations of production.[1] Politics here is not just any sort of politics, but a form of politics which has become distinct from kinship relations and largely freed from religious relations and priestly hierarchies. It is therefore an example which complements that of the Australian Aborigines, amongst whom it is kinship relations which function as relations of production, and that of the Incas, where a politico-theocratic State power organizes the society's infrastructure.

In these various enquiries, my aim has never been to draw up a systematic inventory of the different forms of relations of production encountered in history, so as to construct a typology. Necessary though it may be to construct such a typology, my principal aim here has been to see if this interpretation of the facts offered any theoretical advantages in providing fresh insights into the original logic of the functioning and development of Greek society.

The reader will recall the dispute described in the previous chapter between the advocates of a 'primitive' view of the Greek economy and the proponents of a 'modern', even capitalist view of it. This dispute would now seem to have been settled, thanks in

---

1. I ought to add that there is something subjective about this choice. I have always been passionately interested in ancient Greece, its language, culture and history. I do not know the deeper reasons for this enthusiasm, but excellent Greek teachers must have played a part. Latin and the history of Rome have never attracted me to anything like the same degree.

large part to Edouard Will. However, for the latter the idea that there could have been something like a *Greek* economic system or several such systems, seems to have been rejected as the product of an uncritical, ethnocentric view of the past. My own reading of the Greek data leads me to draw an opposite conclusion. With what data, then, are we concerned?

We still know very little about the development of the productive forces in Ionia and mainland Greece in the seventh and sixth centuries, but what we do find is that the social relations which functioned as relations of production from the fifth century onwards were political relations between citizens and non-citizens, free men and slaves. The reader will recall that *to be a citizen was (almost always) to own a piece of the City's land and, conversely, to be a landowner was almost always to be a citizen.* Granting access to landed property to someone from outside the City was always both an exception and a privilege. To be a citizen, a man (and not a woman) enjoying the rights associated with freedom, meant that one owned land, was eligible for political and judicial offices, took part in the cult of the City's gods and had the honour of belonging to the corps of hoplites so as to defend the City by force of arms.

The manner in which the political functioned as relations of production thus determined a specific division of labour. Free men foreign to the community of citizens (and slaves *a fortiori*) were simultaneously excluded from ownership of land, political responsibilities, ritual activities and the protection of the City's gods. Handicrafts, commerce and banking were confined to the metics. Here we find an initial characteristic of the economic, social and intellectual development of a Greek city such as Athens (this was not the case with Sparta). However, in addition to this contrast between foreigner and citizen, we encounter another in the fact that all free men, be they citizens or metics, could, depending on their wealth, work their own land or have it worked by slaves, work themselves or make slaves work for them. This is a second characteristic of a Greek city. Metics and slaves, though excluded to varying degrees from the administration of the community or *politeia*, were nevertheless indispensable for the functioning and prosperity of Greek *society*.

Thus, it seems that something along the lines of an economic 'system' of classical Greek city-states becomes apparent. The original characteristics and specific 'logic' of these city-states derived from the very nature of the two components of their infrastructure. These two components were, on the one hand, the fact that the productive base was a rural economy, but one becoming more and more open to production for the market and a monetary economy, and secondly and above all, the fact that the social relations organizing and orienting this material base were, from within, political relations. For this reason, because of the original nature of these relations of production, the Greek economy was neither 'primitive' nor 'modern' and undoubtedly had the capacity to reproduce itself as a 'system' — but only *in so far as these political relations were reproduced.*

Thus we can see the error in these opposing viewpoints and the futility of the debate which has divided 'primitivists' and 'modernists', Karl Rodbertus's disciples and followers of Edward Meyer and Rostovtseff, since the end of the last century. For the former, the Greek economy remained 'primitive' since it was essentially based on agricultural production organized within the framework of the *oikos*, that is, a family group, including slaves of course, but remaining largely self-sufficient. For the latter, on the other hand, this economy was far more 'modern' than primitive since only the commercial aspects of its production, the existence of international trade and the more and more generalized use of money — characteristics later found in modern industrial capitalism — could explain both the prosperity and the dominance of Athens. Although after Hasebroeck's work, Meyer's 'modernist' theses have lost much of their impact, so that today the 'primitivist' position appears closer to the truth, it would seem that this debate was from the outset a dead end.

For an economy to be characterized as a 'primitive economic system' it is not enough for it to be organized within a framework of domestic units of production. At least one further condition must be satisfied: that the social relations governing access to resources and allocating social labour power are the kinship relations linking these family units of production. After the reforms of Solon and Cleisthenes, we no longer have such a situation.[2] Nor is it sufficient that an economy be oriented toward a

---

2. Aristotle was not mistaken in this respect since in *The Politics*, having demonstrated how important familial relations were to society, he declared: '... the *polis* is prior in the order of nature to the family and the individual. The reason for this is that the whole is necessarily prior ... to the part. If the whole body be destroyed, there will not be a foot or a hand, except in that ambiguous sense in which one uses the same word to indicate a different thing ...' (Book I, chap. ii, §§ 12-13, translated by Ernest Barker).

distant international market and employ large amounts of money for it to be 'modern', that is, similar to the capitalism governing our own societies. To be considered modern, another condition must be met: production in all sectors — including agriculture — should be oriented towards the market and the producers should be wage labourers, personally free, but constrained to sell their own labour power. Now Greek production for export — even of objects made in runs, such as amphoras — never became 'industrialized', but continued to remain in the hands of artisans. And wage labour by free men played only a minor role compared with that of slave labour.

Thus, the classical Greek economy was a 'political economy' in the literal sense. This determined its fundamental character, its unity and the conditions for its reproduction, in other words, its characteristics of a system having a specific 'rationality' of functioning, its own conditions of appearance and disappearance, determinate capacities for evolution, and consequently its own dynamic. Therefore I cannot agree with the following statement by Edouard Will, over-riding his previous correct and well-supported assertions that the 'principles governing the economy of the Greek cities cannot in any way be reduced to those elaborated by modern economic theorists': 'Thus, the underlying tendency is not toward a rational allocation of the "productive forces" but toward an *irrational division of social labour by virtue of the dignity attributed to man*'[3] Here Will is making a value judgment, using a norm of what 'should' be a 'rational' allocation of the productive forces, a norm *external* to Greek society and history, but one which in fact reflects the apparent principles of the functioning of a contemporary capitalist economy.

Yet Will himself has shown that given the fact that landownership was the exclusive right of citizens, 'working of the land was the most honourable form of work, that which led to *arétè*' (virtue),[4] and thus was more than just work, but 'the essential basis of "well-being", of civic virtue and of man's relationship to the gods'.[5] Landownership was reserved exclusively for citizens in order to prevent them from losing their freedom, from having to depend upon others in order to survive, so that they might preserve their liberty, in short, continue to exist as *citizens*. Thus,

---

3. E. Will, *Le monde grec et l'Orient*, Paris 1972, p. 633.
4. E. Will 1972, p. 632.
5. E. Will 1972, p. 671.

this intimate connection between political relations, landowner-ship and the dignity attributed to agriculture explains the original forms and conditions of the allocation of social labour power in the case of citizens as well as that of metics and slaves. It also explains the conditions governing the distribution of productive forces among the various 'sectors' ('subsistence agriculture, agri-culture for export, handicrafts, mining, commerce and banking) which were to expand with the development of the city. And it was due to the fact that such activities as commerce, handi-crafts and mining rendered the free individual engaging in them *dependent* on others that these activities were considered beneath the dignity of a citizen and were quite willingly left to slaves and foreigners. This situation was not in the least 'irrational'.[6]

However, Will's remark has the merit of drawing our attention to the problems and *contradictions* encountered and developed by such a system and which led to its eventual disappearance. We can understand why for a long time the struggle for *land* and the struggle for *political equality* in this system were only *two* sides of the *same struggle.* Thus, we can also understand why the political struggles amongst citizens for the maintenance and expansion of 'democracy' were a strategic element in the reproduction of the material basis of their social existence, and played such a decisive role not only in Greek ideology but also in the actions of the Greeks. We can understand why the concentration of landed property, or the accumulation of transferable wealth, in short, any form of development toward differences in wealth between free men, threatened the impoverished and often landless citizens with *falling* into a dependence upon *the wealthy or the State* and thus *losing* the very basis of their existence as citizens. 'The condi-tion for a man to be free', said Aristotle, 'is that he be not depend-ent on another' (Rhetoric 1367a 32). Now what was true of the individual was true of the whole city. The individual's desire to

---

6. The reader will appreciate how ambiguous the following assertions are: 'If, on the one hand, the social division of labour was to a large extent affected in terms of traditional and irrational criteria which tend to link types of occupation with types of social status; and if, on the other hand, what we have sometimes been tempted to regard as 'economic policy' actually only consists in the convergence of economic effects of measures which themselves were not economic, we must, in approaching the economies of the Greek cities, rid ourselves of all anachronistic theories and analyse concrete data in the light of mental facts which are not our own.' (E. Will 1972, p. 635.)

continue to exist in independence (*autarkeia*) parallels the city's desire and need to intervene in international trade and in the freely practised commerce of citizens and metics with other cities. But this intervention was only at the level of the importation of staple goods which contributed to the *poor citizens' subsistence* and strategic goods necessary to the city's military power.

Of course in a society largely governed by private property, the State could only intervene within certain limits. But the Greek State possessed more extensive means of intervention than did the State in the most advanced industrial capitalist nations of the nineteenth century. The leasing of its *ager publicus* brought in revenues and it heavily taxed the wealthy metics and slaves. Even the wealthy citizens could hardly refuse the State when it asked them to subsidize liturgies and other ceremonial or military expenses of the city. Furthermore, they had an interest in making such contributions since they brought political honour and prestige. In this way, the poor could live thanks in part to the State subsidies that enabled them to retain their status and take public office. For a long time, they could also expatriate themselves and establish colonies in distant but fertile barbarian lands or along trade routes that it was in the interest of Athens to control. But despite all these possible outlets, the very expansion of the system made continued equality between citizens and between cities increasingly difficult and threatened the very foundations of the economy and society.

Thus, we come to see the structural reasons — those having their basis in the properties of social relations rather than in the will and intentions of individuals — why the conflict between rich and poor citizens would almost entirely prevail over that between free men and slaves in the history and minds of the classical Greeks. For the same reasons, the second conflict (free men/ slaves) which was perhaps the more decisive for the society's eventual fate and for the long-term reproduction of this economy and way of life did not have the same possibility of *becoming politically evident*, and thereby assuming equal importance *in the social consciousness of the time*, or *reaching the same level of development in political practice*. Yet the development of the Greek cities, occasionally a very rapid and profound development as in Athens during the sixth century, resulted in the increasingly extensive use of slave labour in agriculture as well as in all other sectors, including finance. In the fifth and sixth centuries B.C., given the nature of productive technology, slave manpower was probably the main productive force upon which the material life and wealth of the City depended.[7]

Why, except on very rare occasions, did this fundamental conflict never occupy centre stage in the political life, consciousness and social struggles of the Greek cities? First of all, we should remember that for the Greeks (as for the Romans) slavery was taken for granted as part of the 'natural basis' of society and that the *institution* as such was never seriously challenged by either free men or slaves. In fact, among the essential elements of a free man's 'liberty' was the freedom to enslave other men.[8] But the possession of slaves was not merely an abstract of the status of free man attribute, because the slave was an integral and essential part of every free man's *oikos*, his family and his home, and was explicitly acknowledged as such: 'Now the Household, when complete, consists of slaves and free persons ... the first and smallest elements of the household are master and slave, husband and wife, father and children.'[9]

Moreover, according to Aristotle's vivid expression, 'the slave is a part of the master, in the sense of being a living but separate part of his body.[10] Separate like the oxen (also part of the family), but different in that while the slave, like the oxen, is an 'animate

---

7. M. Austin and P. Vidal-Naquet, *Economies et sociétés en Grèce ancienne*, Paris 1972, pp. 32-3.

8. The reader should consult the many searching writings by Moses Finley on this subject and especially his article 'Between Slavery and Freedom', in *Comparative Studies in Society and History* VI (3), April 1964. Finley refers to Aristotle, who wrote in *The Politics* (1333b 38) of the training of citizens for war: 'Training for war should not be pursued with a view to enslaving men who do not deserve such a fate. Its objects should be these — first, to prevent men from ever becoming enslaved themselves; secondly, to put men in a position to exercise leadership ... and thirdly, to enable men to make themselves masters of those who naturally deserve to be slaves.' (translated by Ernest Barker.)

9. Aristotle, *The Politics*, Book I, chapter III, § I, translated by Ernest Barker. Aristotle asserts much the same thing in chapter 2, § 5: 'The first result of these two elementary associations [of male and female, and of master and slave] is the household or family. Hesiod spoke truly in the verse,

'First house, and wife, and ox to draw the plough for oxen serve the poor in lieu of household slaves.' (translated by Ernest Barker).

The same applies to the Romans; see Emile Benveniste, *The Indo-European Language and Society*, translated by Elizabeth Palmer, London 1973, p. 291: 'What constitutes the *familia* is, etymologically speaking, the whole of the *famuli*, the servants who live in the same house. The notion does not coincide with what we understand by "family", which is restricted to those connected by kinship.'

10. Aristotle, *The Politics*, Book I, Chapter VI, § 9.

tool', he is 'endowed with speech'.[11] Above all, he is a living body, a 'corporeal force' at his master's service, subject to his command or to that of an overseer taking his place.[12] This living body 'only reasons in order to fulfil some vague emotion'. It is the body of a human being deprived of any of the qualities of the human personality. The slave is a nobody. He 'belongs' to his masters as part of the latter's 'possessions': 'Of property, the first and most indispensable kind is that which is also best and most amenable to Housecraft; and this is the human chattel. Our first step therefore must be to procure good slaves. Of slaves there are two kinds; those in positions of trust, and the labourers'.[13] This piece of advice was expressed by the author of *Economics*, a rather banal work that some scholars have attributed to Aristotle. These slaves were so indispensable to the lives of every individual and the city that a poor, sick Athenian around 400 B.C., seeing himself deprived of any form of State aid on the pretext that he was too poor to be eligible for any office, 'appealed formally to the Council for reconsideration of his case. One of his arguments was that he could not even afford to buy a slave who would support him, though he hoped he might be able to do so'.[14] This anecdote shows once more that only the existence of slavery, the exploitation of non-citizens, made possible the maintenance of an extremely relative equality between citizens. Thus the two conflicts, between rich and poor and between free men and slaves, enmeshed tightly with each other in a complex and original way, combining the effects of inequality of wealth with those of inequality in status. To be a wealthy citizen meant that

11. See *The Politics*, Book I, Chapter IV, § 2. 'The use which is made of the slave diverges but little from the use made of tame animals; both he and they supply their owner with bodily help in meeting his daily requirements.' (Book I, Chapter V, § 8.)

12. *The Politics*, Book I, Chapter VII, §§ 4-5: '... a master is such in virtue not of owning, but of using slaves. This science belonging to the master is something which has no great or majestic character: the master must simply know how to command what the slave must know how to do. This is why those who are in a position to escape from being troubled by it delegate the management of slaves to a steward, and spend on politics or philosophy the time they are thus able to save.'

13. Aristotle, *The Oeconomica*, p. 335.

14. In 'Between Slavery and Freedom', Finley comments upon a text of Lysias's as follows: 'Here was no theorist but a humble Athenian addressing a body of his fellow-citizens in the hope of gaining a pittance from them. The implications — and the whole psychology — could scarcely be brought out more sharply.' (p. 245)

one possessed large quantities of the two 'true' forms of wealth, land and slaves.

In Athens, at least, after Solon's reforms a citizen could no longer be reduced to slavery except for a serious crime. From that time on debt bondage was abolished and the poor were protected by the law.[15] Slaves could only be imported. They could only be foreigners, preferably Barbarians bought on the market and whose capture was left to other Barbarians — Scythians, Phrygians or other 'native' tribes specializing in and profiting from this activity. Without pressing the point further, we shall simply note that war was a necessary element in the reproduction of these relations of production and to some extent determined the relations between the Greeks and Barbarians and *amongst the Barbarians* themselves. It was a situation similar to that created in Africa 2,000 years later, with the development of the slave trade.

But to be a slave is not simply to be a man living in a foreign city and working in a despised occupation willingly relegated to him (which is the case today with migrant workers in our own societies). Reduced to the state of an animate tool, but one that speaks, the slave is completely eliminated from the human order: he no longer wholly belongs to nature but he is not altogether a part of culture either. The slave is imprisoned within society and the community of free men since he lives in the intimacy of his master's family and is an integral and indispensable part of the latter's *oikos*, of its social and material substance. He is deprived of some of the crucial human attributes. Only the free man living in *his* city, owning and working his own land or having it worked by his slaves, is fully a man. As a landowner and a slaveowner, the citizen 'represents' the society, the realization of a properly human order. This brings us back to our point of departure. Political relations function as relations of production because they give access to the two essential means of production: land

---

15. Finley writes as follows: 'Debt bondage is not the kind of institution which will suddenly fade away and disappear without good reason. It cannot be simply abolished by decree, unless a sufficiently effective power is already installed which will carry out the decrees, and unless there is also a practicable alternative for each class, namely, a substitute labour power for the creditors and guarantees or the emancipated debtors.' ('La servitude pour dettes', *Revue historique du Droit étranger et français* 1965, p. 179.) Finley advances a revealing comparison between this situation and that in South-East Asia, after the colonial authorities had abolished debt bondage. Compare H.N.C. Stevenson, *The Economics of the Central Chin Tribes*, Bombay, pp. 175-88.

and labour. (In capitalist society and the capitalist mode of production, citizenship and political rights do not give any one privileged access to the means of production.)

The specific nature of these relations of production or their political essence placed the slave, in contrast to the free foreigner, the metic, beyond *any* polity, and prevented him from becoming politically conscious of his lot, and from uniting with other slaves in order to take their place in history and collectively engaging in the political struggles which might have one day put an end to their common exploitation. To have organized such struggles and to have had the possibility of imposing a solution that would end their oppression, two conditions excluded by the very nature of the relations of production would have had to be met: first, a large number of slaves would have had gradually to become conscious of themselves as an exploited 'class' and, secondly, they would have had to extend their consciousness through various forms of struggle and to elaborate a viable, all-embracing long-term solution — that is, one that not only seemed to satisfy their own interests but also satisfied those of the whole society. Such a situation would have presupposed a much stronger consciousness and much sharper conflicts than those which enabled the poor citizens to obtain the final abolition of debt bondage in the face of resistance from the wealthy. However, in the latter case the possibility of redress pre-existed in the society. This possibility was provided precisely by slavery, slavery which from then on was to be confined to foreigners and Barbarians, who had to be enslaved in greater numbers than before.

Let us elaborate on these two points, namely, the impossibility for the slaves of *imagining* a way of ending their oppression, and the impossibility of their becoming conscious of themselves as a 'class'. As far as the first is concerned, some criticism of slavery did occur amongst *free* men in Greece. The sophist Antiphon proclaimed that all men are naturally identical and one was not 'genetically' determined to be free or enslaved. We can understand Aristotle's determination to refute such a thesis so contrary to his own.[16] Xenophon even tells us that before the rule of the 'Thirty', some citizens went so far as to maintain that there would be no 'true' democracy until the slaves took part in the governing

---

16. Aristotle, having quoted line 1400 from *Iphigenia in Aulis* — 'Meet it is that barbarous peoples should be governed by the Greeks' — goes on to comment that it contains an assumption 'that barbarian and slave are by nature one and the same.' (*The Politics* Book I, chapter II, § 4, translated by Ernest Barker.)

of the city. And we see how Agathocles in Sicily at the end of the fourth century emancipated all his able-bodied slaves in order to create a better spirit of emulation between slaves and citizens and thus strengthen his city's military potential. However, we know little of the opinions of the slaves themselves. In any case, as Moses Finley has reminded us, proposing the slaves' participation in a city's government and proposing the abolition of slavery itself — an institution acknowledged to be necessary to the material and intellectual life of the free men — are not at all the same thing.

Therefore the second point — the impossibility of slaves becoming conscious of themselves as an exploited 'class' — was more significant and can be explained by the same reasons. First of all, the fact that their masters allowed them to hope for their eventual emancipation was sufficient for many to accept their lot.[17] Resistance by others was principally passive, or semi-active when accompanied by acts of sabotage. But above all, most slaves chose to escape, either individually or collectively, when the external situation permitted. Some slaves even dared to go as far as an armed uprising but were always mercilessly suppressed.

Thus, as J.P. Vernant has pointed out, the opposition between the slaves and their owners, which could not assume the form of a concerted struggle at the level of social and political structures, at

---

17. Aristotle summarizes this principle as follows: 'The element which is able, by virtue of its bodily power, to do what the other element plans, is a ruled element, which is naturally in a state of slavery; and master and slave have accordingly, as they thus complete one another, a common interest ...' (*The Politics*, Book I, chapter II, § 2). However, he proceeds to qualify this judgement a little further on: 'The rule of a master is one kind; and here, though there is really a common interest which unites the natural master and the natural slave, the fact remains that the rule is primarily exercised with a view to the master's interest, and only incidentally with a view to that of the slave, who must be preserved in existence if the rule itself is to remain.' (Book III, chapter VI, § 6.)

In *The Oeconomica* of the Pseudo-Aristotle, we read the following: 'We may apportion to our slaves (1) work, (2) chastisement, and (3) food.... To set the prize of freedom before him is both just and expedient; since having a prize to work for, and a time defined for its attainment, he will put his heart into his labours. We should, moreover, take hostages (for our slaves' fidelity) by allowing them to beget children; and avoid the practice of purchasing many slaves of the same nationality, as men avoid doing in towns. We should also keep festivals and give treats, more on the slaves' account than that of the freemen; since the free have a fuller share in those enjoyments for the sake of which these institutions exist.' (pp. 337, 339.) J. Tricot relates this text to customs in Rome, where it was also forbidden to make slaves work on festive days. Cp. Cicero, *De Legibus*, II 8, 'Pesias in famulis heberato'.

another level played a decisive role in the evolution of ancient Greek society:

> ... the collective opposition came into play, and had a decisive effect, in other terms: it was at the level of the forces of production that the slaves, as a whole and as a social class, manifested resistance to their masters — the same forces of production of which the slaves were precisely the central factor in the economic and technical context of ancient Greece. At this level, as the use of slave labour became general, the conflict between the slaves and their owners became the fundamental contradiction of the slave mode of production. In this system, in which overall technical progress was blocked or at least markedly held back, the spread of slavery was clearly the only way to develop the forces of production. But at the same time the slaves' opposition to their masters, their resistance, their inevitable reluctance to perform the tasks allotted to them, impeded progress and imposed tighter and tighter limits on output. Moreover, when it came to increasing productive capacity, multiplying the numbers of slaves could not be continued indefinitely without endangering the stability of the social system as a whole. Thus we can say that, after a certain point, the conflict between the slaves and those who used them became the fundamental contradiction of the system even though, as Parain pointed out,[18] it did not emerge as the principal contradiction.[19]

Here again we find the same structural reason, namely, the fact that the relations of production are internal to the political relations. This fact had two distinct effects and determined two complementary but opposed modes of development in the contradictions of the system: on the one hand, the contradictions between free men were *directly* visible at the *political* level and could be the object of explicit political action and change; on the other hand, the contradictions between slaves and free men could only appear on the political level indirectly and could *not* become the object of direct political action on the part of the slaves.

However, J.P. Vernant's analysis enables us to point out the existence of another fundamental structural relation, a close relationship between the actual 'mode' of development of the productive forces, both material and intellectual, and the nature of the social relations which functioned in the City as relations of

---

18. The reference here is to Charles Parain's remarkable article: 'Les caractères spécifiques de la lutte des classes dans l'Antiquité classique', *La Pensée* 108, April 1963, pp. 3-25.

19. Jean-Pierre Vernant, 'The Class Struggle' [1965], reprinted in *Myth and Society in Ancient Greece*, translated by Janet Lloyd, Brighton 1980, pp. 14-15.

production. Recognized by many historians of Antiquity, this close relationship is clearly outlined by Will when he states that in Greece 'production was never governed by worries about productivity in any branch of activity since it was paralyzed by archaic conceptions of a religious and moral nature ... The non-productive spirit of the individual worker found its corollary in the cities' policy when handling, most often indirectly, economic matters.'[20]

In Greece, the thought of free men, men having the means and time to cultivate themselves, was drawn more to 'pure' know-ledge, the theoretical and speculative sciences, than to applied science and technical innovation which could have made possible 'the production of more by producing differently', and could in the long run have changed the material and intellectual relation-ship with nature, the relationship which Marx spoke of as a 'generator of myth'. It is perhaps too much to speak of a 'techn-ological stagnation' of Greek society in the fourth century, for without the development of the material and intellectual produc-tive forces, any society risks becoming gradually and unwittingly stagnant and turning in on itself, becoming less able to cope with the effects of internal conflicts or the attacks of neighbouring and more dynamic societies.[21]

Analysis of the case of ancient Greece provides us with a new element in support of the thesis advanced in chapter 1, whose validity I tried to establish with respect to the Mbuti Pygmies, namely, that within the infrastructure of any society there exists a network of *unintentional* relations between the productive forces and the social relations of production constituting the infrastruc-

---

20. E. Will 1972, p. 672. Will demonstrates that the so-called 'industrial enter-prises' of the Greeks, such as the armoury of Lysias and his brother Polemarchus, were only apparently such, for they arose out of the multiplication of a number of small artisanal workshops which used handicraft methods, and not those of mass production, to produce goods (p. 653).

21. This was the case with Roman society, which ended up by being no longer able to resist the invasions of the barbarians whom it had dominated and manipu-lated, and whose culture it had modified, for so many centuries. But Roman society had become a huge empire in which the productive forces of classical Antiquity underwent their greatest development — in agriculture, mining, communications, public works, armaments, and so on. This may well have been due to the fact that from the time of the Republic on, the Romans had had forms of large-scale landed property known as *latifundia*, which employed slaves much more extensively than the (by comparison) relatively modest enterprises of the Greek cities had done, and to the fact that commodity production had attained previously unknown levels.

ture, which acts upon all the other levels and aspects of social reality.

To be more exact about what we mean by 'unintentional relations' we should recall that these are relations of order based on the inherent properties of the social relations (and in this case of the relations of production and the productive forces). These properties, being properties of 'relations', exist whether or not the individuals living within them and acting to reproduce them are conscious of them. Such objective properties of social relations constitute the 'unintentional' content of social reality, but this unintentional content is not socially inactive or passive. It 'act'. It determines a range of causes and effects which neither originate from nor are based upon the consciousness or will of social actors, be they individuals or collectivities. These unintentional properties can never *cease existing* and acting as long as the social relations which they express *continue to exist*. In no way does this mean that these relations do not evolve under the influence of human beings' conscious actions or that the understanding of these relations has no bearing on the process of their evolution. It only means that when human beings produce changes in social relations, they do so by transforming their properties, not by 'creating' them.

A society is not a subject, and social actors are always in determinate relations. If certain individuals within a society are in some way or to some extent aware of the existence and nature of the inherent properties of their social relations, they can either exploit or counteract their effects more or less successfully, but they can only abolish these effects by abolishing the social relations which cause them, in other words, only by profoundly, indeed radically, transforming their society. The analysis of these networks of unintentional causalities has sometimes been called the analysis of 'structural causality'. However, these concepts are often enveloped in an air of mystery, which gives the impression that social structures have the capability or power to act and reproduce themselves without any form of human action. To avoid this, I prefer to talk of the analysis of the 'effects of a structure'.[22] Social structures only act by virtue of and through the individual and collective actions daily carried out by men to reproduce or modify their material and social conditions of existence. The properties of these structures are the invisible and

22. See above, chapter 1, p. 30.

unintentional foundation of social reality, the basis of necessity in which the actions of men acquire their ultimate meaning, find the full measure of their efficacy and exhaust the entirety of their social effects.

In the case of Greek society we are confronted with a veritable network of distinct effects of the productive forces and the relations of production which converge and mutually reinforce one another. We have already seen that the very nature of the relations of production makes it difficult, even impossible for the slaves to become politically conscious of themselves and to organize an *all-out* struggle for the abolition of slavery. At the same time the effect of the same relations of production on the development of the forces of production can be seen in the lack of real interest by the dominant classes and trained minds in the search for technological innovations which could have increased the productivity of labour and offered a real possibility of employing fewer slaves for an identical amount of work.

Had the Greek slaves wanted and attempted[23] to free themselves through revolt, the only objective conditions for the abolition of slavery they would have found in their society at that time would have been ephemeral and glorious dreams, ideas without the means of becoming reality, a utopian vision. Marc Bloch, Verlinden, and Georges Duby have shown that there were still many slaves throughout the European countryside during the seventh and eighth centuries A.D. and that they played an important role in the domestic economy and in agricultural production.[24] Incapable of being imposed through the struggles of a revolutionary class conscious of itself, the disappearance of slavery in Western society could only be an extremely slow, 'unending' process. And it is not in the least surprising to find that its disappearance often stemmed from initiatives on the part of the masters themselves who suppressed slavery in their own interest, in order to substitute more profitable and less brutal forms of personal dependence, since the latter required less effort to control individuals and organize their labour — while it induced

---

23. As the Roman slaves had done on many occasions — in 217, 196, 185, 139, 104, up until the famous revolt of Spartacus from 73 to 71 BC. There were no such revolts under the Empire.

24. Marc Bloch, 'Comment et pourquoi finit l'esclavage antique', *Annales ESC* 1947, pp. 430-43; C. Verlinden, *L'esclavage dans l'Europe médiévale.* I: *Péninsule ibérique, France*, Ghent 1977. Georges Duby, *Guerriers et paysans, VIIe-XIIe siècles*, Paris 1973, pp. 41-3.

them to work and cooperate to a greater degree.[25] This only appears paradoxical to those who project anachronistic and ethnocentric images of the bourgeois revolution of 1789 or of the Bolshevik revolution on to the resistance against their masters by the slaves of antiquity. Such projections have no bearing on an understanding of the logic of the 'political economy of slavery'.

In conclusion, the economy of a Greek city during the classical period was a coherent whole, even in its contradictions.[26] As I see it, the source of both this coherence and these contradictions was the same and was to be found in the fact that political relations functioned as relations of production. If Edouard Will had considered things in this perspective, he could never have written: 'When the modern historian tries to reconstruct 'the Greek economy' or less ambitiously that of a *polis*, he sets himself a factitious task, since this economy, if conceived of as a totality, was non-existent, being but a sum of the activities performed in the various sectors and not a coherent organism conceived of as such.'[27]

25. Furthermore, it was within the very large slave-run enterprises that management difficulties were most severe. Dion Chrysostom gives us a picture of the slaveowner as being forced to subject his slaves to an implacable discipline, to constant surveillance, and always threatened with seeing them escape, fall ill and so on (see Charles Parain 1963, p. 16). It is also worth noting that the colonate system, often employed by the big Roman landowners to replace slavery, represented a return to small-scale agricultural exploitation, which thereby imposed new limits on the development of the productive forces.

26. Let me emphasise that my notion of a 'Greek city' bears a strong resemblance to Athens and only a very slight one to Sparta. On this point, see V. Ehrenberg, *L'État grec*, Paris 1976.

27. E. Will 1972, p. 631. In fact, Will, to whom we owe so much, advances theoretical conclusions which fall short of his own analyses, for he continues to see the 'political' and the 'economuc' as two separable and separate social 'realities', rather than as functions which may be articulated with each other within the same social relations. Thus, when he writes (p. 432) that 'a well-balanced understanding of the Greek *polis* of the classical period therefore requires that we distinguish carefully between the *political* structures, which only concern the citizens, and the *socio-economic* structures, which include and transcend them', he is clearly right at the level of the institutions and the categories which the Greeks employed to refer to, and think about their social relations. But his formula serves to obscure the fact that at the level of functions the political relations function from within as relations of production, and it thereby threatens to impose upon us the ideas the Greeks constructed of themselves and their social relations.

An earlier version of this text, translated by Anne Bailey, was published under the title 'Politics as "infrastructure": an anthropologist's thoughts on the example of classical Greece and the notions of relations of production and economic determination', in J. Friedman and M.J. Rowlands, *The Evolution of Social Systems*, London 1977, pp. 13-28.

Part Four
Estates, Castes and Classes

7

Estates, Castes and Classes

Reading the special number of *Recherches Internationales* (*84*, 1975) devoted to 'forms of exploitation of labour and social relations in classical Antiquity', and especially the general introduction[1] and Zelin's and Finley's contributions, has led me to reconsider the real implications of the terms estate, caste and class.

For Zelin, in the beginning, estate and class coincide. Classes are estates: estates function as classes. Then the development of the material and social conditions of society produces the gradual separation of a reality of classes and a reality of estates. This separation arises from the fact that free individuals, citizens for instance, lose their fortunes and therefore proceed to take their place alongside slaves and dependants in the various labour processes. As these individuals fall, so too do certain slaves rise, becoming rich and powerful (bankers, for instance), and sometimes possessing slaves and dependants themselves. Those citizens who find themselves obliged to practise 'servile' trades, whilst still belonging to their own estate and retaining some of its privileges and obligations, begin to form a class with all those individuals who, regardless of their social or ethnic origin, occupy the same place in the production process, reduced here to the various 'labour processes'.

This emergent class first of all exists 'in itself', as a new and

---

1. Written by J. Annequin, M. Clavel-Lévêque and F. Favory.

objective aspect of reality. Gradually, as certain of its elements, issued from various different 'estates', become conscious that they share the same fate and a common set of interests, the class begins to exist 'for itself' and to recognize itself as such. Zelin places great emphasis, moreover, on the multiplicity of forms of dependence in ancient societies. He presents his taxonomic contribution as if it were an indispensable theoretical instrument, and one which might instil order in the minds of historians. In fact, apart from the advantage to be gained from distinguishing more clearly between the different forms of dependence existing in Antiquity — for which there was no need to have recourse to Euler's circles — this article quite simply fails to pose the basic problems which the topic raises.

First of all, to assert that, in the beginning, class and estate coincided, is to advance a formula whose apparent clarity may be shown upon closer examination to be based upon a misconception. Individuals belong objectively to the same class if they occupy the same place in the process of *production*. The initial error committed by many historians is to take the *labour* process for the *production* process, thereby confusing the place of individuals and groups in production with their involvement or non-involvement in various labour processes. Thus it is that certain slaves (bankers or barbers), themselves able to own slaves, occupied the same place as free men in the division of *labour*. Some historians, Moses Finley and Pierre Vidal-Naquet among them, with reason deduce from this that the slaves did not constitute a class in the modern and narrower sense of the term. To claim otherwise is to reduce the relations of production to just one of their three aspects — the labour process — thereby disregarding the other two: the relations of individuals and social groups *to the means* of production, and their relations with the products of labour, *with the results* of the labour process.

Now, everyone knows that the owner of slaves, without even having to figure in the labour process insofar as he can be replaced by his steward (*epitropos* or *villicus*), enjoys permanent control over the conditions of production, since he owns them, just as he owns the results (products or services) of his slaves' labour. It is for this reason that the argument that some citizens occupied the same position in the labour process as slaves in no way proves that they were beginning to form a class together with them. For citizen and slave did not enjoy anything like the same relation to the product of their labour: a slave's gains did not

belong to him and his master could deprive him of them whenever he wished.

An even more significant point is that many historians still
hold, to my mind wrongly, that the division of labour 'explains'
the relations of production, whereas in fact every division of
labour receives its *material content* from the existing productive
forces, and its *social form* from the relations of production. One
therefore has to explain why it was that amongst the Greeks, in
certain cities fifth-century Athens (but not Sparta — where land
and slaves belonged to the State), only the citizens had access to
the land, whilst foreigners, who were free men but not citizens, in
principle did not have it.[2] It is this fact which enables us to
perceive the nature of the division of labour, since exclusive
access to the land made agriculture the *preserve of citizens*, who
cultivated their plots themselves or could arrange for slaves to
take their place if they had the means to do so. This replacement
concerns the labour process, but does not involve any alteration
in the other two aspects of the place of citizens in the agricultural
production process — their relations with the land (and with the
instruments of production) and their relations with the results of
agricultural labour.

It is because they are citizens that individuals and their family
group (*oikos*) have access to the land, and not *vice versa*. At any
rate, this was the basic principle to which, from the time when it
was first established, only a few, very rare exceptions were known.
Several centuries had to pass before the land of a city such as
Athens could be alienated to foreigners.[3] In principle, then, and
over a very long period of time, belonging by birth to a 'community' (*koinōnia*) of citizens, to a *polis*, conferred upon an individual (a man) access to land, without this right being founded upon

2. This should not be taken to mean that all citizens were landowners.
Within the *demos* of classical Athens, a significant number of citizens — including
artisans, tradesmen and agricultural day labourers — had no land. But we should
not forget that when the Greeks, founded colonies, they often did their utmost to
make them into Cities of Equals, cities of citizen-landowners with equal-sized
plots. See David Asheri, *Distribuzioni di terra nell'antica Grecia*, Turin 1966.

3. On these various points and on the problem of the metics' access to the
land, see Moses Finley, *Studies in Land and Credit in Ancient Athens. 500-200 BC*, New
York 1973. See also the articles by J. Pečirka, 'Land Tenure and the Development
of the Athenian Polis', in *Geras Studies presented to George Thompson*, Prague 1963,
pp. 183-201 and 'The Formula for the Grant of ἔγκτησις in Attic Inscriptions', in
Acta Universitatis Carolinae, Prague 1966, which shows just how rarely the right to
acquire a plot of land in the City was granted in the fifth and fourth centuries.

labour. One has to acknowledge that relations which in an ethnocentric fashion seem to us to be 'political', function as relations of production. By reserving the land of the City for citizens alone, they turn agriculture into an activity apart, since it is exclusively reserved for them (or their slaves) and is thus an activity placed at the very pinnacle of a hierarchy of economic activities, the lowest of which is trade, especially trade in money (banking activities and usury). The fact that agriculture was the principal form of production in Antiquity and the Middle Ages does not by itself suffice to explain its importance and its social status for an Athenian citizen of the early epochs of the city. One must take into account the fact that the citizen has access to the land *as a private proprietor*, and that he works it or has it worked for him in complete *independence* from the other citizen-proprietors.

Agriculture is valued because it makes it possible to reproduce a citizen's material *independence* from others, whilst all forms of artisanal activity or trade obviously make individuals materially and therefore socially dependent upon their clientele. Artisanal activity and trade thus appear, by contrast with agriculture, to be activities which jeopardise the liberty of the citizen and contradict his privileged status as a free man, one who, in Aristotle's famous definition, 'does not depend upon another in order to subsist'. It can be seen why these activities were, preferably, left to free foreigners (metics) or slaves, and why a landless citizen, obliged to engage in such occupations in order to live, thereby compromised his position in society.

Since belonging to a city was a fact of birth, it was kinship relations which served to reproduce the estates.[4] Now, as I have shown in the previous chapter, membership of an estate did not simply entail the possibility of impossibility of enjoying access to the land, but at the same time conferred or withheld the right to practise the city's cults and to benefit or not from the protection of its divinities, together with the rights to bear arms, fill judicial magistracies and hold political office. It is an anachronism to refer to ancient Greek citizenship as purely and simply a 'political' relation, since that is to use a term which, in capitalist society, designates activities and social institutions

---

4. With respect to the Roman world, see the article by J. Maurin, 'Esclavage, parenté et cité', *Bulletin de l'Association Guillaume Budé*, 1975, pp. 221-30 and the article by B. Cohen, 'La notion d'*ordo* dans la Rome antique', *Bulletin* . . .1975, pp. 257-82.

distinct from the relations of production and functioning predominantly as 'superstructures'. (Such at any rate was the situation in the nineteenth century, for in numerous capitalist nations the State is now itself proprietor and producer, and intervenes persistently and directly in many other ways in the economy's functioning.)

In short, the characteristic feature of the social and economic organization of certain cities of classical Antiquity was the existence of a hierarchy of social groups, estates, whose members would either reserve for themselves or else renounce certain activities, material and non-material, depending upon whether they did or did not belong by *birth* to a local *community* which combined town and country, agricultural and urban activities. The hierarchy of estates therefore constituted the social form within which a kind of division of labour was developed and material production was effected. It constituted the form of social relations of production since it functioned as such, but at the same time it directly assumed many other functions. If the relations between the estates are relations of domination and exploitation — and in this they resemble class relations, since there are only class relations if there exists a dominant social group which exploits the labour of other social groups — nevertheless, strictly speaking, the estates are *not* classes.

Like classes, estates are forms of *domination and exploitation of human beings* which correspond to *another* level of the development of the productive forces and material wealth. This is why in *The German Ideology* (1845-46), Marx took so much care to distinguish between estates and classes, and showed how the bourgeoisie, as an estate in feudal society with purely local interests, was gradually transformed into a *class* existing first 'in itself', as a new force in the national realities which was gradually becoming conscious of itself, of its own interests, of its weight, and gradually opposing itself to the old feudal society from which it had emerged. From a class 'in itself' it was becoming a class 'for itself'.

Thus, when in 1848 in the *Communist Manifesto* Marx speaks of the estates of ancient society and of the Middle Ages, sometimes employing the word 'estate' (*Stand*: estate), and sometimes the word 'class', he is not so much contradicting or repudiating his earlier analyses as seeking to *tear off* the veil of illusions which surrounded the estates in Antiquity and in the Middle Ages, to *make them appear* as what, despite a tendency to obscure this aspect, they also were: relations of domination and exploitation of some human beings by others, corresponding, like every social form of production, to a determinate level of development of the productive forces, to a specific material base.

I do not believe Marx held that in Antiquity there were classes *hidden behind* the estates or *contained* in them, and which would gradually become distinct from them. In employing the word 'classes' to designate the estates, Marx wanted to present a different image of them from the one they had in the dominant ideology of these societies, as well as in the works of the historians who uncritically took these representations from Antiquity and the Middle Ages as their starting-point. He wanted to show that they were not, as had formerly been believed, more or less harmonious relations, but relations of oppression and exploitation, relations not founded *only* upon ideas (religious or otherwise) but reflecting also a determinate material base, corresponding to a definite level of development of material and intellectual productive forces. There are therefore *two* uses of the word 'class' in Marx. One of these designates *specific* historical realities, namely, the social groups born of the development of the capitalist mode of production and the dissolution of the feudal mode of production. These are classes in the 'strict' sense of the term. The other designates historical realities *analogous* to the classes of capitalist society, but distinct from them, and is therefore a usage which is not specific, and which is in some sense *metaphorical,* since the term subsumes only the resemblances and not the differences.[5]

The existence of classes in the *strict* sense of the word presupposes the *juridical* equality of all a society's members, together with their material and social inequality in their relations to the conditions and operation of the production process. In capitalist society, individuals may either own or not own the material conditions of production, and if they do not, then to subsist they must work for those who do. These different relations to the material conditions are *sufficient* to *constrain* some work *for* others, and this material constraint has no other direct justification.

Apart from this material and impersonal dependence and submission within the production process, the worker owes the capitalist nothing, for he has no direct religious, political or familial obligation to him. Outside production, capitalists and workers are in principle equal, and this equality in principle is recognized

---

5. For the two uses and meanings of the word 'class' in Marx, see the Appendix.

by the law. In societies with estates, this equality in principle *does not exist* and is in the last analysis *unthinkable*, save on a purely abstract plane, as we find in the case of certain Stoics, who posited the natural equality of human beings regardless of their race. In societies with estates, inequality is sanctioned by law, is legal and legitimate, as a fact inscribed in the laws of nature — a nature which includes both human beings and gods. This does not mean that law creates inequality but that it sanctions and codifies it.

In order for 'genuine' classes and class relations to be constituted, the distinctions between estates must therefore be *abolished*, since the *genesis* of classes is a *process involving the dissolution* and finally the *abolition* of estates. Of course this process did go on in Antiquity, where it was linked to the development of commodity production and the accumulation of monetary wealth, together with increased use of slaves in production. But it was several times thwarted and checked by the struggles of the poor, who had fallen into a state of dependence upon the rich and been condemned to debt bondage. When the poor struggled and indeed enjoyed partial success at the time of Solon's and Cleisthenes's reforms[6] it was with the aim of preserving or restoring their *status* as *free* men in relation to the rich and the powerful who threatened them; it was in some sense to shelter the estates from the *economic* movement — the concentration of land ownership and the accumulation of large monetary fortunes. But these reforms are to be explained predominantly in terms of a logic of estates and not in terms of a logic of classes in the modern sense of the word.

This ceaselessly reaffirmed vitality of the estates and their privileges — estates consciously maintained despite the economic and social processes which were slowly undermining them — was to give a new impetus to the enslavement of 'barbarians'. Oppression of the latter preserved the estates and ensured the expansion of the population and the production which threatened them. However, this was a provisional solution since, from the time of Alexander up until the fall of the Roman Empire, the role of the Cities was progressively eroded, whilst the functions assumed by the estates and their hierarchies within the Cities disappeared simultaneously. Yet the estates themselves did not disappear.

---

6. See Pierre Lévêque and Pierre Vidal-Naquet, 'Clisthène l'Athénien', *Annales littéraires de l'Université de Besançon* 65, 1964, and chapter 2, 'Isonomie et démocratie' (pp. 25-32), in particular.

They became an institutional framework of an increasingly formal kind, interfering less and less with the polarization of society between the rich (and powerful) and the poor (and dependent) groups which, in spite of their differences in status, enjoyed (as Moses Finley has shown)[7] progressively similar conditions of life. Finley goes on to observe that this process of polarization was intensified with the transition from the Republic to the Roman Empire and that in the long term it would perhaps have led to a society divided into *genuine* classes, rather than into estates, had it not been checked, and then to some extent halted, by the Germanic invasions and the break-up, then the disappearance, of the Roman Empire.

This break-up enabled the local communities (Celtic, Iberian and so on) to recover some of their vigour, while the Germanic invasions brought with them *other* forms of property and *communitarian* social organization, which also featured *private* property in livestock, in arms, and often in cultivatable land. Through the *convergence* of these processes linked with the break-up of Roman society and the Roman slave state, communitarian forms of property and social organization were once more able to win, or to win back, ground from Antiquity's forms of private property and from the large-scale use of slaves in production. Historical movement was once again tending to draw the societies of the West towards the birth of a new division into hierarchized estates, whose formal codification would occur much later, in the eleventh and twelfth centuries, at a time when the first leap forward of the European economy occurred, when the seigniorial mode of production was definitively consolidated,[8] being based upon a development of productive techniques which favoured

---

7. See Finley, 'Between Slavery and Freedom', *Comparative Studies in Society and History* VI (3), 1964 pp. 233-49. It is interesting to compare Finley's position with that of Niebuhr, which Marx was later to espouse in the *Grundrisse*: 'In one passage Niebuhr says that the Greek writers writing in the period of Augustus had great difficulty with, and misunderstood the relation between patricians and plebeians, confusing this relation with that between patrons and clients, because they "wrote at a time when *rich and poor were the only true classes of citizens*; where the needy person, *no matter how noble* his ancestry, required a patron, and where the millionaire, *even if he were a freed slave*, was sought out as a patron. *They could hardly find a trace of inherited dependency-relations [Anhänglichkeit] any longer.*" ' (pp. 400-401 of the German edition, Berlin 1953; p. 501 of the English edition, Harmondsworth 1973; the last three emphases are mine.)

8. For these points, I have relied upon two books by Georges Duby: *Guerriers et paysans — VIP-XIP siecles*, Paris 1973 and *The Three Orders*, Chicago 1980.

small and medium units of agricultural exploitation rather than large ones. However, several centuries were to pass before this 'feudal' society would generate from within itself the conditions for the emergence of genuine 'classes'. This would require a new and more substantial development of commodity production and international trade. The bonds which tied the peasants to their local communities (to which their lords belonged in the same sense as they themselves did) and which subjected them to their lord and his suzerains both had to be dissolved. Artisanal and industrial production, and the communes, would also have to be freed from the constraints and privileges of other communitarian structures, such as the guilds and corporations.

The estates were therefore not classes. But it was in fact their development which created the material and social conditions for the emergence of classes. The estates themselves were, in my view, the result of the development of social forms which had existed previously, namely, tribal or inter-tribal communities within which hereditary hierarchies of kinship groups had emerged that mutually *excluded each other* in the conduct of the various material and social activities which produced and reproduced their society. One example of this development is that which led to the formation of the caste system in India.[9] The relations between orders or between castes, through their multi-functional nature, resemble kinship relations in numerous 'primitive' societies. They constitute, however, relations of a new type, distinct from kinship but which control it by subordinating it to their own reproduction (caste endogamy, determination of the marriage rules which reproduce citizenship, *connubium* of Roman citizens, *contubernium* of slaves, and so on).

---

9. It is worth noting that Marx used the word 'caste' (*Kaste*) on several occasions to refer to estates, in Antiquity and the Middle Ages. And in the *Grundrisse* we find the following interesting use of the word:

> The tribes of the ancient states were founded on two different principles, either on kinship ties [*Geschlechtern*], or on occupation of the soil [*Orten*]. Kinship tribes preceded the locality tribes in time and are almost everywhere pushed aside by them. Their most extreme, strictest form is the institution of castes [*die Kasteneinrichtung*], separated from one another, without the right of inter-marriage, and with quite different status [*Würde*]; each with an exclusive, irrevocable occupation.'

(p. 381 of the German edition, p. 478 of the English edition and pp. 76-7 of *Pre-Capitalist Economic Formations*, edited by E.J. Hobsbawm, translated by Jack Cohen, London 1964; translation modified.)

It therefore serves no purpose at a theoretical level if one calls estates 'classes-estates' or 'estates-classes', nor, above all, if one asserts that classes originally coincided with estates, since estates cannot *in principle* function as classes. This would merely be a way of dodging the fundamental problem: explaining what estates are *before* they give birth to the conditions for class formation. Only an analysis of this sort would enable us to shed some light upon the historical process of their genesis within older societies and more 'primitive' communities. For this reason, in order to explain the genesis of hereditary hierarchies which become hierarchies of 'estates' within a society, one should look to anthropology, rather than economics or history, for analytical instruments, hypotheses and models.

What approach should be adopted so as to shed some light upon the genesis of a division into estates? Zelin puts forward two sorts of reasons for such a division. In pre-capitalist and, *a fortiori*, archaic and ancient societies, the '*juridical*' has enormous weight in the fashioning of social relations. Furthermore, *extra*-economic constraints, armed violence among them, explain the subordination of certain social groups to others.

It is obvious enough that recourse to armed violence can explain the appearance of slavery and many other forms of personal dependence. But force alone will not serve to organize production. In order to go beyond simple pillage, whether episodic or not, one must add to it a social organization of production.

Nevertheless, to account for the formation of orders and for their logic, it is not sufficient to place the emphasis upon the formation of various forms of servitude (slavery, serfdom and so on). In Marx's eyes:

> Slavery, bondage etc., where the worker himself appears among the natural conditions of production for a third individual or community ... is always secondary, derived, *never* original, although [it is] a necessary and logical result of property founded on the community and labour in the community.[10]

> Slavery and serfdom are ... only further developments of the form of property resting on the clan system. They necessarily modify all

---

10. Karl Marx, *Grundrisse*, p. 395 of the German edition; pp. 495-6 of the English edition.

of the latter's forms. They can do this least of all in the Asiatic form.[11]

If one accepts this highly plausible hypothesis regarding the secondary character of slavery and serfdom, the genesis of estates (and castes) must be explained *without* invoking slavery and serfdom — social relations which develop on the basis of organized communitarian structures (or possibly not — as was often the case in Black Africa), according to a hierarchy of estates or castes. Prior to the large-scale use of slavery and serfdom in production, there exists familial slavery, which *does not yet decisively modify* either the conditions of production or the social structure, but which will be a form *well-adapted* to subsequent developments in production, in the accumulation of material riches and social inequalities. Of course, one must distinguish between the enslavement of a member of one's own society and that of a foreigner. In the case of foreigners, physical constraint is generally required at the outset in order to *detach* these individuals from the community to which they belong. And it will be necessary from then on to *maintain* them in that state, even though, in addition to the violence, there is the material constraint of being deprived of every means of subsistence and production.[12] Just the opposite occurs when *debts* oblige a member of one community to sell either himself or a member of his family, for a limited period or in perpetuity, to his creditor. In this case, the material constraint contained in the relations of these individuals to the conditions of production *precedes* the intervention of physical constraint — which may, moreover, never be employed if the indebted individuals 'voluntarily' place themselves in slavery.

---

11. Karl Marx, *Grundrisse*, p. 392 of the German edition; p. 493 of the English edition.

On the problem of slavery in Greece, the reader should consult Yvon Garlan's recent book on the subject, *Les esclaves en Grèce ancienne*, Paris 1982. In his conclusion, Garlan, who had read the present book in manuscript, expressed his general agreement with my analysis of the use of the two concepts of class in Marx. Indeed, he reiterated my formula, affirming that in Antiquity there were no 'classes hidden behind the orders or contained in them, and which gradually became distinct from them'. It is worth noting in passing that some anthropologists owing their allegiance to Marxism, such as Claude Meillassoux, have sought to refute Louis Dumont's arguments in *Homo Hierarchicus* by discovering hidden classes in the castes of traditional India. See Claude Meillassoux, 'Y a-t-il des castes aux Indes?', *Cahiers internationaux de Sociologie* LIV, January–June 1973, pp. 5-29:

Analysis of the genesis of estates and castes (two systems of
social hierarchy which were probably developed under different
conditions and at different periods within fairly similar archaic
communities — at any rate if one limits oneself to the example of
those prehistoric populations which were the ancestors of the
Indo-European peoples) must therefore be conducted *without
referring* either to slavery or serfdom, which were later developments. Furthermore, a Greek or Roman slave did not, strictly
speaking, belong to any estate. He belonged to the family or lineage which owned him, and the use he was put to was first and
foremost a matter of private law. He was outside official human
society, whilst of course being a significant element in real human
society.[13]

We must therefore try to identify the economic *and* the non-
economic reasons which could have given rise to a division of
society into estates, i.e. into a series of social groups amongst
which the different material *and* non-material activities necessary
to the reproduction of their society are *distributed*. To each of these
activities and functions there is attached a set of values, a *status*
determining the *rank* which the groups and the individuals that
adopt them occupy in the social hierarchy, statuses and ranks
which are hereditary or which increasingly tend to become so.

As far as the economic reasons are concerned, they must be
sought both in a given state of development of the material and
intellectual productive forces, and in the nature of the relations of

---

'In our perspective, castes only appear as an ideological veneer which conceals
social reality by spreading the social divisions across a formal hierarchy,
drowning the relations of exploitation among them ... The so-called 'caste
system' thus represents the perpetuation and adaptation of status relations and
ideology to a class society which is unceasingly changing under the effect of its
own contradictions and external impacts, as a means of domination in the
service of the dominant classes, which are themselves transformed. Agrarian in
origin, the status organization of Indian society crumbles before the emerging
industrial society.'

I hope that I shall not be misunderstood here. I do not mean to question the
hypothesis that religion, in India as elsewhere, legitimized, if it did not mask,
numerous forms of oppression and exploitation. Nor would I dispute that the
development of modern, industrial capitalist society helps to dissolve the ancient
social organization, already profoundly mutilated by centuries of pillage and
colonial despotism, and in which individuals originating from different castes or
from outside the castes altogether, are today involved together in the formation of
new social relations which are in fact class relations. However, the problem with
which we are concerned is not contemporary India but its point of departure,

production and the corresponding forms of property. By way of example, one could investigate the economic basis of what Marx called 'the ancient mode of production'. This mode of production depended, as far as its material base was concerned, upon various forms of small-scale agriculture, stockbreeding and small artisanal workshops, and upon an original combination of communitarian and private forms of ownership and use of the soil. This originality did not consist merely in the existence of private ownership of the soil, but also in the relation of *subordination* of this property to its owners' membership of a community of free men. To understand the economic reasons for the formation of estates, prior to the development of the slave mode of production, in the Greek, Etruscan or Latin Mediterranean world, one must therefore explain the reasons for this separation of private from collective property, and for the maintenance of the subordination of this private property to communitarian property and to the reproduction of communitarian social relations. We can more clearly appreciate now than in the nineteenth century that the formation of these cities of free men claiming equality in law arose out of the dissolution of the local aristocracies, whose dominance was, however, never totally eliminated, and which had been built up, either through internal development or through conquest, upon the very basis of communal property —

---

namely, ancient India. What interpretation should be given of the caste system, of its nature and therefore of its origin and evolution over the centuries? With respect to this traditional India, Meillassoux asserts that the caste system masked class relations, with three dominant classes — the seignorial class, the clerical class and the merchant class — variously exploiting the last class, that of the Sudra. Thus, for Meillassoux the four Varna defined in the Rig Veda are classes. And these classes, he holds, correspond to the notion of estate; these 'classes-estates' are concealed and 'drowned' in a system of statuses and castes which derive from them and at the same time mask them. It is easy enough to see that this analysis renders Marxism 'safe', since dominant and dominated classes have been discovered, hidden in the heart of a social system which is exotic and apparently quite different from our own.

12. 'The fundamental condition of property resting on the tribal system which is originally formed out of the community) — to be a member of the tribe — makes the tribe conquered by another *propertyless* and throws it among the *inorganic conditions* of the conqueror's reproduction, to which the conquering community relates as its own. Slavery and serfdom are thus only further developments of the form of property resting on the tribal system. They necessarily modify all of the latter's forms.' (*Grundrisse*, p. 391 of the German edition, p. 493 of the English edition: translation modified).

13. See Jean-Pierre Vernant, 'Class Struggle' [1965], in *Myth and Society in Ancient Greece*, pp. 1-19.

a property which these aristocracies, without ever having actually abolished it, had more and more put to their own use.[14]

As a general hypothesis regarding the economic reasons for the formation of ancient estates (and even of castes), one could perhaps argue as follows. They are a transformation in social organization, a *codification* of new relations of domination corresponding to the *partial* dissolution of *communitarian* forms of ownership of the soil and the means of production, involving communal labour and use (drainage and irrigation systems, various forms of collective management and control of the conditions of production in agriculture, stockbreeding, fishing, mining and so on), but responding to the purpose of limiting this process of dissolution, of *maintaining in existence* and sometimes even of *reconstructing* the communitarian relations, of subordinating the new economic and social development to the reproduction of communitarian relations.[15] In restricting access to the land to 'citizens', the Athenian legal codes based themselves upon the ancient principle of the tribal or village communities, according to which an individual only has *rights* over a territory and its resources if he is a member, by birth or by adoption, of the community which claims them as its property.

The estates are therefore not classes in the modern sense of the word, either 'in themselves' or 'for themselves'. They are relations of domination and subordination arising out of the *partial* dissolution of communitarian relations of production, based upon forms of property and production which, whether slowly or rapidly, were distinguished and separated from more ancient communitarian forms and which are opposed to them *without being able to abolish them*. They slowly dissolve them but they cannot liberate themselves by attacking them head on. The contradiction and *the paradox of these new forms of property and society* is that they can only be reproduced *by reproducing at the same time* the communitarian forms to which they are opposed, because they remain *materially*, *socially* and *juridically* subordinated to these forms. Materially, because the life of the majority cannot be lived without having

---

14. Marx had an inkling of an analogous mechanism when he said of the Roman patricians: 'Since the patrician represents the community in a higher degree, he is the *possessor* or the *ager publicus* and uses it through his clients etc. (and also appropriates it little by little).' (*Grundrisse*, p. 382 of the German edition, pp. 478-9 of the English edition.)

15. This hypothesis is forcefully advanced by Robert A. Pastug in his article, 'Classes and Society in Classical Greece', *Arethusa* 8 (1), 1975 pp. 85-117.

access, for stockbreeding, agriculture and domestic artisanal production, to common resources — land, heaths, forests, water-courses and so on. Socially and juridically, because belonging to local groups organized in communities composed of kinship groups (*genos, gens*, lineage and so on) larger than the nuclear family still constitutes the preliminary social condition for the great majority to secure their material conditions of existence.

There are therefore profound relations between these economic bases and the other elements of social life — predomin-ance of kinship relations more extended than associations of nuclear families, many different forms of solidarity and mutual aid (religious, military and cultural) — which are combined with the material constraints so as to form quite diverse modes of life, in all of which, however, the archaic principle of the domination of the local community over its members *is still asserted.*

'Extra-economic reasons' closely associated with, and depend-ent upon, the economic ones are also involved, and these *constrain* certain social groups to *submit* to others. But this submission may have seemed to both parties to be a way of *cooperating* in order to reproduce a reality which transcended them and enabled them to live — namely, the ancestral community, which was a com-munity understood and lived as their 'Common Weal'. All of these constraints, including the readiness to consent to a division apparently *advantageous to all,* may account for the formation and the maintenance — the conscious reproduction — of the estates. It should be readily apparent now how differently I interpret the manner in which extra-economic constraints may be held to explain the original characteristics of the relations between the estates and the forms of oppression and exploitation they contain. It is not, as Zelin claims, because 'the juridical' has 'more import-ance' in archaic societies, where all activities seem subject to a complex codification and ritualization. The juridical is above all an expression, a coherent formulation, of principles of social practice. It is neither its source nor its foundation.

Nor is the juridical, as Zelin (in the wake of so many others) has asserted, primarily the effect of physical violence. Armed force has never been sufficient to *engender stable* social systems. The strongest component in the power possessed by a particular estate or caste in its domination of others is not physical force or armed violence, indispensable though they may be. The most potent component arises from the consent of the dominated to their domination. This consent has its source in subjective and objective reasons which constrain the dominated without the dominant compelling their adherence either through the threat of arms (warriors) or through their knowledge and power (priests, Brahmins). Did not Marx and Engels vigorously oppose Bakunin and the anarchists over their argument that classes and the State, having no other basis but violence, could therefore immediately be 'abolished' by that selfsame violence? The state cannot be abolished; it will disappear or 'wither away' when, through the struggles and endeavours of men, its economic, social and historical *raisons d'être* have disappeared.

These considerations have prompted me to reassert that it is a strategic priority, in history and anthropology, to search *elsewhere* than in physical violence or in the alleged 'greater importance of the juridical' for the reasons, both economic and non-economic, which have permitted distinctions and hierarchies to be generated *with* the consent of a society's members. These reasons would also serve to explain how it is that these hierarchies, prior to being differences between individuals, were first distinctions between social *groups* to which the individuals belonged by birth and which reproduced themselves at the same time as the kinship relations. Finally, one must seek the reasons why these groups came to consider their *mutual exclusion* from various material *and* non-material activities to which different values and social importance were attached, to be an *advantage for all* and not solely for the groups standing at the top of the social hierarchy. This is the perspective to adopt in attempting to reconstitute the process of caste formation in ancient India and to analyse this system's conditions of reproduction up until the modern epoch.[16]

---

16. The particular interest of the caste system is likewise that it displays in a quite spectacular fashion the role of the taboos which surround the performance of each social activity and which restrict it to specific social groups, to the exclusion of all the others. The production of these prohibitions is therefore one of the actual conditions for the specializations of each social group with respect to hereditary tasks. The caste system's originality consists in the existence of a system of philosophico-religious representations, of a theory hierarchizing all social activities and all the social groups which perform them in terms of a graduated scale of degrees of purity or impurity. This is a system in which 'political' power, wielder of physical force and armed violence, has to subordinate itself to religious power, and receives it legitimation from it. In so-called primitive segmentary societies, there are not in general any exclusive claims to the majority of the material and social activities which each group must produce in order to reproduce itself. Each segment, whether it is or is not a local group and/or a kinship group, has the competence and the right to participate in the hunt (if they are hunters) or to

The birth of 'estates' and 'castes' had above all to be 'legitimate', rather than the result of an act of violence to which people consented in the long term only because they had no choice — a legitimate birth which combined the power of objective reasons and of the subjective interpretations individuals and groups gave to it. A birth which was historically 'necessary', inasmuch as it combined and accumulated the determinant force of new conditions which had arisen and developed over a long period without anyone being aware of them on the one hand, and on the other, the force of conscious wills, which had arisen from the attempts of thought to interpret these new realities and from the effects of these interpretations upon life. But for these forces to have added up without the use of violence always being the decisive factor, it was necessary for the material and social conditions, whether already operative or emergent, to appear in the collective consciousness interpreting them as an advantage (or 'progress', as people would say from the eighteenth century onwards), rather than as a decline or as the irreversible disappearance of an older and better order. Among the procedures involved in this birth, legitimacy must have prevailed over arbitrariness.

To take the analysis of these processes further, one would therefore have: a) to have systematic recourse to anthropology, which possesses a wide range of data from numerous existing societies divided into estates or castes and which are *today* undergoing rapid mutation (India is the most telling instance of this); and b) to be able to analyse the role of thought in the genesis of new social relations, the role of the production of interpretations

---

practise agriculture (if they are agriculturists). It has the competence to marry off its members and to transmit their goods. When particular groups are specialized in certain tasks to the exclusion of others, these are usually concerned with ritual practices intended to reproduce (by means which are to our eyes imaginary) the community *as such* and in its relations with *the universe.* Moreover, it is usually beginning with this domain (the religious interpretation of the world and the religious practices to which it gives rise) that a social division of labour develops — the bear hunt, for example, being restricted to certain groups or individuals who are in possession of magico-religious powers. The codification-legitimation of the division of tasks between the various social groups, together with their unequal valorization within a huge system of religious representations constructed upon the opposition between the pure and the impure, is in some respects the application to a complex society of a mechanism present in societies with much simpler material bases. In *The Savage Mind* Lévi-Strauss himself embarked upon a comparison of the section system of the Australian aborigines and the caste system of Indian society.

of reality which bring in their train the consent of the dominated to their own domination.

Through this twofold approach, which involves critical consideration of anthropology's materials and analyses and the development of a materialist, non-reductionist theory of the role of thought in the (trans)formation of social relations,[17] we may hope to advance several steps in our analysis of ancient and medieval societies, and in our analysis of the societies with estates, castes and classes which coexist today — in the East and in the West — and which are in a state of mutation and transition towards new forms of social organization.

The formation of estates and castes was linked to a real development of the productive forces such that numerous social groups were able to abandon all productive, material tasks in order to devote themselves exclusively to war, prayer and rites. But the assignment of a given task to a given group was almost certainly never the *direct* effect of a realization that tasks had to be *divided* if the *material* capacity to act upon nature was to be developed. The division was conceived in terms of an interpretative system of the universe and society, and above all of the invisible powers which are presumed to oversee its reproduction. Hence the materially and technologically *arbitrary* nature of many aspects of the division of labour in pre-capitalist societies with estates or castes.

17. See above, chapters 3 and 4.

Appendix

A Note on the Two Uses and Two Meanings of the Word 'Class'
in Marx

The notion of class in Marx has for decades been the object of
bitter controversies which, it seems, are still unresolved (in spite
of the flood of articles and books which it has provoked). This
being the case, the best method to adopt here is, I believe, to
return to those writings by Marx in which the words *Stand* (estate)
and *Klasse* (class) are actually employed, as to analyse their
theoretical context more precisely.

This rereading has shown me that Marx utilizes the word
'class' with two different intentions, thereby conferring upon it
two meanings which are sometimes contrasted with each other.
First, a restricted meaning designating the social groups which
constitute modern capitalist society, and between which exist
relations of domination and exploitation founded *exclusively upon
the distinct place of these groups in the capitalist process of production,*
that is, both upon their situation with respect to the means of
production and the results of the labour process, and upon their
role in the labour process itself. In short, classes are social groups
which are in a relation of domination and exploitation with
respect to each other for exclusively *economic* — material and
social — reasons. It is in this sense that the classes of modern
society are not estates. They arise out of the decomposition of
feudal society, and they are contrasted with the estates, since they

replace the latter when these have disappeared, either of their own accord or under the impact of social revolutions.

In its second sense, the concept of class is utilized in a generic fashion, that is, in such a way as to subsume both the estate and castes of pre-capitalist societies and the classes of capitalist society. This generic use has the effect of obliterating the specific differences between estate, caste and class, and of making it seem as if Marx employs these terms indiscriminately to designate the estates of pre-capitalist state societies, ancient or feudal. We find these two uses of the concept of class both in *The German Ideology* (1845-46) and in *The Communist Manifesto* (1848) but in inverse proportion. In *The German Ideology*, great care is taken to distinguish between estate and class, and it is the specific concept which is dominant. In the *Manifesto*, a polemical work, the generic concept dominates. The emphasis is there deliberately placed upon the existence of classes and the role of the class struggle in history. One has to wonder what can have led Marx, who was habitually so careful to avoid an anachronistic use of concepts, to employ the notion of class in a generic sense, to blur the difference between it and the notion of estate and, as a consequence, to generalize to other epochs and societies a concept which strictly speaking may only be applied to modern capitalist societies (and of course, nowadays, to societies which claim to be socialist).

My response would be that Marx was led to substitute the term 'class' for 'estate' and to treat the two terms as equivalent because he wished to bring out two ideas: that estates — like classes — were based upon relations of exploitation and oppression, and that their emergence and disappearance corresponded to different stages in the development of the production of the material conditions of existence, whatever might be the often largely illusory explanation given of itself by each society and epoch.

In short, for Marx the capitalist mode of production, as it developed, demonstrated for the first time in the history of humanity the determinant role of the development of the productive forces and the relations of production in the evolution of society and history. It was the new awareness of this determinant role, up until then partially obscured or denied, which brought to light the often largely illusory character of the interpretations each society made of itself and the universe. Marx's historical materialism is nothing other than the generalization of these theoretical perspectives to all previous and subsequent epochs in humanity's history. It was this that Marx achieved in *The German Ideology*.

> In the whole conception of history up to the present this real basis of history has either been totally disregarded or else considered as a minor matter quite irrelevant to the course of history. History must, therefore, always be written according to an extraneous standard ... With this the relation of man to nature is excluded from history and hence the antithesis of nature and history is created. The exponents of this conception of history have consequently only been able to see in history the spectacular political events and religious and other theoretical struggles, and in particular with regard to each historical epoch they were compelled to *share the illusion of that epoch*. For instance, if an epoch imagines itself to be actuated by purely 'political' or 'religious' motives, although 'religion' and 'politics' are only forms of its true motives, the historian accepts this opinion. (*The German Ideology*, in K. Marx/F. Engels, *Collected Works* Volume 5, London 1976, p. 55.)

And here is the general formula for historical materialism:

> The fact is, therefore that definite individuals who are productively active in a definite way enter into these definite social and political relations. Empirical observation must in each separate instance bring out empirically, and without any mystification and speculation, the connection [*Zusammenhang*] of the social and political structure [*Gliederung*] with production. (*The German Ideology*, p. 35.)

In treating estates as classes, Marx was not trying to discover classes hidden behind, or contained within the estates. He was not trying to cause something else to be seen but rather to allow facts already known to historians (and ethnologists) to be viewed in another way. He was trying to find other reasons than those which the historical actors had been able to advance. At the linguistic level, the use of the word 'class' in Marx is not only ambivalent but ambiguous, and this ambiguity will always exist, since it is inscribed in his texts. On the plane of conceptual analysis, however, the ambiguity dissolves once one has reconstructed the texts in terms of their context and recovered the logic of Marx's approach, the precise nature of his questions and answers.

I shall now present some evidence to substantiate this interpretation.

I — The Origin of the Concept

Marx did not invent the concept of class. He inherited it from two separate lines of descent, namely, that of the French and English economists (Quesnay, Smith, Ricardo), and that of the historians (mainly French) of the bourgeoisie (Guizot, A. Thierry, etc.).

Marx's Letter of 5 March 1852 to Joseph Weydemeyer:

> As to myself, no credit is due to me for discovering either the existence of classes in modern society or the struggle between them. Long before me bourgeois historians had described the historical development of this class struggle and bourgeois economists the economic anatomy of the classes. What I did that was new was to demonstrate: 1) that the *existence of classes* is merely linked to *particular historical phases in the development of production*; 2) that class struggle necessarily leads to the *dictatorship of the proletariat*; 3) that this dictatorship itself only constitutes the transition to the *abolition of all classes* and to a *classless society*.
> (Marx/Engels, *Selected Correspondence*, Moscow 1975, p. 64.)

A few references from the economists

> —— F. Quesnay: 'The Nation is reduced to three classes of citizens, the productive class, the class of proprietors and the sterile class.' (*Tableau économique de la France*, 1758).

> —— A. Smith: 'These are the three great, original, and constituent orders of every civilized socety, from whose revenue that of every other order is ultimately derived.... [the proprietors of land] are the only one of the three orders whose revenue costs them neither labour nor care, but comes to them, as it were, of its own accord, and independent of any plan or project of their own.' (*The Wealth of Nations* (1776), Harmondsworth 1970, pp. 356-7.)

> — D. Ricardo: 'The produce of the earth — all that is derived from its surface by the united application of labour, machinery and capital, is divided, among three classes of the community; namely, the proprietor of the land, the owner of the stock or capital necessary for its cultivation, and the labourers by whose industry it is cultivated.' (*On the Principles of Political Economy and Taxation* London 1817, p. iii).

II — Some Texts in Which the Concept of Class has a Specific Meaning and in which Estate and Class are *Distinct* Concepts Referring to *Different* Historical Realities and Epochs

The German Ideology (1845-46)

'Out of the many local communities of citizens in the various towns there arose only gradually the middle *class*. The conditions of life of the individual citizens became — on account of their contradiction to the existing relations and of the mode of labour determined by this — conditions which were common to them all and independent of each individual.... With the setting up of intercommunications between the individual towns, these common conditions developed into class conditions.' (p. 76.)

'By the mere fact that it is a *class* and no longer an *estate*, the bourgeoisie is forced to organize itself no longer locally, but nationally, and to give a general form to its average interests.' (p. 90.)

'The independence of the state is only found nowadays in those countries where the estates have not yet completely developed into classes, where the estates, done away with in more advanced countries, still play a part ...' (p. 90.)

'The difference [between class and] estate comes out particularly in the antagonism between the bourgeoisie and the proletariat.' (p. 79.)

The Communist Manifesto (1848)

'We see, therefore, how the modern bourgeoisie is itself the product of a long course of development, of a series of revolutions in the modes of production and of exchange.

Each step in the development of the bourgeoisie was accompanied by a corresponding political advance of that class. An oppressed class under the sway of the feudal nobility, an armed and self-governing association in the medieval commune; here independent urban republic (as in Italy and Germany), there taxable 'third estate' of the monarchy (as in France), afterwards, in the period of manufacture proper, serving either the semi-feudal or the absolute monarchy as a counterpoise against the nobility, and, in fact, corner-stone of the great monarchies in general, the bourgeoisie has at last, since the establishment of modern industry and of the world market, conquered for itself, in the modern representative state, exclusive political sway.'

(*The Revolutions of 1848*, Harmondsworth 1973, p. 69.)

'In proportion as the bourgeoisie, i.e., capital, is developed, in the same proportion is the proletariat, the modern working class,

developed — a class of labourers, who live only so long as they find
work, and who find work only so long as their labour increases
capital.'
(*The Revolutions of 1848*, p. 73.)

Finally, we should not forget that in the historical process which
transforms the bourgeoisie from an estate into a class, there is a
moment, an epoch, when it is already objectively a class 'in itself',
but not yet one 'for itself'; it does not yet have consciousness of
itself as such and still behaves like an estate subordinated to the
nobility and the clergy:

Economic conditions had first transformed the mass of the people
of the country into workers. The domination of capital has created
for this mass a common situation, common interests. This mass is
thus *already a class* as against capital, but *not yet for itself*. In the
struggle, of which we have pointed out only a few phases, the mass
becomes united, and constitutes itself as a class for itself. The interests it defends become class interests. But the struggle of class
against class is a *political* struggle.

In the bourgeoisie we have two phases to distinguish: that in
which it constituted itself as a class under the regume of feudalism
and absolute monarchy, and that in which, already constituted as
a class, it overthrew feudalism and monarchy to make society into
a bourgeois society. The first of these phases was the longer and
necessitated the greated efforts. This too began by partial combination against the feudal lords.

Much research has been carried out to trace the different historical phases that the bourgeoisie has passed through, from the
commune up to its constitution as a class.'
(*The Poverty of Philosophy* (1847), in K. Marx/F. Engels, *Collected
Works* Volume 6, London 1976, p. 211; emphases added.)

III — Some Texts in which the Concept of Class is Employed in a General Sense and in which Class and Estate become Equivalent Terms

The German Ideology

'The class relations between citizens and slaves are ... completely
developed [in Antiquity].' (p. 33.)

'The third form [of property] is feudal or estate property ... the
hierarchical structure [*Gliederung*] of landownership, and the

armed body of retainers associated with it, gave the nobility power over the serfs. This feudal organization was, just as much as the ancient communal property, an association against a subjected producing class; but the form of association and the relation to the direct producers were different because of the different conditions of production.' (pp. 33-4.)

'... in the heyday of feudalism ... the division [*Gliederung*] into estates was certainly strongly marked ...

The grouping of larger territories into feudal kingdoms was a necessity for the landed nobility as for the towns. The organisation of the ruling class, the nobility, had, therefore, everywhere a monarch at its head.' (p. 35.) 'Particularly in the relations that have existed hitherto, when one class always ruled, when the conditions of life of an individual always coincided with the conditions of life of a class, when, therefore, the practical task of each newly emerging class was bound to appear to each of its members as a *universal* task ...' (pp. 289-90.)

The Communist Manifesto

'The history of all hitherto existing society is the history of class struggles.

Freeman and slave, patrician and plebeian, lord and serf, guild-master and journeyman, in a word, oppressor and oppressed, stood in constant opposition to one another, carried on an uninterrupted, now hidden, now open fight, a fight that each time ended, either in a revolutionary reconstitution [*Umgestaltung*] of society at large, or in the common ruin of the contending classes.' (p. 68.)

'In the earlier epochs of history, we find almost everywhere a complicated arrangement [*Gliederung*] of society into various orders [*Stände*], a manifold gradation of social rank [*Stellungen*]. In ancient Rome, we have patricians, knights, plebeians, slaves; in the Middle Ages, feudal lords, vassals, guild-masters, journeyman, apprentices, serfs; in almost all of these classes, again, subordinate gradations [*Abstufungen*].

The modern bourgeois society that has sprouted from the ruins of feudal society has not done away with class antagonisms. It has but established new classes, new conditions of oppression, new forms of struggle in place of the old ones.

Our epoch, the epoch of the bourgeoisie, possesses, however, this distinctive feature: it has simplified the class antagonisms. Society as a whole is more and more splitting up into two great hostile camps, into two great classes directly facing each other: bourgeoisie and proletariat.' (p. 68.)

And Engels added the following note to the English edition of 1888:

'That is, all *written* history. In 1847, the pre-history of society, the social organization existing previous to recorded history, was all but unknown ... With the dissolution of these primeval communities society begins to be differentiated [*Spaltung*] into separate and finally antagonistic classes.' (pp. 67-8 n. 13.)

Capital

'The class struggle in the ancient world ... took the form mainly of a contest between debtors and creditors, and ended in Rome in the ruin of the plebeian debtors, who were replaced by slaves. In the Middle Ages the contest ended with the ruin of the feudal debtors, who lost their political power together with its economic basis. Here, indeed, the money-form — and the relation between creditor and debtor does have the form of a money-relation — was only the reflection of an antagonism which lay deeper, at the level of the economic conditions of existence.'
(*Capital* Volume 1, Harmondsworth 1976, p. 233.)

It would be interesting to compare these texts, as well as the conclusions which I have drawn from them with the interpretations to be found in authors such as Georg Lukács (see 'Class Consciousness', in *History and Class Consciousness* (1923), translated by Rodney Livingstone, London 1971, pp. 46-83); Nicos Poulantzas (see *Political Power and Social Classes*, translated by Timothy O'Hagan *et al.*, London 1973); or Louis Althusser (see Louis Althusser and Etienne Balibar, *Reading Capital*, translated by Ben Brewster, London 1970).

INDEX

Radical Thinkers ▼